Beginning Oracle WebCenter Portal 12c

Build next-generation Enterprise Portals
with Oracle WebCenter Portal

Vinay Kumar

Daniel Merchán García

Apress®

Beginning Oracle WebCenter Portal 12c

Vinay Kumar
Rotterdam,
Netherlands

Daniel Merchán García
Greater London,
United Kingdom

ISBN-13 (pbk): 978-1-4842-2531-8
DOI 10.1007/978-1-4842-2532-5

ISBN-13 (electronic): 978-1-4842-2532-5

Library of Congress Control Number: 2016961815

Managing Director: Welmoed Spahr
Lead Editor: Nikhil Karkal
Technical Reviewer: Nanda Kishor
Editorial Board: Steve Anglin, Pramila Balan, Laura Berendson, Aaron Black, Louise Corrigan, Jonathan Gennick, Robert Hutchinson, Celestin Suresh John, Nikhil Karkal, James Markham, Susan McDermott, Matthew Moodie, Natalie Pao, Gwenan Spearing
Coordinating Editor: Prachi Mehta
Copy Editor: Karen Jameson
Compositor: SPi Global
Indexer: SPi Global
Artist: SPi Global

Distributed to the book trade worldwide by Springer Science+Business Media New York, 233 Spring Street, 6th Floor, New York, NY 10013. Phone 1-800-SPRINGER, fax (201) 348-4505, e-mail orders-ny@springer-sbm.com, or visit www.springeronline.com. Apress Media, LLC is a California LLC and the sole member (owner) is Springer Science + Business Media Finance Inc (SSBM Finance Inc). SSBM Finance Inc is a **Delaware** corporation.

For information on translations, please e-mail rights@apress.com, or visit www.apress.com.

Apress and friends of ED books may be purchased in bulk for academic, corporate, or promotional use. eBook versions and licenses are also available for most titles. For more information, reference our Special Bulk Sales–eBook Licensing web page at www.apress.com/bulk-sales.

Any source code or other supplementary materials referenced by the author in this text are available to readers at www.apress.com. For detailed information about how to locate your book's source code, go to www.apress.com/source-code/. Readers can also access source code at SpringerLink in the Supplementary Material section for each chapter.

Printed on acid-free paper

Daniel Merchán García (Dedications)
I dedicate this book to my family, my amazing mum, my lovely sister, my awesome brother and,
of course, my dad... I miss you, but somehow I know that you are proud of me.
Many thanks to my friends who are always there for the good and the bad moments.
My workmates who are always there for 1, 2, 3, 4... drinks after work,
a special mention to Maria, who is an infinite source of happiness and
positive energy and Pedro, who hates the pigeons and I do not understand why.

Vinay Kumar (Dedications)
I dedicate this book to my family, parents who inspired and motivated me.
Special thanks to my beautiful wife Saumya for continuous support and
lovely son Vedansh for making me cheerful always.
I would also like to thank my siblings, who always stood beside me and
to all those people who motivated me knowingly or unknowingly.

Contents at a Glance

Contents

About the Authors

Vinay Kumar is an Oracle ACE and technology evangelist. He has extensive experience in designing and implementing large-scale projects in Oracle Enterprise Technologies. He has implemented multiple Enterprise Portals on the Web and intranet using Oracle WebCenter Portal/ADF and open source. He is a technology advisor, trainer, and architect. He loves exploring emerging solutions and applications mainly related to Oracle Middleware and open source. He is the top contributor in the WebCenter forums at OTN. He loves spending his time mentoring, writing technical blogs (www.techartifact.com), publishing white papers, and maintaining a dedicated education channel at YouTube for ADF/ Webcenter.

Find his views at @vinaykuma201.

Daniel Merchán García is an Oracle ACE associate specializing in Oracle WebCenter Technologies with over 6 years of experience in Enterprise Portal Technologies. He has implemented dozens of Enterprise Portal solutions around the world by using Oracle WebCenter technology.

He is a technical leader who loves to help others to learn and understand the Oracle Fusion Middleware. In addition, he is an active member of the Oracle Community Forums and he always shares the knowledge through his personal blog based on Oracle WebCenter. Suite.

Find his views at @dmerchang.

Acknowledgments

A lot of time went into this book. However, without the help of others, this would have been harder. Two years ago, in an Oracle Open World, we had been talking about the possibility of writing an Oracle WebCenter Portal book. Finally, we are here, the book is in your hands and we are happy to see that our efforts may help others to learn and understand Oracle WebCenter Portal a little bit more.

We want to thank all of the Oracle WebCenter Community that trusts in our Oracle WebCenter Portal knowledge.

Thanks to the Apress Media staff who has given us the opportunity to publish this book.

Thanks to our Technical Reviewer Nanda Kishor who has provided very good suggestions.

Thanks in general to everyone who shares the technology knowledge with everyone to make IT simple.

CHAPTER 1

■ ■ ■

Introduction to Enterprise Portals

Before starting to describe the new functionalities offered by Oracle WebCenter Portal 12c, it is very important to understand the concept of Enterprise Portal and the differences between them and a regular website.

What Is an Enterprise Portal?

An Enterprise Portal can be defined as a **secured single entry point to multiple applications.** In other words, it is a Framework for integrating information, people, and processes across organizational boundaries.

Typically, Enterprise Portal displays personalized applications and information aggregated from multiple back-end sources, under a unified access point.

Portals may also serve as a collaboration environment for users, whether they are employees, team members, customers, or business partners.

The pillars of an Enterprise Portal are the following, as shown in Figure 1-1:

- **Single Sign-On**: Portal provides Single Sign-On capabilities for allowing the end users to access all the organizational information, processes, and collaboration tools only if the user is initially authenticated.

- **Integration**: A Portal is usually a Framework that offers tool for integrating data and information from back-end services such as REST, SOAP, Databases.

- **Federation**: Integration is usually done via WSRP Portlets (Web Service Remote Portlet).

- **Personalization**: Offers the content and the data personalized to the user who is logged into the Enterprise Portal based on the roles associated with the user.

- **Customization**: Users with appropriate privileges can customize the pages and components that they want to show or hide in their personal pages or dashboard.

- **Access Control**: Limits the access to the Portal Services based on the roles of a user.

- **Enterprise Search**: Advanced search capabilities for searching and displaying the content from multiple data sources.

© Vinay Kumar and Daniel Merchán García 2017
V. Kumar and D. M. García, *Beginning Oracle WebCenter Portal 12c*, DOI 10.1007/978-1-4842-2532-5_1

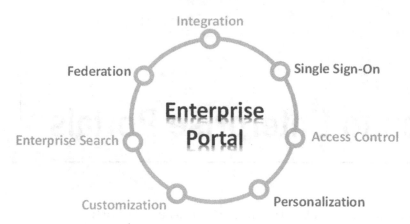

Figure 1-1. *Pillars of an Enterprise Portal*

■ **Note**   Enterprise Portals are also called **Web Portals** because the access to the presentation is made via Web Interface.

Typically, Enterprise Portals are used for two types of solutions:

- **Intranet Portals**: This type of portal offers to the employees or users within an organization a unique way to access to all of the required information.

- **Extranet Portals**: Transactional Portals that integrate Social Capabilities and Collaboration.

Enterprise Portal versus Website

An Enterprise Portal can be easily confused with a regular website. However, an Enterprise Portal is much more than a simple website.

A **website** usually refers to a collection of web pages, images, and videos addressed, relative to a common URL.

However, an **Enterprise Portal** is a gateway for accessing secure information, content, forums, etc.

The following table shows some of the key differences between Portals and Websites.

Concept	Portal	Website
Access	Public and Private	Public
Content	Extensive and unfocused	Focused
Collaboration	Full of Collaboration Capabilities	Limited collaboration tools
Integration	Integrates information of multiple systems via components such as Portlets / Mashups consuming REST, SOAP, or Database data	Marketing automation integration for a continuous, seamless visitor experience across different channels and devices
Transactional	Yes	No
Analytics	Yes (basic gathering)	Yes (granular analytics)

Which One to Choose?

The decision for using a website or an enterprise portal depends on the requirements of the business.

Typically, Enterprise Portals have Web Content Management functionalities for contributing and publishing web content like a website. However, they are usually very limited and without any intelligence if it has to be compared to a marketing website solution.

The best solution is mixing both solutions:

- Expose your Web Marketing Assets through a website.

- Only portal members can see their personal business data via an Enterprise Portal.

■ **Caution**   Enterprise Portals are built on top of heavy Frameworks, which are slower than a regular website for delivering Web Content Information.

Introduction to Oracle Fusion Middleware

As defined by Oracle:

> *Oracle Fusion Middleware is the digital business platform for the enterprise and the cloud. It enables enterprises to create and run agile, intelligent business applications while maximizing IT efficiency through full utilization of modern hardware and software architectures.*

Basically, the Oracle Fusion Middleware is a family of applications that runs On-Premise or On-Cloud, which covers all the needs that an organization can have.

This book focuses on the capabilities and features included in the Oracle's Enterprise Portal solution offering called **Oracle WebCenter Portal** (Figure 1-2).

Figure 1-2. *Oracle WebCenter Portal Login Page*

Oracle WebCenter Portal is not just a part of Oracle Fusion Middleware; it is also a part of the Oracle WebCenter Suite that comprises:

- **Oracle WebCenter Content**: The ECM (Enterprise Content Management) solution for content management and business processes driven by documents.

- **Oracle WebCenter Portal**: The Enterprise Portal solution to make agile the creation of intranet and extranet collaborative portals.

- **Oracle WebCenter Sites**: The WCM (Web Content Management) solution for marketing websites.

■ **Note**   Oracle WebCenter Portal 12cR2 (12.2.1.x.x) is the release covered in this book. It is the evolution of Oracle WebCenter Portal 11gR1 (11.1.1.x) and the other older solutions called Oracle Portal and WebLogic Portal.

The WebCenter Suite is a complete Digital Experience solution for Marketing, Portal. and Content Management (Figure 1-3).

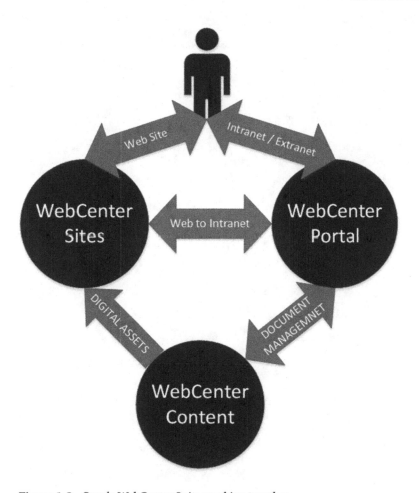

Figure 1-3. *Oracle WebCenter Suite working together*

CHAPTER 2

■ ■ ■

Introduction to Oracle WebCenter Portal 12c

Portal is a software/framework that provides a platform to integrate and bring together heterogeneous process/data. It provides a medium to make connections to multiple sources. WebCenter Portal networks span an entire enterprise in a secure way with a process-oriented security framework. Portal can be used to bring information from multiple sources and unite them in a single platform. It helps in search, navigation, personalization, notifications, and information integration. It also empowers applications with collaborations, administration, and task management features.

Nowadays business requires more agility and innovation to compete with the ever-increasing market pressure and to sustain growth. Earlier traditional ways of building applications needed changes. Frameworks should provide rich interfaces with collaboration features and support for indulging users more interactively. Portal provides an easy and feasible environment to build process-oriented applications rapidly. WebCenter Portal enables user to build applications by uniting multiple building blocks. It also provides in-built configurable building blocks.

WebCenter Portal is a product from Oracle and is on the future path of WebLogic Portal. It also extends features of WebLogic Portal. WebCenter Portal provides some common features out of box for example content management, business process integration, and SOA integration. It is also enriched with different layout, template, skins, and runtime data control features. Following are out-of-box WebCenter Services:

- Social collaboration Services – User productivity can be maximized by using User collaboration features. Portal users can work together more efficiently using collaboration.

- People Connection Services – Portal provides services like social network to connect within organizations. For example, Facebook, LinkedIn.

- Discussions Forums – It provides the ability to create and participate in discussions. Using discussion service, it is easy and fast to create forums in Portal. This is an embedded version of Forums provided by Jive Software.

- Announcements – This feature allows users to post, personalize, and manage announcements in WebCenter Portal.

- Instant Messaging and Presence (IMP) – It enable chat features in Portal. It provides the ability to observe the online presence status of other authenticated users (whether online or offline) and to contact them.

- Blog – User can use blogging functionality within the context of an application/Portal.

© Vinay Kumar and Daniel Merchán García 2017
V. Kumar and D. M. García, *Beginning Oracle WebCenter Portal 12c*, DOI 10.1007/978-1-4842-2532-5_2

- Wiki – It is a self-service community and content-oriented publishing service. Organization-based wikis can be easily created using this service.

- Document/Content management – WebCenter Portal makes application powerful with full support of enterprise content management. It consists of ADF built task flow (content manager), which manages documents from Oracle WebCenter Content management (UCM) using RIDC libraries. This service has full functionalities of WebCenter content management. It allows you to perform all actions, which can be done in WebCenter Content ADF user interface. It manages and stores documents, allows content upload, folder creation and management, versioning, and so on.

- Links – This service provides the feature to read, access, and map web-based information using URL-based links. Attaching a link in wiki, blogs or discussion forums can be good use cases for this.

- Page – Users can build pages in Portal. It provides the ability to create and manage pages at runtime.

- Tags – It provides the ability to assign one or more relevant keywords or tag with any page or document, which will help in search processes in Portal. This feature is similar to the del.cio.us website or any other tagging website. Internally it uses secure enterprise search features to fetch content based on tags.

- Events – Events helps to schedule meetings, appointments, and other types of collaborations. To use this feature, separate calendaring servers, for example Beehive, need to be installed.

- Mail` – Mail enables integration with IMAP and SMTP mail servers to enable users to perform simple mail features, such as reading, writing, and deleting messages with attachments.

- Search – It helps to search tags, services, an application, or an entire site. This will use Oracle **Secure search Enterprise** product. All the searches using Search Task flow will take place within WebCenter Portal using SES.

- Worklist – It provides a personal, at-a-glance view of business processes. This includes requests for document review and other types of business process reviews that come directly from enterprise applications.

WebCenter Portal 12c (12.2.1) is the latest version of WebCenter Portal. There are some changes in 12c compared to the previous version of WCP 11g. This chapter introduces you to the differences between WCP 11g and 12c and all new features of WCP 12c.

Concepts/Architecture

WebCenter Portal delivers right information to right people through role-based access control. It integrates content through mashup or reusable components for enabling business functions. It gives you great interfaces for managing Portal, information, and supports all devices.

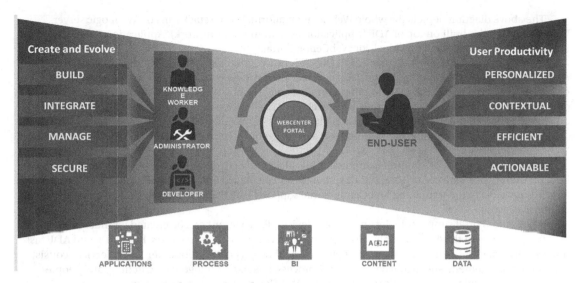

Figure 2-1. *Conceptualizing WebCenter Portal concepts*

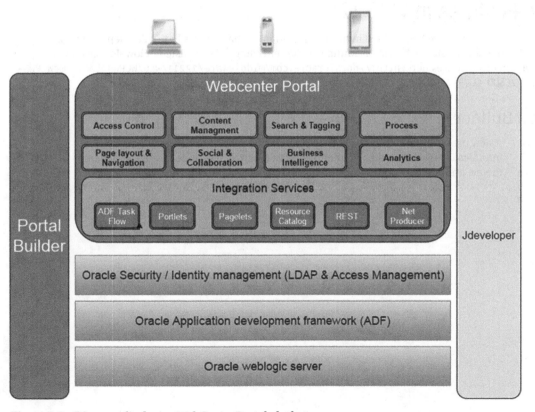

Figure 2-2. *Diagram displaying WebCenter Portal platform*

The above diagram depicts the whole WebCenter platform. Whole stack runs on WebLogic server. WebCenter Portal is built on top of ADF (Application development framework). Application Development Framework (ADF) is the building block for WebCenter Portal.

All built-in task flows are built using ADF. Out-of-box task flow customization is also achievable in ADF using **MDS** layer. WebCenter Portal has a new nice user interface for managing administrative tasks of WebCenter Portal and is called WebCenter Portal builder console. WebCenter Portal builder asset development will be done through round-trip development with JDeveloper. WebCenter Portal assets can be downloaded and edited in JDeveloper and later deployed to WebCenter Portal.

WebCenter Portal contains out-of-box assets and pluggable components, which can be deployed to WebCenter library.

ADF Task Flow and data control components use REST and SQL data sources. Business objects can be built on web service data control or other data sources and displayed into user interfaces using custom or out-of-box visualization templates. WebCenter Portal supports HTML5 templates, which means it provides a responsive layout.

WebCenter Portal supports tablet and mobile devices. Page variant can be created for different devices.

Integration with third-party applications can be achieved by portlets, pagelets, REST API, and ADF task flow. Security of Portal is managed by WebLogic security through OPSS. WebCenter Portal services consist of content management, social and collaboration, process, business intelligence, searching, and people connections, etc. Role-based security is supported in WebCenter Portal.

New Features in WCP 12c

Multiple new features have been added in this release. Some of the features have been deprecated or removed in the new version. Changes according to different categories are listed below. Please read in details about new features here: http://docs.oracle.com/middleware/12211/wcp/WCPWN/toc.htm#WCPWN-GUID-D852C8DD-CD7B-412E-B42D-94F7882ECCFA

Portal Builder

- A new user interface is designed for Portal administrator. Portal console user interface is rebuilt for edit and administration features. It is built based on bootstrap theme, and has a responsive layout that is supported in tablets UI as well.

Figure 2-3. *New Admin console of portal builder*

- There is lesser number of portal roles. Viewer and Participant roles are removed. It helps to speed up portal creation.

- New and easy WebCenter Portal administration console that includes a better user-oriented experience with familiar concepts for existing WebCenter Portal customers.

- New feature of draft pages. Portal Administrator can create pages at runtime and save pages in draft stage to publish later.

Figure 2-4. *Draft new pages*

- Two new HTML5 responsive templates: Mosaic and Unicorn with ALTA template.

- New device-setting features for optional rendering of portal in specific group of devices.

- New process of import and export portal life cycle that enables easy export/import and backup for portal in different environments. This will restore the environment with minimum downtime. Deploy is a new feature, which enables portal to deploy to different environments from portal builder console including portal content, assets, and shared libraries. More information about this will be discussed in Chapter 6.

Figure 2-5. *Deploy portal environment*

- Create/Edit of Page: Page can be created and edited on Web.

- Changes since the last deployment are clearly displayed prior to propagation.

- Deploy is a new feature to manage a portal life cycle easily. In earlier version, users had to export portal assets and libraries separately and then import all separately in different environments. With this feature, Portal managers can deploy portals in a self-service manner.

- New user interface is built for Pagelet producer configuration. WebCenter Portal Administrator can configure pagelets.

- A new Content Manager Task flow that supports managing and viewing documents in Content Server. Content Manager Task flow in 12c (based on ADF RUI) replaces Document Explorer task flow in 11g. User interface is more intuitive and better. User experience is better in content manager task flow. New security on content added. It allows users to use all features of WebCenter content by using this task flow.

- Portal 12c also supports Native HTML5 tags, including integration with camera, geospatial, and phone.

- It also supports consuming and producing REST APIs (ADF REST DC with JSON Descriptors).

- All portal deployments can be audited. That means that all deployment can be verified by respective users. The details can be viewed after a deployment completes.

Development Environment

- There is an out-of-box content presenter template in WebCenter Portal. By using this, users can create a responsive content presenter that adjusts to the width of the browser. This supports mobile and tablet devices.

- Process of custom-shared library development and deployment is simplified. New JDeveloper template is provided by WebCenter Portal that make easy process for building custom components, such as task flow, managed beans, and data control. It helps to deploy ADF task flows as shared libraries directly to WebCenter portal server.

- There is new page performance analyzer that shows how much time that individual components take to display on a portal page, as well as the overall time taken to display a page. This new tool is useful for developers who do first-level performance analysis.

■ **Note**   Now WebCenter spaces is renamed as **WebCenter** portal. WebCenter spaces administration console is renamed as WebCenter portal builder.

One of the biggest changes in WCP 12c is that there is no WebCenter portal framework application. There is only one environment for building portals, that is, portal builder (earlier called as WebCenter spaces). Existing users who are currently on WebCenter portal framework and want to migrate to WCP 12c need to migrate first to 11.1.1.8 or 11.1.1.9 portal builder application.

Deprecated Features in WebCenter Portal

- Polls have been deprecated in WCP 12c. If we migrate polls from 11g, it should be handled by a custom solution.

- Document Explorer task flow is deprecated in new version.

- Sub portals are also missing in WCP 12c. For migration from 11g, separate portals should be made instead of sub portals.

- Personalization features are also missing. Personalization engine includes scenarios and conductor architecture to give personalized experience in portal. For migrating from 11g, this design (conductor/scenarios) needs to be removed and the custom solution should be built to handle this.

- SharePoint JCR Adapter is missing in new version. This is used for making connection with SharePoint and WebCenter portal.

- Web Clipping Provider that is used to clip part of web page (HTML) and display in portal is missing in new release.

- Recent Activities Portlet to display recent activities of user is also deprecated.

- Analytics & Activity Graph Engine are deprecated in WCP 12c. Also worklist services are missing in new version.ytics and worklist services are also missing in new version.

CHAPTER 3

■ ■ ■

Oracle WebCenter Portal 12c Administration

Portal Administrator manages all portal administration-related activities in the Portal server console.

WebCenter portal can create multiple portals in the portal browser. Administrator can manage various portal-related activities at runtime. That's why WebCenter Portal 12c is also called the runtime portal.

Common activities of portal administrator are:

- Create, edit, and delete portal.

- Create, edit, and delete pages.

- Add, update, and modify content of page.

- Preparing connection to discussions forum, documents, portlets, activities, etc.

- Managing security for portal environment.

- Managing device settings for other devices.

- Adding custom task flow in the resources catalog.

- Managing portal assets, that is, page template, skin, content presenter, visualization template, page styles, pagelets, data sources, etc.

- Managing delivery management for portal, assets, and portal content, etc. Deploy is a feature that allows/supports/provides/regulates delivery management of portal in different environments.

WebCenter Portal server consists of the following common terminologies.

- **Home Portal** - The home portal is the area where users have access to their profile, available portals, portal templates, and documents, and they can customize certain elements of their own.

- **Portal Composer** – With portal composer, Administrator can create, edit, and delete pages via Page Editor. Portal composer will be in the portal administration console. In the portal administration console, the administer can create, edit, and delete portals. The administrator can manage all activates of portals. Portal composer can also manage runtime customization using Oracle Metadata Services (MDS).

© Vinay Kumar and Daniel Merchán García 2017
V. Kumar and D. M. García, *Beginning Oracle WebCenter Portal 12c*, DOI 10.1007/978-1-4842-2532-5_3

- **Portal template** – Template is a tool for enforcing a standard layout and look and feel across multiple pages or within a region. When the template changes all pages that are based on that template are automatically changed as well. It gives a base-user interface for your new portal such as header, footer, navigation, etc. Users can use available built-in templates or create custom templates.

- **Pages** - Portal consists of prebuilt pages with the following categories.

- **System pages** – System pages are pages that offer a ready-to-use set of customizable utility pages, such as the Login page, error page, Self-Registration page, etc. Additionally, the tools and services offered by WebCenter Portal each have an associated system page to provide a user interface to the tool such as the Document, Discussion page, etc. These pages can be customized at runtime and restored back to the default state by deleting all page customizations. Administrator can create page variants for some of the System pages.

	System Pages			
General				
Security				
Tools and Services	**Name**	**Variants**	**Last Modified**	**Actions**
Attributes	About WebCenter Portal Display information about WebCenter Portal		Modified by:system 5/5/2015	Customize | Restore Default
System Pages	Activities Displays application and social networking activities for current user		Modified by:system 4/15/2015	Customize | Restore Default
Business Role Pages	Activity Stream Displays application and social networking activities		Modified by:system 5/30/2015	Customize | Restore Default
Personal Pages	Analytics Gather information on usage metrics and performance		Modified by:system 4/8/2015	Customize | Restore Default
Device Settings	Announcements Enables users to view and manage announcements for a portal		Modified by:system 5/30/2015	Customize | Restore Default
	Discussions Enables users to view and manage discussion forums for a portal		Modified by:system 5/30/2015	Customize | Restore Default
	Documents Enables users to view and manage documents for Home portal		Modified by:system 5/30/2015	Customize | Restore Default
	Documents Enables users to view and manage documents for a portal		Modified by:system 5/30/2015	Customize | Restore Default
	Error Encountered Error Encountered		Modified by:system 5/30/2015	Create Page Variant | Customize | Restore Default

Figure 3-1. *System Pages*

- **Business Role pages** – These are pages that can be populated with information of relevance of a particular business role. Visibility and order of pages can be set here.

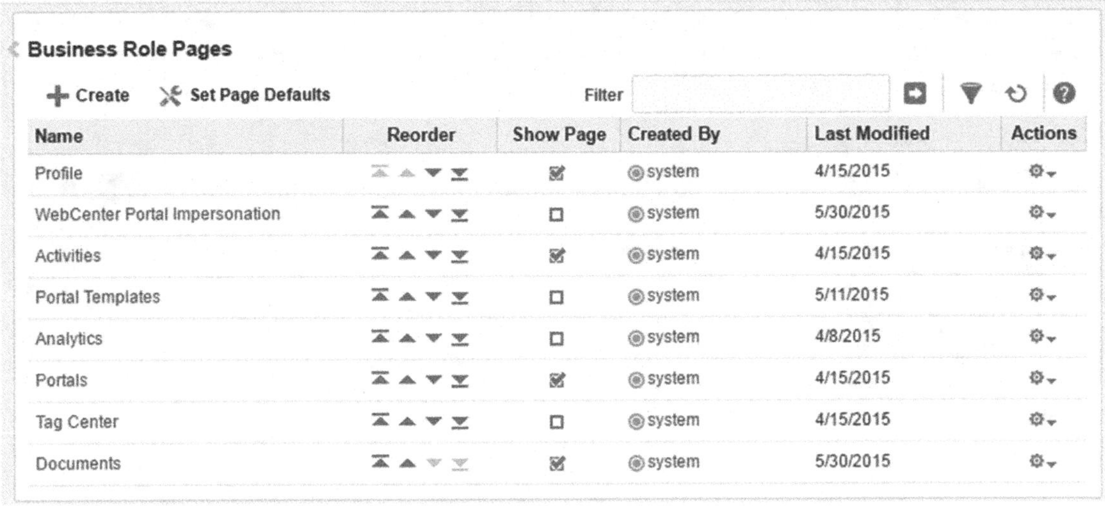

Business Role Pages

✛ Create   ✂ Set Page Defaults   Filter [   ] ▣ ▽ ↻ ❓

Name	Reorder	Show Page	Created By	Last Modified	Actions
Profile	⊼ ▲ ▼ ⊻	☑	⊙ system	4/15/2015	⚙▾
WebCenter Portal Impersonation	⊼ ▲ ▼ ⊻	☐	⊙ system	5/30/2015	⚙▾
Activities	⊼ ▲ ▼ ⊻	☑	⊙ system	4/15/2015	⚙▾
Portal Templates	⊼ ▲ ▼ ⊻	☐	⊙ system	5/11/2015	⚙▾
Analytics	⊼ ▲ ▼ ⊻	☐	⊙ system	4/8/2015	⚙▾
Portals	⊼ ▲ ▼ ⊻	☑	⊙ system	4/15/2015	⚙▾
Tag Center	⊼ ▲ ▼ ⊻	☐	⊙ system	4/15/2015	⚙▾
Documents	⊼ ▲ ▼ ⊻	☑	⊙ system	5/30/2015	⚙▾

Figure 3-2. *Business Role Pages*

- **Portal pages** – These are pages that can be added in portal by portal manager or administrator to contribute to the portal functionality. Users can also consume custom task flows or portlets in these pages.

- **Portal Assets** - Assets are reusable components that define structure, layout, and look and feel of the portal. Some of the portal assets are template, skin, content presenter, task flow, page style, layouts, pagelets, datasources, data controls, visualization templates, etc.

- **Resource Catalog** – These are portal assets that expose components and connections that are added to a portal. Resource catalog is useful to populate pages, page templates, and task flows. Shared libraries (custom task flow in design time) deployed in WebLogic can be added, and later these task flows can add to the portal page for custom functionality.

- **Tools and Services** – Tool and services console provides the medium to make back-end connection for collaboration and communication with other systems. Admin can make a connection to the back-end server for portlets, pagelets, and documents, etc. Administrator can enable built-in services in portal-like documents and search mechanisms for those specific to the portal. Portlets connections can also be configured from this console.

Creation of Portal

To create a portal in a portal browser, make sure the portal server is up and running.

1. Navigate to URL "host:port/webcenter." Click on create portal on portal browser.

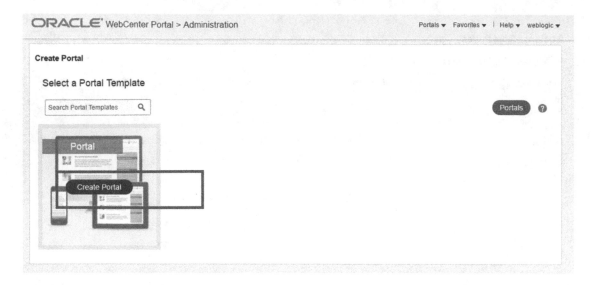

Figure 3-3. *Create portal in portal browser*

2. Provide portal title, description as Title as "Frolic Insurance," and description as "Insurance."

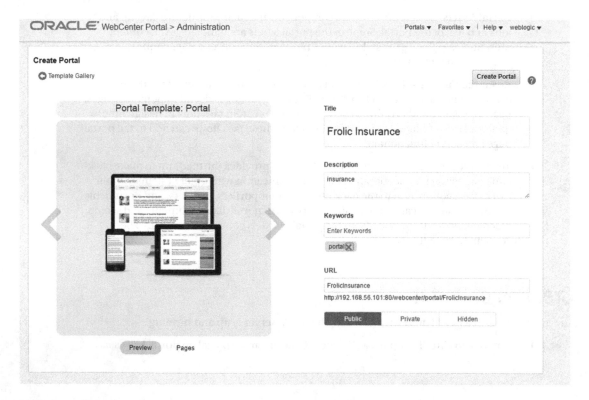

Figure 3-4. *Create portal in portal browser*

3. Portal security can be set to either public, private, or hidden. Default security is public.

4. Click on Pages tab to create portal pages. Provide comma-separated page names in "Add more Pages" section as in Figure 3-5. This will create pages in portal with standard navigation.

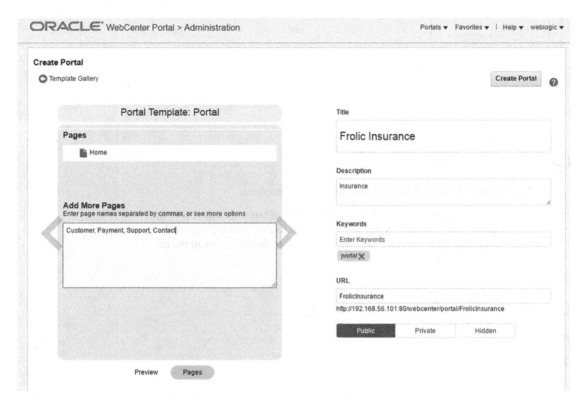

Figure 3-5. *Creating portal pages*

5. Click on Create Portal.

6. Portal is created with pages. Composer is open to edit the portal (Figure 3-6).

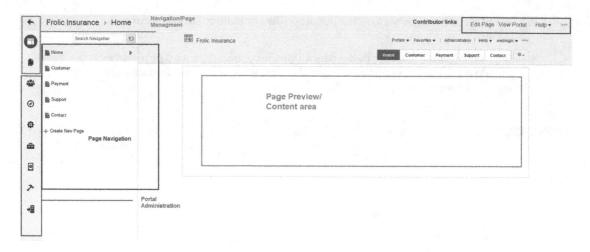

Figure 3-6. *Portal composer*

7. Figure 3-6 shows different sections in page composer.

8. Now click on view portal on top-right section of page in contributor link section. This will display portal with default template and pages with standard navigation. Now let's add some richer user interface features in portal.

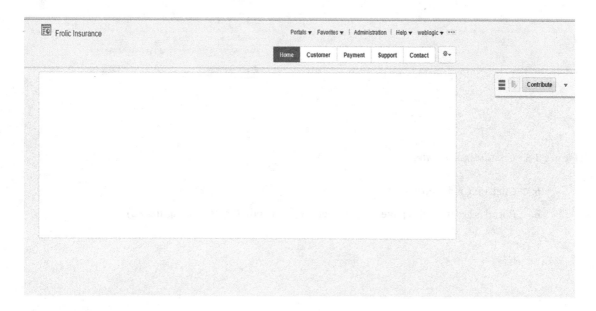

Figure 3-7. *Default portal view*

Portal-Specific Administration

To change the look and feel of a portal, edit the page template and skin.

1. In portal composer, click the setting icon.

Figure 3-8. *Portal setting Icon*

2. Go to the page template and change out-of-box page template to "Mosaic."

3. Go to skin and select skin to "Mosaic."

4. Change the copyright message.

5. Change default language to "English."

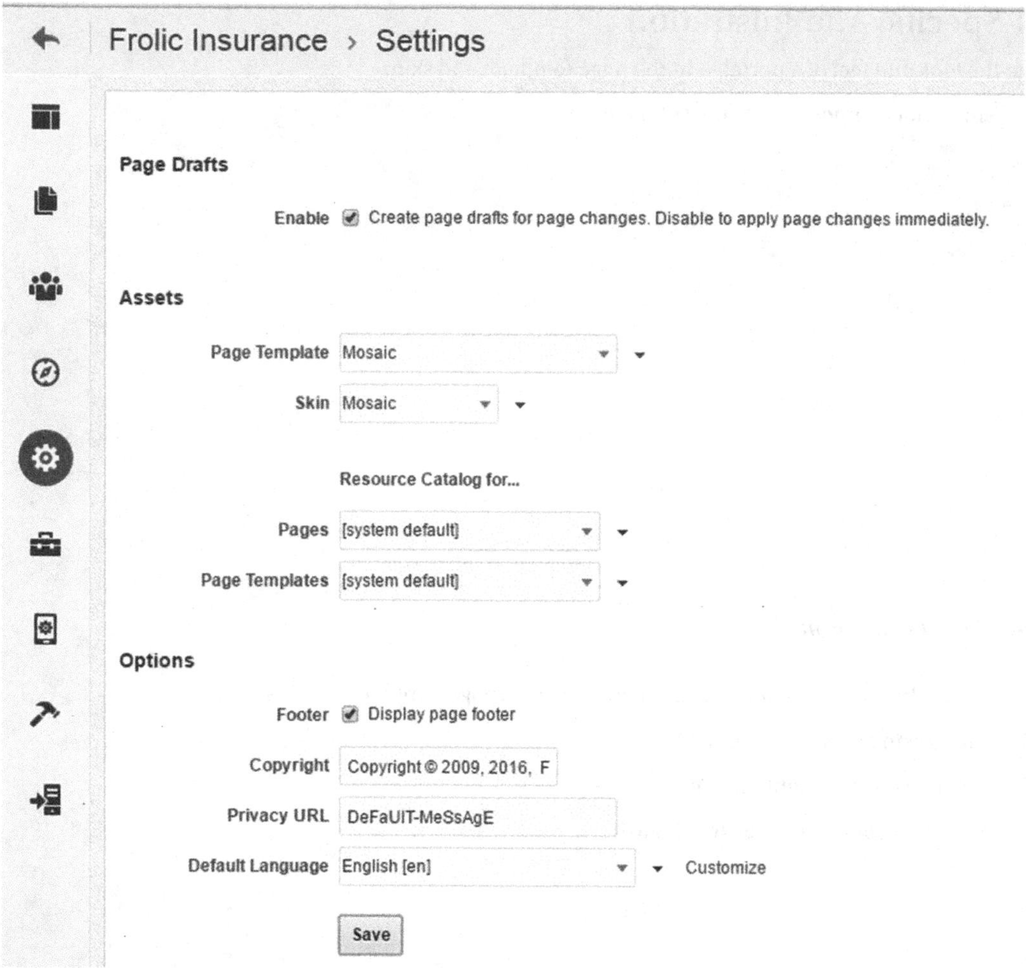

Figure 3-9. *Portal setting*

6. Click save and view portal.

Figure 3-10. *Frolic insurance portal*

7. Click on the Settings icon. Change the portal Icon, Logo, and Preview Image by uploading a new image.

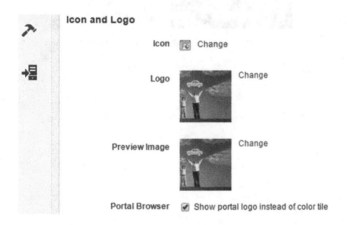

Figure 3-11. *Portal logo*

8. Click the back icon in setting page.

Figure 3-12. Portal back icon

9. Portal logo and icon is updated with the uploaded image.

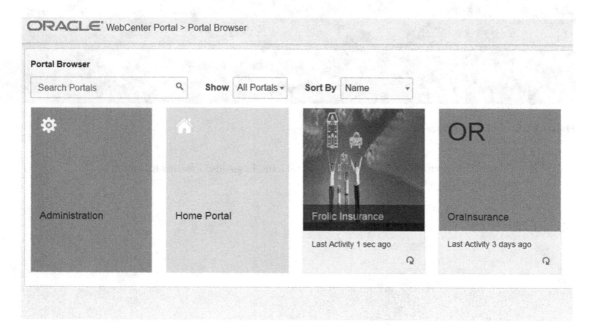

Figure 3-13. Portal browser image

We will discuss each feature available to the portal manager or moderator.

Icon	feature	Details
	Back	Returns to the Portal Browser page.
	Pages	Manages page navigation, page creation, reordering page structure, and more.
	Drafts	Manages the drafts for this portal. By default, every modification will create a draft that must be approved.
	Security	Sets security on the portal, such as access level, defining roles and permissions, and managing membership.
	General	Modifies general settings of the portal, such as the title (name) and description, and to perform general actions on the portal, such as closing the portal, adding RSS feeds, or deleting the portal.
	Settings	Specifies settings that define the look and feel of the portal.
	Assets	Manages the assets for the portal such as page templates, resource catalogs, skins, and more.
	Device Settings	Use this page to manage devices and device groups in a device-enabled portal.
	Tools and Services	Enables and disables tools and services operating in the portal, such as Announcements, Discussions, Documents, Events, and Lists.
	Deploy	Use this page to deploy, redeploy, and propagate a portal to a target server.

Security

Click the security icon. Default roles are visible, that is, "portal manager," "Authenticated-user," and "Public-User." Permission for each role can be modified. New Role specific to portal can be created in security section. Portal access can set to public, private, or hidden. Public portal can be accessible by URL without authentication. Private portal needs membership and list in available portal list. Hidden also needs memberships and doesn't list in available portal list.

Figure 3-14. *Portal Security*

Administrator can also see members of specific portals. People and groups can be added to a portal. Different roles can be assigned in members tab. We will look into the advanced security settings in Chapter 10.

Figure 3-15. *Portal Members*

Portal Assets

Click the Assets icon. This page allows the administrator to define the portal-specific assets like page template, skin, content presenter, page styles, task flow, etc. When portal is exported, all portal-specific assets are also exported. Administrator can make custom template, skin, and other assets developed through jdeveloper available to specific portal. Datasources based on REST or SQL can be created.

Figure 3-16. *Assets-specific portal*

Device Setting

Click on the Device Settings icon. This page shows the list of device families that can have variant pages in this portal.

Tools and Services

Click on the tool and services icon. This will display all enabled services in the portal. While enabling service, there is a message mentioning set roles for particular services.

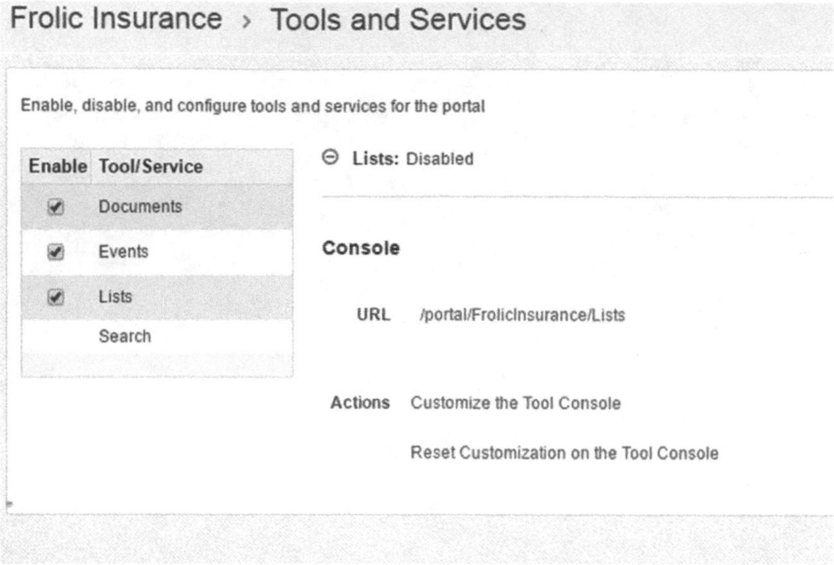

Figure 3-17. *Tools and services*

Deploy

This is a new feature in WebCenter Portal 12c. It allows users to publish a portal to a target server (that will act as the delivery environment). Click on deploy icon. Select the target server and other options for deployment on the deploy page. Administrator can deploy shared libraries, portal assets, and content with portal. This will make portal deployment process better in comparison to the previous version.

After the portal is deployed, the status of deployment is displayed on a status page. History of the portals can also be viewed.

■ **Note** Deploy icon will not be visible unless users are granted the application-level permission Portal Server-Deploy.

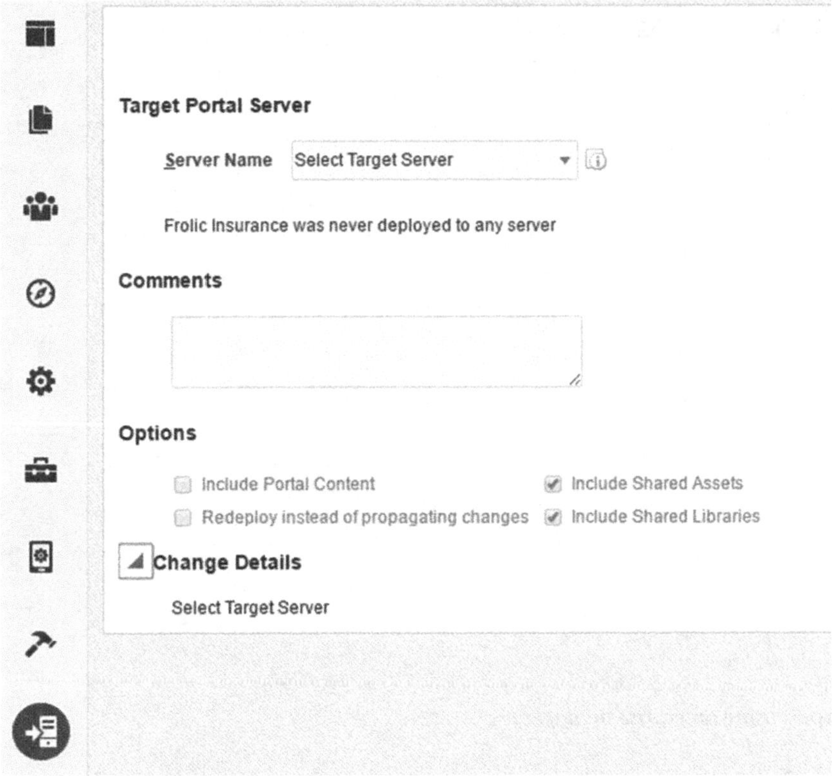

Target Portal Server

Server Name   Select Target Server   ▼ ⓘ

Frolic Insurance was never deployed to any server

Comments

Options

☐ Include Portal Content   ☑ Include Shared Assets
☐ Redeploy instead of propagating changes ☑ Include Shared Libraries

◢ **Change Details**

Select Target Server

Figure 3-18. Portal deploy options

Administrator can also deploy portal from one environment to another using wlst command by import and export process.

```
Export wlst command syntax

exportWebCenterApplication(appName='webcenter', fileName='myAppExport.par',
connectionFileName='connection.properties')
Import wlst command syntax

importWebCenterApplication(appName='webcenter',fileName='myAppExport.par')
```

There is one more option to export and import whole WebCenter application using Enterprise manager.

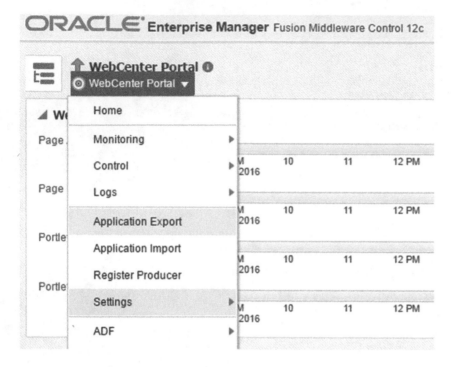

Figure 3-19. *Application export using Enterprise manager*

Pages

This manages the pages, page navigation, and structure.

1. Click on page icon. Click on create new page.

2. Select a page style as portal.

3. Provide page name and review information and click on create page.

Figure 3-20. *Portal-specific pages*

New page will open in edit mode. Portal manager can add content to this page. After creating the new page, there will be new notifications in draft icon. Portal manager needs to publish this page. Subpages can also be created inside pages. Select page and create new subpage, making the current page as parent. This will also reflect in the navigation menu.

Draft

Click on draft icon. There is a newly created page named "policy" in draft stage. This page will not be visible in the portal to the users until it is published in the draft section. Select the newly created page and click on publish.

Figure 3-21. *Publish in portal*

WebCenter Portal Administration

Navigate to the url "Host:Port/webcenter/portal/admin."

There are multiple options for setting generic WebCenter portal configurations that are not specific to one portal.

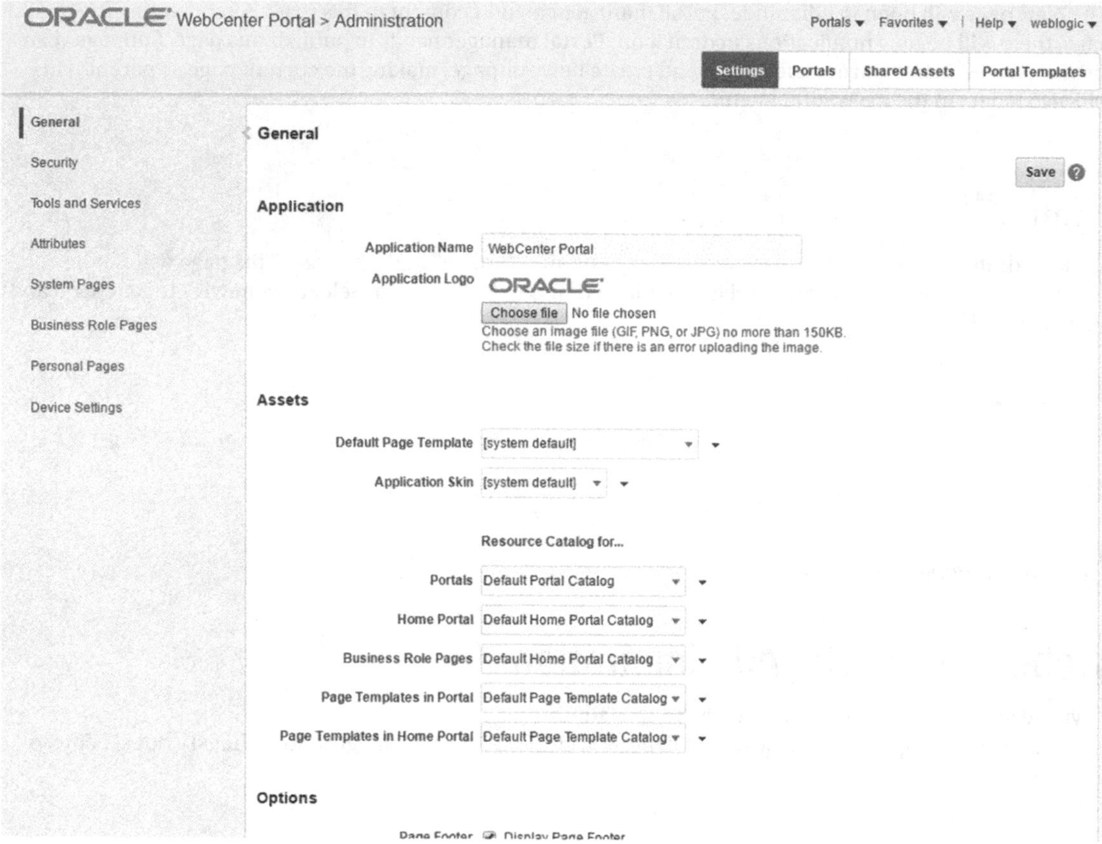

Figure 3-22. *WebCenter Portal administration*

General – In general tab, users can change Application name and application logo. There are options of changing the default page template, application skin, session timeout, etc.

Security – Administrator can manage user role assignments. New role can be created that will be applicable to whole WebCenter Portal not specific to one portal. By default, all users who log in to WebCenter Portal are granted the Authenticated-User role. Click Grant Access to assign users to other application roles or to grant administrative privileges.

Tools and Services – Portal Administrator can configure search with Oracle secure enterprise search. Different portal connections can be configured: for example, people, portlet, portal server, and external application connections.

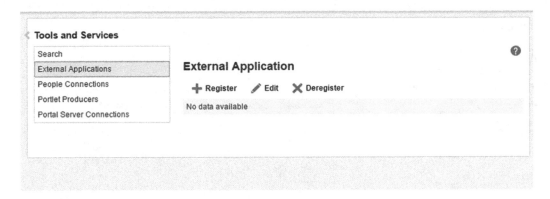

Figure 3-23. *Tools and services in portal administration*

Attributes – Attributes store information. It is like a variable/placeholder, which manages values globally and portal specific: for example, created date, description, etc. In addition to these built-in attributes, portal moderators can add custom attributes that are unique to the portal and its characteristics to specify additional portal information.

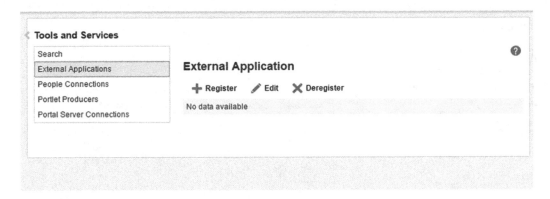

Figure 3-24. *WebCenter Portal attributes*

Attributes can be accessed using the following expression:

```
#{WCAppContext.application.applicationConfig.customAttributes[attributeName]
```

Device Settings – Device settings and related features control exactly how your portal pages are rendered on different devices. Device settings can be configured only at the application level and not at the portal level. Administrators can add support for a new type of device or device group or change the way portal pages are rendered on certain devices.

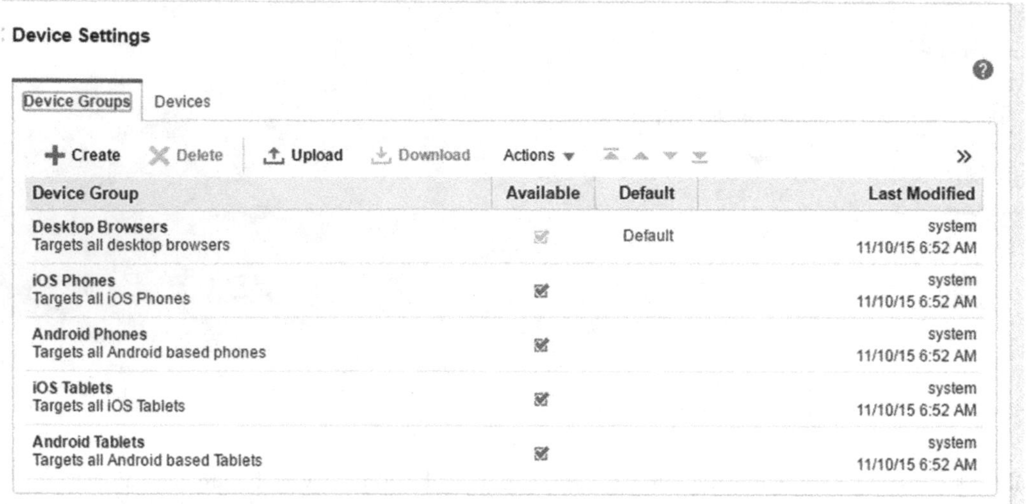

Device Settings

Device Groups | Devices

+ Create | ✕ Delete | ⬆ Upload | ⬇ Download | Actions ▾ | ⤒ ▲ ▼ ⤓ | »

Device Group	Available	Default	Last Modified
Desktop Browsers Targets all desktop browsers	☑	Default	system 11/10/15 6:52 AM
iOS Phones Targets all iOS Phones	☑		system 11/10/15 6:52 AM
Android Phones Targets all Android based phones	☑		system 11/10/15 6:52 AM
iOS Tablets Targets all iOS Tablets	☑		system 11/10/15 6:52 AM
Android Tablets Targets all Android based Tablets	☑		system 11/10/15 6:52 AM

Figure 3-25. WebCenter Portal device settings

CHAPTER 4

■ ■ ■

Portal Asset Development

WebCenter Portal offers different development strategies. One of them is via portal assets development. Assets in WebCenter Portal are different reusable building blocks that make Web Portal together. Web Portal comprises different components like css, page template, Navigation component, Page styles, task flow, content presenter, etc. All these are called Portal Assets. WebCenter Portal (WCP) gives various out-of-box assets that can be used to build a rich user interface portal. These assets are customizable and editable within each portal for specific requirements.

Following are assets in WebCenter Portal:

- Page Templates

- Resource Catalogs

- Skins

- Page Styles

- Content Presenter

- Task Flow Styles

- Layouts

- Pagelets

- Task Flows

- Data Visualizations

- Visualization Templates

- Data Controls

- Business Objects

- REST Data Sources

- SQL Data Sources

Out-of-box assets are the main pillar for portal development. It is very useful for quick and easy portal development. If these assets don't fit business requirements, then either editing or building new assets is possible using JDeveloper.

© Vinay Kumar and Daniel Merchán García 2017
V. Kumar and D. M. García, *Beginning Oracle WebCenter Portal 12c*, DOI 10.1007/978-1-4842-2532-5_4

These should be created in JDeveloper and later deployed to WebCenter Portal. Page templates, skins, layouts, page styles, Content Presenter templates, and Visualization templates are WebCenter Portal assets that can be used to create or modify asset applications in JDeveloper:

- Layouts define structure of a page, such as the number and relationship of columns, and are part of a page's page style.

- Page Styles define the layout of a newly created page, and may also dictate the type of content the page supports.

- Page Templates define a reusable outer overview of the page, on which multiple pages can be developed.

- Skins define the appearance and look and feel, including colors and fonts, of a specific portal or the entire application.

- Visualization Templates determine the layout of content in a task flow that is created at runtime. Visualization templates can also include objects that can be bound to any data visualization that is added to the task flow.

- Content Presenter Display Templates define templates for display content from enterprise content management; in our case it is WebCenter content.

Other WebCenter Portal assets that are not mentioned above can't be created or edited in JDeveloper. Figure 4-1 shows design and runtime WebCenter Portal Assets.

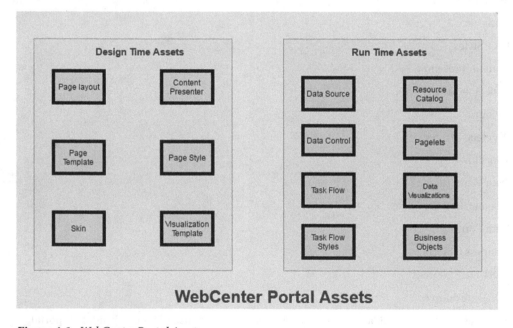

Figure 4-1. *WebCenter Portal Assets*

Setting Up JDeveloper Environment for Asset Development

- Download and install JDeveloper 12.2.1.1.

- Install WebCenter extension from update center.

- From the Help menu, select Check for Updates.

- On the Source page, select Search Update Centers. Check JDeveloper extensions from the following link – *http://www.oracle.com/ocom/groups/public/@otn/ documents/webcontent/156082.xml* .

- Check **Oracle Fusion Middleware Products** and **Official Oracle Extensions and Updates** check box and then click Next.

- From the generated list, search for the **WebCenter Core Design Time** and **WebCenter Framework and Services Design Time** extensions, select them, and then click Finish.

- When prompted, restart JDeveloper.

Create WebCenter Portal Asset Application

1. Create a new application as WebCenter Portal Asset Application.

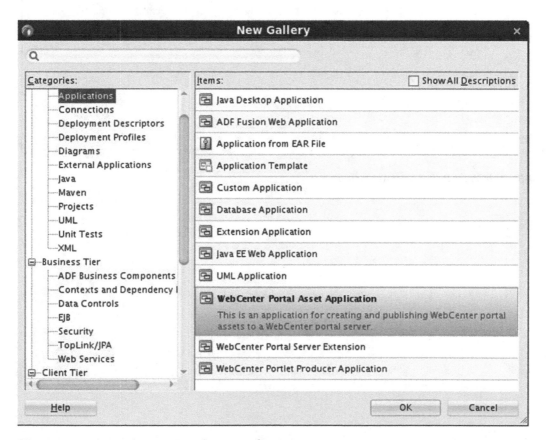

Figure 4-2. *Create WebCenter Portal Asset Application*

2. Provide **Application Name, Directory path,** and **Application Package Prefix**.
   Click next and enter **Project Name** in the wizard.

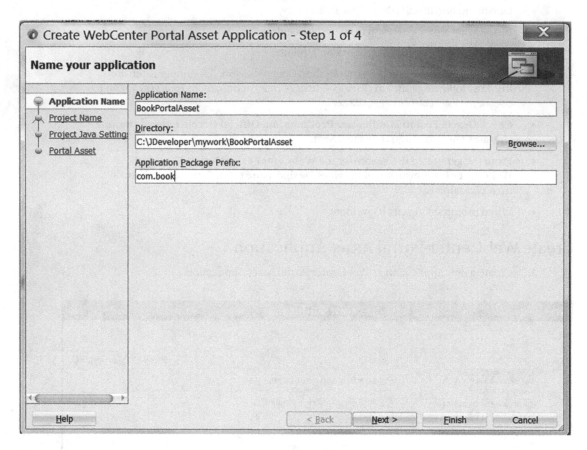

Figure 4-3. *WebCenter Portal Asset Application*

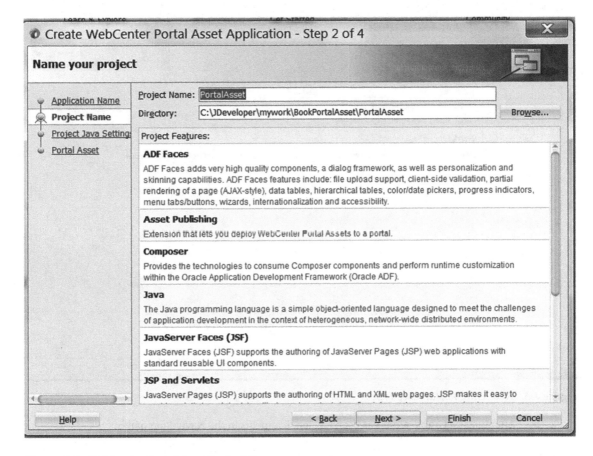

Figure 4-4. *WebCenter Portal Asset Project Name*

3. Click Next and provide optional Project Java Setting and then click Next.

4. Select the Asset Type (for example, Page Template), the Directory where the asset will be created, and click Finish.

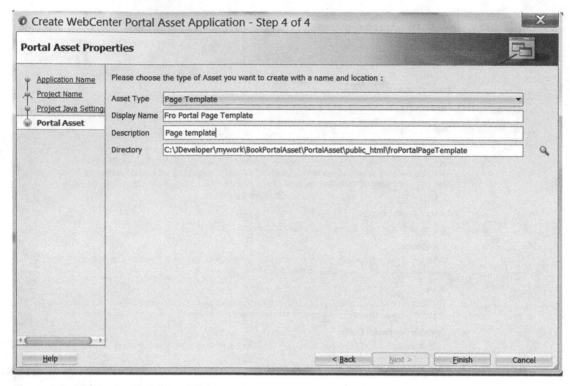

Figure 4-5. *WebCenter Portal Asset Type*

5. After the asset application has been created, it appears in the Navigation pane.

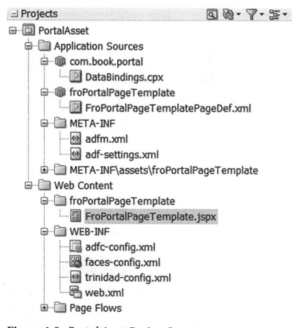

Figure 4-6. *Portal Asset Project Structure*

6. When WebCenter Portal asset application is created, the following message will be displayed in the Log Messages window, and required .jar files are added to the workspace.

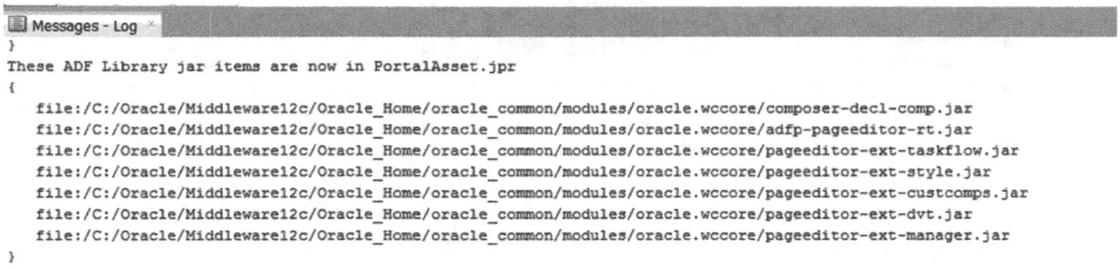

```
Messages - Log ×
}
These ADF Library jar items are now in PortalAsset.jpr
{
    file:/C:/Oracle/Middleware12c/Oracle_Home/oracle_common/modules/oracle.wccore/composer-decl-comp.jar
    file:/C:/Oracle/Middleware12c/Oracle_Home/oracle_common/modules/oracle.wccore/adfp-pageeditor-rt.jar
    file:/C:/Oracle/Middleware12c/Oracle_Home/oracle_common/modules/oracle.wccore/pageeditor-ext-taskflow.jar
    file:/C:/Oracle/Middleware12c/Oracle_Home/oracle_common/modules/oracle.wccore/pageeditor-ext-style.jar
    file:/C:/Oracle/Middleware12c/Oracle_Home/oracle_common/modules/oracle.wccore/pageeditor-ext-custcomps.jar
    file:/C:/Oracle/Middleware12c/Oracle_Home/oracle_common/modules/oracle.wccore/pageeditor-ext-dvt.jar
    file:/C:/Oracle/Middleware12c/Oracle_Home/oracle_common/modules/oracle.wccore/pageeditor-ext-manager.jar
}
```

Figure 4-7. *Portal Asset Project Structure*

7. Above-mentioned .jar files get added to application for providing the following features:

   • Asset Publishing - Allows you to publish an asset application to WebCenter Portal.

   • Page Editor - Lets you consume page components and perform runtime customizations within the Oracle Application Development Framework (Oracle ADF).

   • Customization Components - Also lets you consume Composer components and perform runtime customizations within the Oracle Application Development Framework (Oracle ADF).

8. After an asset application has been created, you can change the values for asset-specific properties, such as displayName and the Description, by editing the **assetDef.xml** file under META-INF/assets/<assetName>.

9. Double-click the FroPortalPageTemplate.jspx file to open the page template in the editor.

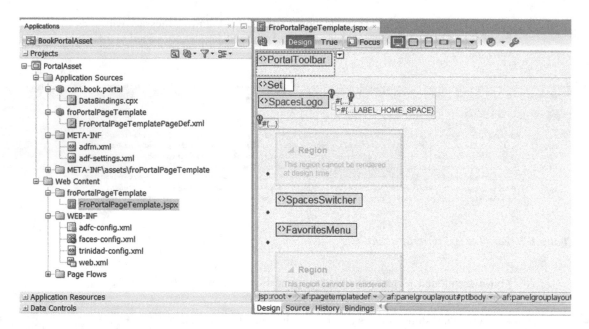

Figure 4-8. *Page Template in design mode*

10. For making the desired template, replace the contents of this page with the structure. For example, add the bootstrap template theme.

Create Portal Connection with JDeveloper

After the creation of any assets, it can be deployed to WebCenter Portal as a global shared asset or to a specific portal. For publishing assets to portal, there should be a connection between the portal and JDeveloper. WebCenter Portal server connection dialog is used to configure the connection to a portal environment.

Make connection as an application resource or as an IDE connection to reuse in multiple portal assets applications.

1. In the Application resources area, right-click on connections and select New connection-> WebCenter Portal Server Connection.

Figure 4-9. *New WebCenter Portal Connection*

2. Provide Connection Name, Host, Port, and security credentials in WebCenter Portal Connection wizard.

3. Click on test connection. If successful then click OK. Successful IDE connection for WebCenter Portal is created.

WebCenter Portal Server Connection

Creates a connection to a Portal Server. This connection is used to publish portal assets.

Create Connection in: ○ Application Resources   ● IDE Connections

Name:

```
WCP12c
```

Host:

```
http://192.168.1.74
```

Port:

```
8888
```

Service Path:

```
/rest/api/v1/resourceIndex
```

Username:

```
weblogic
```

Password:

```
••••••••
```

Test Connection

Status:

```
Portal Server Connection Successful.
```

Help   OK   Cancel

Figure 4-10. WebCenter Portal Connection wizard

4. Once IDE connection is created successfully, the connection name is displayed in Resources ➤ IDE Connections pane. By expanding connection name, shared assets and all portals in WebCenter Portal gets listed.

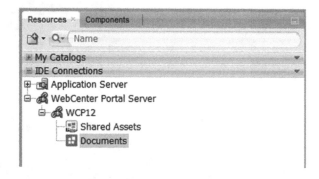

Figure 4-11. Shared assets and Portal name list

WebCenter Portal Assets Publishing

Once Portal assets is created and ready for deployment, it can be deployed to WebCenter Portal in two ways:

- Deploying portal assets application in WebCenter Portal server directly from JDeveloper using WebCenter Portal server connection.

- Deploying asset application AAR file and later importing manually in WebCenter Portal.

Deploying Application from JDeveloper

1. Right-click portal asset application and click on **Deploy** and select default deployment profile.

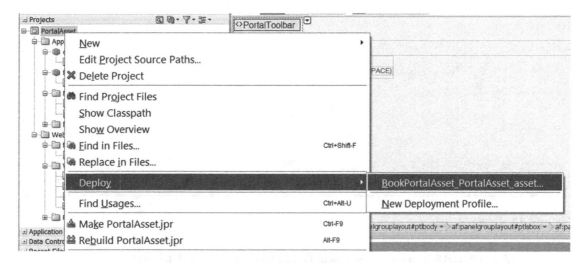

Figure 4-12. *Deploy Portal assets*

2. In **Deployment Action**, select **Deploy to WebCenter Portal**.

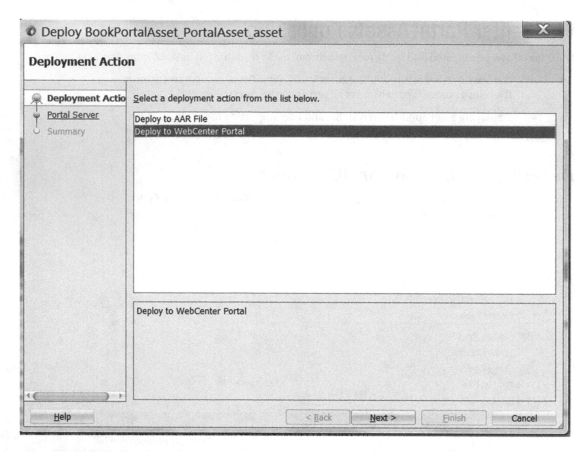

Figure 4-13. *Deploy Action*

3. Select **Portal Server** connection name (WCP12 here) and expand it. Select deployment as Shared Assets or specific to portal. Click Next.

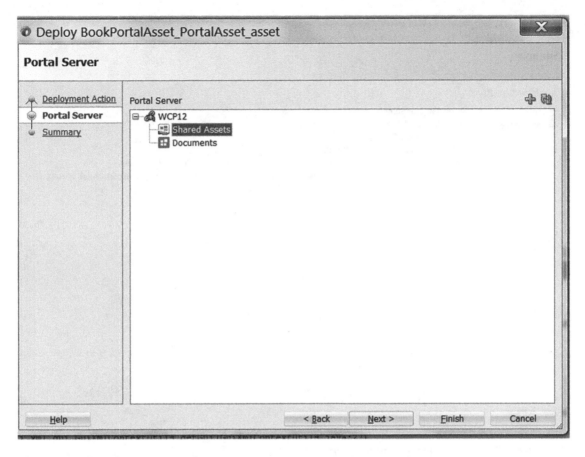

Figure 4-14. Portal server connection

4. Click Summary to view summary of your deployment selections before deploying.

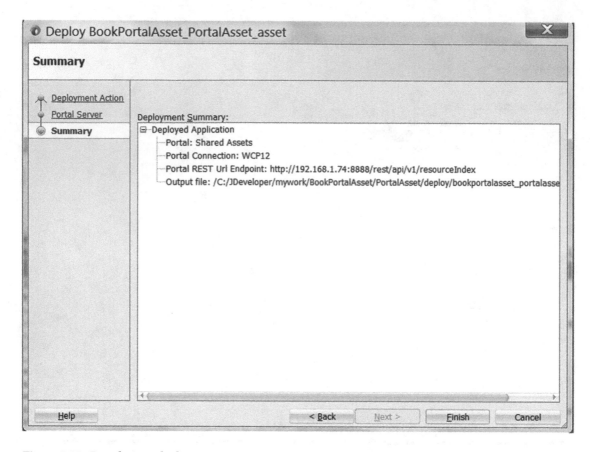

Figure 4-15. *Portal server deployment summary*

5. View in Deployment Log pane and check the status of the deployment. You can also click on the target URL of the Portal Server to view the recently deployed assets.

```
Deployment - Log
Q                              ■ -
[11:03:26 PM] ----  Deployment started.  ----
[11:03:26 PM] Target platform is Standard Java EE.
[11:03:26 PM] Running dependency analysis...
[11:03:26 PM] Deploying profile...
[11:03:26 PM] Exporting assets.
[11:03:27 PM] Wrote AAR file to C:\JDeveloper\mywork\BookPortalAsset\PortalAsset\deploy\bookportalasset_portalasset_asset.aar
[11:03:29 PM] Successfully published shared asset "Fro Portal Page Template" with response status 201 and message: "Created".
[11:03:29 PM] Successfully updated shared asset "Fro Portal Page Template" with response status 200 and message: "OK".
[11:03:29 PM] Target URL -- http://192.168.1.74:8888/webcenter/portal/admin/assets
[11:03:29 PM] Elapsed time for deployment:  3 seconds
[11:03:29 PM] ----  Deployment finished.  ----
```

Figure 4-16. *Deployment log*

6. Click on target URL to check whether newly created asset is deployed on portal or not.

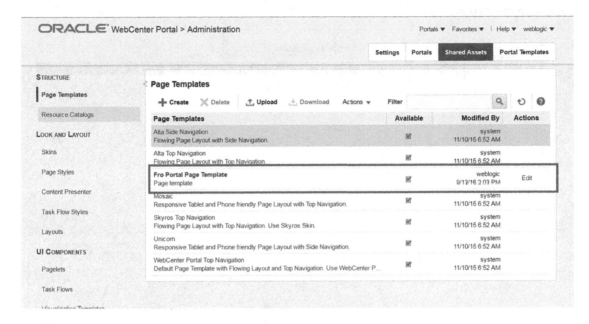

Figure 4-17. *WebCenter Portal Shared Assets*

Deployment of Assets Using AAR file

1. For deploying WebCenter Portal application as AAR file, select default deployment profile as before. In **Deployment Action** select **"Deploy to AAR File."**

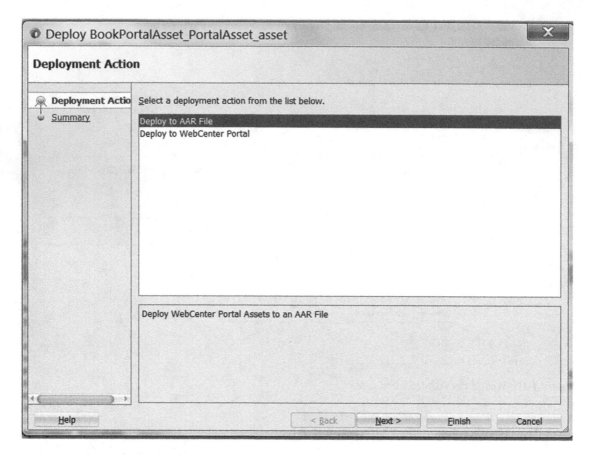

Figure 4-18. *Deploy to AAR file*

2. Click Next and finish. AAR file will be generated in file system. See path in **Deployment – Log pane**.

Figure 4-19. *Deployment Log pane – AAR file*

3. Use importWebCenterResource WLST command to import asset in the portal.

    `importWebCenterResource(appName, fileName, [resourceType, spaceName, server, applicationVersion])`

    appName - For WebCenter Portal, the name is always webcenter.

    filename - Name of the archive file that you want to import.

    resourceType - It is optional and defines the type of assets. Valid options are pageTemplate, contentPresenter, pageStyle, navigation, resourceCatalog, skin, taskFlow, mashupStyle, dataControl, device, deviceGroup.

    spaceName – It is optional. And it defines the name of the portal into which the asset is to be imported.

    Server – Name of managed server where WebCenter Portal is deployed.

    applicationVersion - It is the version number of application and is optional.

For example, the following command imports a page template from an .AAR file into a portal named "MyPortal."

```
wls:/weblogic/serverConfig>
importWebCenterResource(appName='webcenter',fileName='myPageTemplateExport.aar',
spaceName='MyPortal', resourceType='pageTemplate')
```

Similarly **exportWebCenterResource** command exports a specific asset into **.AAR** file.

Runtime Asset Development

Assets that cannot be developed and edited in JDeveloper can be created and edited in runtime in WebCenter Portal console.

Following are the assets that can be configured at runtime, for example:

- Resource Catalogs
- Pagelets
- Task Flow
- Data Control based on Web Service type
- REST Data Sources
- SQL Data Sources

Creating Data Source

WebCenter Portal supports two types of data sources, by which data can be retrieved and presented on the portal Page.

- **REST Data Source** – This data source can be configured by providing a REST API URL that can be internal or external.

- **SQL Data Source** - This data source can be configured by providing data source **JNDI** name and password for data source.

REST Data Source

1. Navigate to URL as `http://Host:port/webcenter/portal/admin/assets`. In Data Sources click REST Data Source.

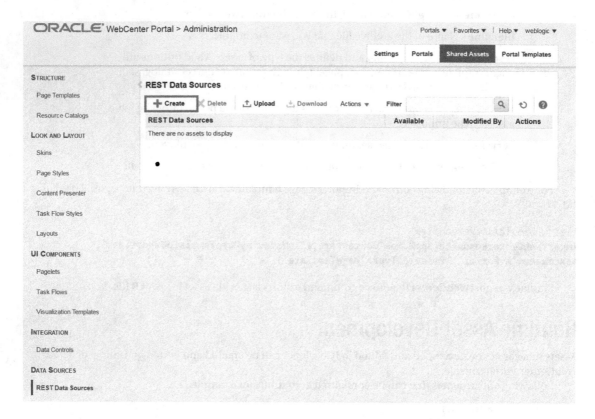

Figure 4-20. *Data control Assets*

2. Provide Data control name and Resource Path. Select Data Source Return type, whether XML or JSON. User can also provide proxy or authentication information and test.

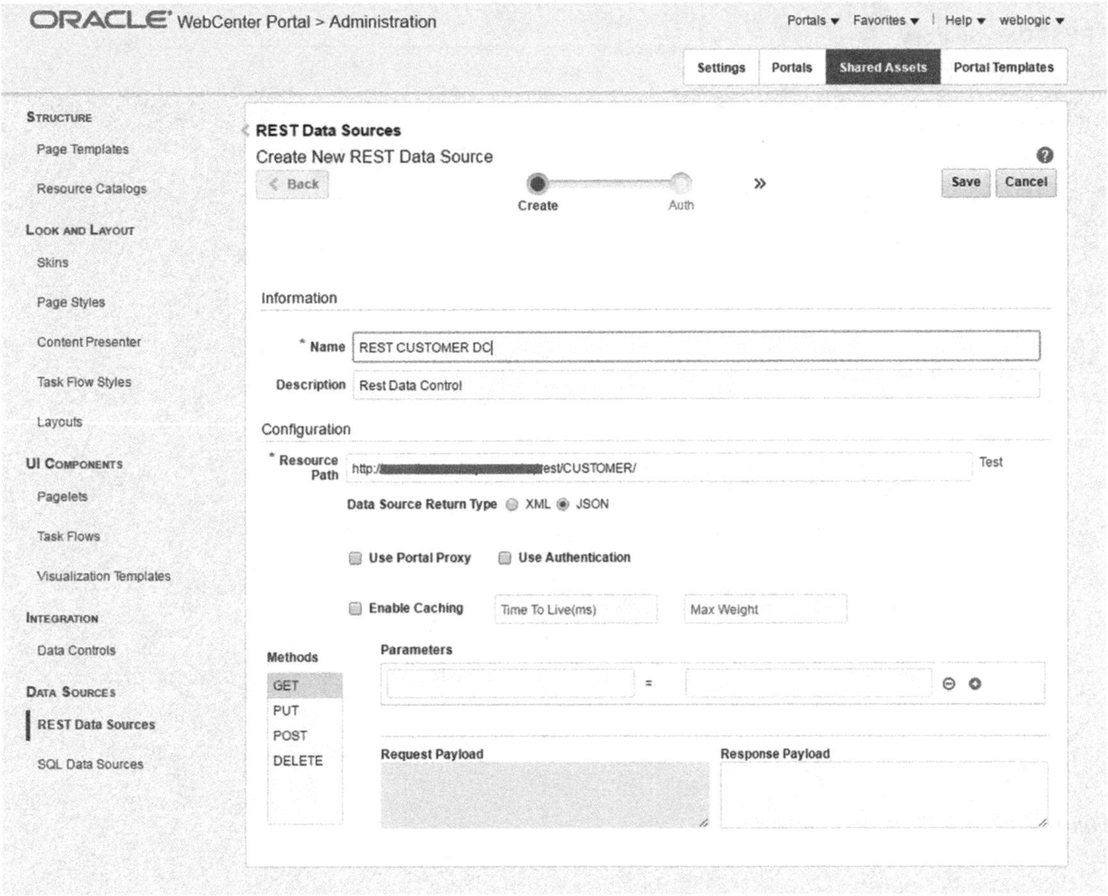

Figure 4-21. *Create REST DC*

3. If test is successful, click Save.

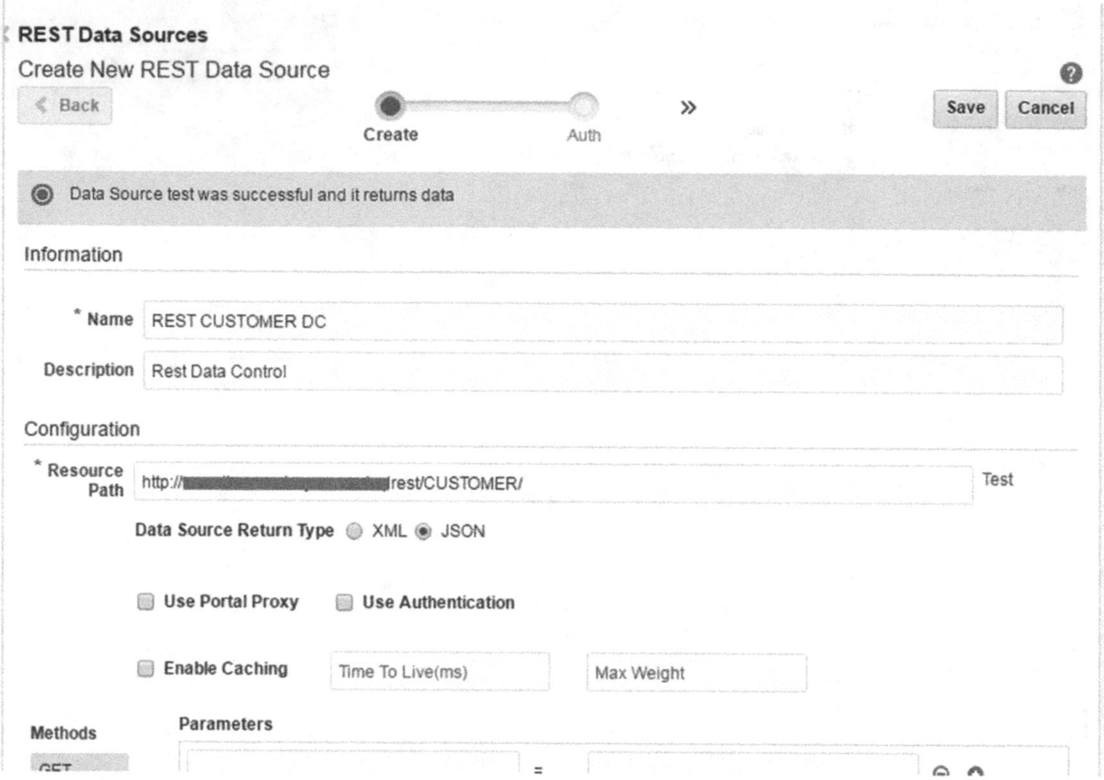

Figure 4-22. REST DC Test successful

SQL Data Source

1. In Data source section in assets page, click on SQL data source and click on create.

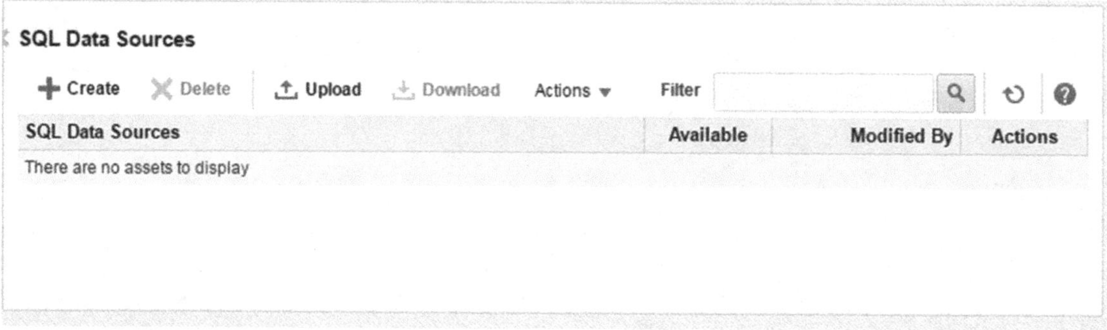

Figure 4-23. SQL DC

2. Provide Data source **Name, Description, JNDI name, and Password**. In the example provided, Database Schema is the same as default WebCenter Portal schema.

■ **Note** WebCenter Portal uses database schema to store portal-specific information like user, roles, portal information, and members of a specific portal, etc.

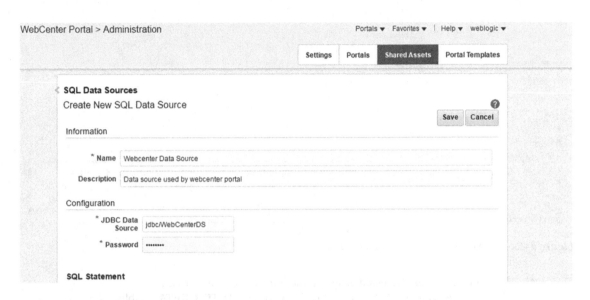

Figure 4-24. *Create SQL DC*

3. Data source can also be tested using another query, which fetches information about portal, portal display name, description, etc., from **WC_SPACE_HEADER** table.

Figure 4-25. *Test SQL DC with portal information*

4. Data source can also be tested using another query, which fetches information
   about all users, name, GUID, email, etc., from **WC_AS_ACTOR_DETAIL** table.

■ **Note** Besides *WC_AS_ACTOR_DETAIL* and *WC_SPACE_HEADER* tables, there are other tables that
contain information specific to WebCenter Portal Console. *WC_PEOPLE_CONN_CONNECTION* table stores
information about user's connection list, GUID, and relations. It is worth checking out WebCenter schema to
retrieve all portal information. ADF business component can also be created over this schema and used in a
custom ADF Task Flow to deploy on WebCenter Portal.

SQL Data Sources

Create New SQL Data Source

Save Cancel

Information

* Name Webcenter Data Source

Description Data source used by webcenter portal

Configuration

* JDBC Data Source jdbc/WebCenterDS

* Password ••••••••

SQL Statement

Select * from WC_AS_ACTOR_DETAIL

Hint: Use :bind-name to refer to bind variables in the SQL Statement

☐ **Updatable**

Test

ACTIVITY_ACTOR_DETAIL_ID	ACTOR_ID	DISPLAY_NAME	ACTOR_NAME	EMAIL
d9cb71a9-3f1a-4ec5-a78b-8ec39ab6cc...	9CB3423079A01...	bob	bob	
6d7c34ba-523f-4217-a2e8-fb20cf26c7e8	D21E2C40799C...	Julia Wilson	julia	
2a0b0160-e621-4e06-a4e7-b10cb8f1c...	617CA19074581...	weblogic	weblogic	

Figure 4-26. *Test SQL DC with portal information*

> 5. After successful test, click on Save. SQL DC gets created in portal and can be used later.

Now SQL and REST DC are created in the portal. These data sources can be used in business object, runtime Task Flow, or visualization template to display content by REST API or SQL source in portal pages. These data sources can be configured at runtime. No coding is required in JDeveloper. Built-in visualization templates or custom visualization templates can use these data sources to fetch content.

CHAPTER 5

■ ■ ■

Working with Pages and Navigation

Chapter 3 introduced some basic concepts about administering Portals by using WebCenter Portal Administration Console (Figure 5-1).

Figure 5-1. *WebCenter Portal Pages Administration*

In this chapter we will offer an in-depth view about the following items:

- **Pages:** Understand the concept of Page and learn how to create, configure, and publish pages within a Portal.

- **Navigation:** An overview about how to develop / code the navigation of a Portal in the Page Template.

What Is a Page?

Maybe the question can sound trivial. However, it can be confusing to understand all the components that are involved during the creation of a WebCenter Portal Page.

© Vinay Kumar and Daniel Merchán García 2017
V. Kumar and D. M. García, *Beginning Oracle WebCenter Portal 12c*, DOI 10.1007/978-1-4842-2532-5_5

There are four WebCenter Portal Asset Concepts involved in a Page:

- Page Template
- Page Style
- Layout
- Page (itself)

The **Page Template** defines a consistent Look and Feel (usually header and footer) for the Pages that are part of a specific Portal (Figure 5-2).

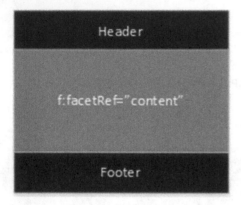

Figure 5-2. *Page Template defines the Header / Footer and a placeholder where the information will be displayed*

It must contain a placeholder / facet called **content that will be the editable area.**

The **Layout** establish the structure / grid of the facet **content** (e.g., two columns, three columns, etc.) (Figure 5-3).

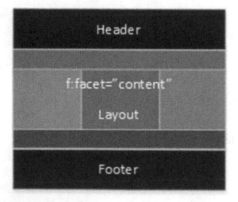

Figure 5-3. *Sample of Page using a Layout with extra header / footer and 3-column grid*

Each part of the grid has to contain an editable area to allow Portal Administrators to *Add Content / Components on to a page.*

A **Page Style** introduces the concept of templating a specific configured Page to allow end users to create similar Pages using a specific Layout and specific components preconfigured like Task Flows, Portlets, etc.

By default, a **Page Style** uses the following Portal components:

- Uses the **Page Template** that is currently configured for the current Portal.

- Uses a certain **Layout** (grid) for the body content (Figure 5-4).

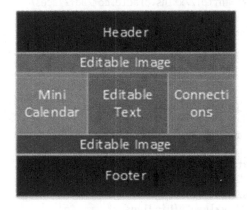

Figure 5-4. *Sample of Page Style with two preconfigured components and some Text / Image Editable empty area to be filled*

All the Page Styles included in the Out-of-the-box installation of WebCenter Portal allow the users to do the following:

- Change the Layout in Runtime.

- Add / Edit / Remove components configured or preconfigured (coming from the Page Style).

To fully understand each part of the concepts learned before, let's analyze the following code of a Page created based on an Out-of-the-box Page Style (Press Summary).

```
<?xml version='1.0' encoding='UTF-8'?>
<jsp:root version="2.1" xmlns:af="http://xmlns.oracle.com/adf/faces/rich"
xmlns:cust="http://xmlns.oracle.com/adf/faces/customizable" xmlns:f="http://java.sun.com/
jsf/core" xmlns:jsp="http://java.sun.com/JSP/Page" xmlns:trh="http://myfaces.apache.org/
trinidad/html">
  <jsp:directive.page deferredSyntaxAllowedAsLiteral="true"/>
  <jsp:directive.page contentType="text/html;charset=utf-8"/>
  <f:view>
    <af:document id="docrt" title="#{pageDocBean.title}">
      <f:facet name="metaContainer">
        <trh:meta content="#{bindings.SEO_KEYWORDS}" name="keywords"/>
      </f:facet>
      <af:form id="f1" usesUpload="true">
        <af:pageTemplate id="T" value="#{bindings.shellTemplateBinding.templateModel}">
```

```
                <f:facet name="content">
                    <af:panelGroupLayout id="pgl1" inlineStyle="replace_with_inline_style"
                    layout="scroll" styleClass="replace_with_scheme_name">
                        <af:declarativeComponent id="dclay" viewId="#{pageDocBean.layoutViewId}">
                            <f:facet name="top">
                                <cust:showDetailFrame background="light"
                                contentStyle="overflow:hidden;" displayHeader="false" id="sdf1"
                                showMinimizeAction="none" showResizer="never" stretchContent="false"
                                text="#{uib_o_w_s_r_DefaultGroupSpaceCatalog['CONTENT_PUBLISHER_
                                IMAGE.BOX_TITLE']}" xmlns:cust="http://xmlns.oracle.com/adf/faces/
                                customizable">
                                    <af:region id="img1" value="#{bindings.contentpublisherimage1.
                                    regionModel}"/>
                                </cust:showDetailFrame>
                            </f:facet>
                            <f:facet name="area1">
                                <cust:panelCustomizable id="pcarea1" layout="auto">
                                    <cust:showDetailFrame background="light"
                                    contentStyle="overflow:hidden;" displayHeader="false"
                                    id="sdf2" showMinimizeAction="none" showResizer="never"
                                    stretchContent="false" text="#{uib_o_w_s_r_DefaultGroupSpaceCatalo
                                    g['CONTENT_PUBLISHER_STYLED_TEXT.BOX_TITLE']}" xmlns:cust="http://
                                    xmlns.oracle.com/adf/faces/customizable">
                                        <af:region id="header1" value="#{bindings.
                                        contentpublisherheader1.regionModel}"/>
                                    </cust:showDetailFrame>
                                    <cust:showDetailFrame background="light"
                                    contentStyle="overflow:hidden;" displayHeader="false"
                                    id="sdf3" showMinimizeAction="none" showResizer="never"
                                    stretchContent="false" text="#{uib_o_w_s_r_DefaultGroupSpaceCat
                                    alog['CONTENT_PUBLISHER_TEXT.BOX_TITLE']}" xmlns:cust="http://
                                    xmlns.oracle.com/adf/faces/customizable">
                                        <af:region id="txt1" value="#{bindings.
                                        contentpublishertext1.regionModel}"/>
                                    </cust:showDetailFrame>
                                </cust:panelCustomizable>
                            </f:facet>
                        </af:declarativeComponent>
                    </af:panelGroupLayout>
                </f:facet>
            </af:pageTemplate>
        </af:form>
    </af:document>
  </f:view>
</jsp:root>
```

■ **Note**   To inspect the source code of a Portal Page (Select the Page in the Pages Administration view,

click ![▶] (Page options) and then Page Information ➤ Source tab). Here you can see the Page and Page Definition source code.

The **Page Template** is referred by:

```
<af:pageTemplate id="T" value="#{bindings.shellTemplateBinding.templateModel}">
```

This is the Out-of-the-box way to refer to the configured Page Template in the Settings of the Portal or to the Page Template configured in the settings of the Page (if selected one different from the *Portal Default*).

■ **Caution**   When developing new Page Styles, please do not refer statically to a Page Template within the af:pageTemplate tag. Copy from an Out-of-the-box Page Style to replicate the same mechanism to allow changing Page Templates dynamically using Portal Administration Console.

The **Layout** is referred by the following part of the code:

```
<af:declarativeComponent id="dclay" viewId="#{pageDocBean.layoutViewId}">
```

This code makes the Layout customizable and it can be changed in Runtime by the Portal Administrator (Figure 5-5).

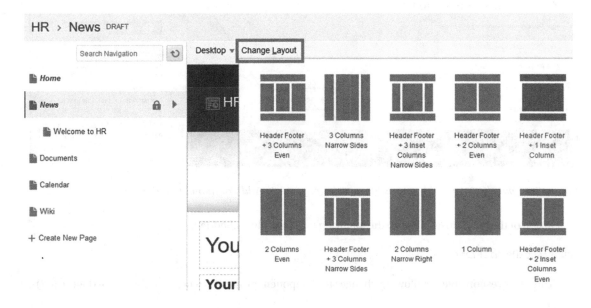

Figure 5-5. *Change Layout available for Portal Administrators*

■ **Caution**   Please, do not forget to include the Declarative Component for allowing the Change Layout functionality in your Page Styles.

The editable areas where *Add Content* are shown is because the presence of the following Oracle Composer tag:

```
<cust:panelCustomizable id="pcarea1" layout="auto">
```

This tag makes an editable area when editing a Portal Page (Figure 5-6).

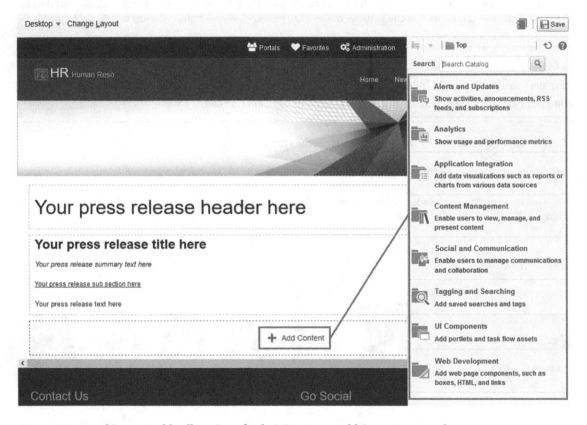

Figure 5-6. *panelCustomizable allows Portal Administrator to Add Components to the page*

Inside of the panelCustomizable, the following tag is usually embedded:

```
<cust:showDetailFrame>
```

This tag is responsible for allowing changes to Component properties when editing a Page (Figure 5-7).

Figure 5-7. showDetailFrame *allows the Portal Administrator to administrate and change the configuration of the components*

■ **Note** After adding a new Component using *Add Component*, it automatically generates a snippet of code like this:

```
<af:showDetailFrame><af:region/></af:showDetailFrame>
```

The af:region is the component (Task Flow or Portlet) added to the page.

In case of developing from JDeveloper, developers will need to wrap the components with af:showDetailFrame to make them configurable in Runtime by administrators.

How Can I Create a Page Style Base on a Page?

In Chapter 4 we learned how to create the different Portal Assets using JDeveloper.

However, it is possible to create Page Styles from configured Pages using the Administration Tools.

As a Portal Administrator, a Page can be configured with some Text Style, Image components, or components such Task Flows that we want to reuse to allowing other users to create similar pages.

Instead of populating the Text areas with real information, let them with descriptive information that the user can use for completing the information (Figure 5-8).

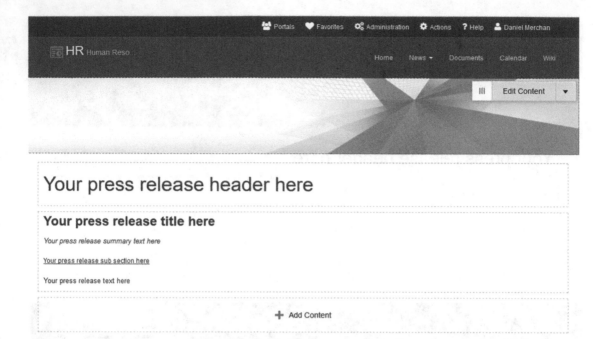

Figure 5-8. *Press-Release Page ready to be templated as Page Style to be reused. It includes Image header, Text Header, Body Text, and an additional Placeholder to add other components if needed*

For example, a new Page Style can be created, based on the existing Press-Release Page Style. Follow the next steps for doing so:

- Click **+ Create New Page** and then select *Press-Release Page Style*.

- Add some editable components from the Resource Catalog. The editable components are found in **Content Management** folder (**Image, Styled Text, Text**).

- Compose the page as desired and add some sample text.

- Save the page and then click ▶ (Page Options) and Save as Page Style.

Once the Page is ready to be "Templated" then click on ▶ and *Save As Page Style* (Figure *5-9*).

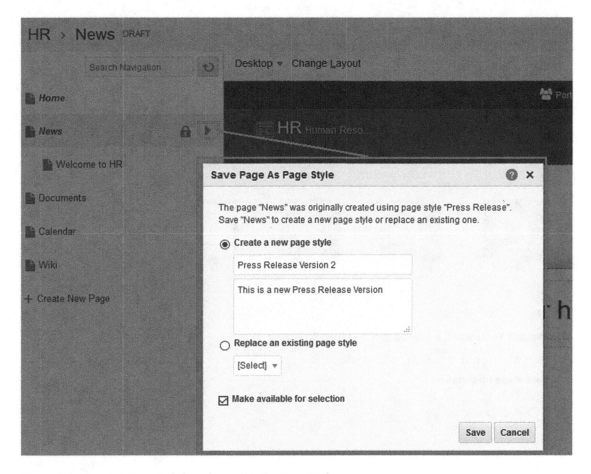

Figure 5-9. *Create a Page Style based on a existing Page Dialog*

Now, the new Page Style can be used when creating new pages (Figure 5-10).

Figure 5-10. *List of available Page Styles to be used*

■ **Tip** Go to the Administration of Assets ➤ Page Styles ➤ Your new Page Style ➤ Actions ➤ Edit Properties. Here you can change the property Icon URI for changing the ICON displayed within the page style.

Types of WebCenter Portal Pages

Oracle WebCenter Portal consists of four different types of Portal Pages.

Type	Description
System Page	Set of **pre-built** pages that are included **Out-of-the-box** in a WebCenter Portal Installation. For example: Page Not Found, Unauthorized page, Search page, WebCenter Portal Welcome Page, etc. In addition, there are some pre-built pages with some of the Portal Services components preconfigured. For example: Documents Page is already set up to display the content related to the Portal, including this page.
Business Role Page	Pages that are targeted for a **specific type of audience** / role. Usually this type of page is accessed from the Home Portal, but it can be used for sharing information across multiple Portals via Page Link (more information later on Working with Portal Pages). For example: Activities page, Documents page, Analytics page, Profile page, etc.
Personal Page	Pages created by the end users that **only are available though the user's Home Portal**. For example: Any custom page created by the end users will appear under Personal Page.

Relationship between Portals and Pages

The location of the pages is strongly linked to the Portal hierarchy.

Depending on the type of page, they are stored and located in different parts of the WebCenter Portal Architecture (Figure 5-11).

- **System Pages** are part of the webcenter.ear (pre-seeded pages).

- **Business Role Pages** and **Personal Pages** are on the level of the Home Portal. It means that they can be exposed in the Home Portal and also across the new created Portals. They are stored in the MDS (Metadata Repository).

- **Portal Pages** are scoped locally to the Portal that belong to and stored in the MDS (Metadata Repository).

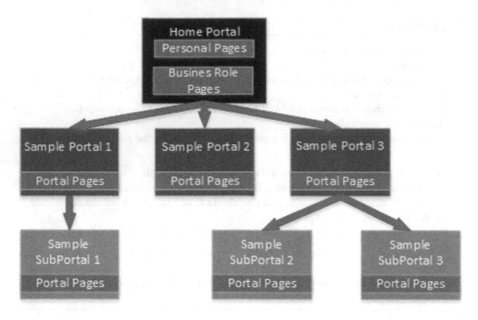

Figure 5-11. *Portal Hierarchy and Pages*

■ **Note**　The Home Portal is the base Portal that Oracle WebCenter Portal brings Out-of-the-box. It exposes all the Business Role Pages and Personal Pages created that the user has access to.

In addition, the created Portals / Subportals can have links to the Business Role Pages, and they will be displayed only if the user has the needed roles assigned.

Working with System Pages

A Portal Administrator can access the System Pages table by navigating to Administration ➤ Settings ➤ System Pages (Figure 5-12).

As commented before, System Pages are pre-seeded pages and configured with WebCenter Portal components that are already in use by the system or can be used within the Portals that we are creating.

The Oracle documentation only talks about System Pages. However, it can be split into two different types of System Pages.

- System Pages that are already in use by the Platform such Login Page, Error Page, or Self-Service Registration.

- Pages including Portal Services preconfigured that can be used in the new Portals created by the Portal Administrator. Pages such Documents, Discussions, Announcements, etc.

The following table shows a summary of the Out-of-the-box pages offered by WebCenter Portal and what an Administrator can do on them:

Table 5-1. *System Pages*

Page Name	Type	Description	Operations
About WebCenter Portal	System Page	Page used to show the About WebCenter information.	Customizable
Activities	Portal Service Page	Page configured to display the Activity Publisher and the Activity Stream for tracking activities for the Home Portal.	Customizable
Activity Stream	Portal Service Page	Appears by default on the Home page in the built-in portal template. It displays the activities for the current Portal.	Customizable
Analytics	Portal Service Page	Includes the Overall Analytics Task Flow for checking the usage of the Portals.	Customizable
Announcements	Portal service Page	It has preconfigured the Announcements Task Flow for displaying the latest announcements of the current portal.	Customizable
Discussions	Portal Service Page	Shows the discussion manager Task Flow.	Customizable
Documents	Portal ServicePage	Configured to display the documents of the current logged user. It is used in the Home Portal.	Customizable
Documents	Portal Service Page	Configured to display the documents of the current portal.	Customizable
Error Encountered	System Page	It is the default page shown when an unexpected behavior occurs in WebCenter Portal. Highly recommended to customize.	Create Page Variant and Customizable
Events	Portal Service Page	This page shows the current events for the current portal.	Customizable
Lists	Portal Service Page	The page is preconfigured with the List service allowing users to create lists and milestones and share it with other users.	Customizable
Members	Portal Service Page	Displays the member for the current portal.	Customizable
No Pages Accessible	System Page	It is the default page shown when a page is not accessible. Highly recommended to customize.	Create Page Variant and Customizable

(*continued*)

Table 5-1. (*continued*)

Page Name	Type	Description	Operations
Page Not Found	System Page	It is the default page shown when a page is not found in the system. Highly recommended to customize.	Create Page Variant and Customizable
Portals	Portal Service Page	Shows the list of portals that can be accessed by the current logged user.	Customizable
Portal Templates	Portal Service Page	Configured to display the list of Portal Templates available.	Customizable
Profile	Portal Service Page	Displays the profile gallery for the current logged user.	Customizable
Public Portals	Portal Service Page	The same as the Portals page, but it shows only the Public Access portals.	Customizable
Resource Viewer	System Page	This page is used internally by WebCenter Portal for rendering resources from the WebCenter Services. Please, do not customize or modify this page.	Customizable
Search	Portal Service Page	Page used for displaying Search Results.	Customizable
Self-Registration	System Page	It is the page displayed to the user when registering for an account.	Create Page Variant and Customizable
Self-Service Membership	Portal Service Page	Page configured to display the component that allows the registered users to request access to specific private Portals.	Customizable
Sign In	System Page	This page came from previous versions of WebCenter Portal and it displays the same page for Login as the *Welcome Page.*	Create Page Variant and Customizable
Tag Center	Portal Service Page	Allows the user to search pages and documents tagged by another user.	Customizable
Task Flow Editor	System Page	Used for customizing Task Flows. Please, do not customize or change this system page.	Customizable
Task Flow Viewer	System Page	Used for displaying Task Flows when exposed in a Portal Navigation instead of embedded into a Page. Please, do not change this internal system page.	Customizable

(*continued*)

Table 5-1. (*continued*)

Page Name	Type	Description	Operations
Unauthorized	System Page	Page displayed to the user when trying to access to a protected resource without the proper rights. Highly recommended to customize.	Create Page Variant and Customizable
Unavailable	System Page	Page displayed when a Portal is inactive, deleted, or offline (Unavailable). Highly recommended to customize.	Create Page Variant and Customizable
User Profile	Portal Service Page	Displays the profile galley of the other users.	Customizable
WebCenter Portal Welcome Page	System Page	The page displayed when an unauthenticated user arrives to WebCenter Portal. It shows the Login and Self-Registration links. Highly recommended to customize.	Create Page Variant and Customizable
Wikis	Portal Service Page	Page with the legacy Documents Explorer for managing Wiki Documents.	Customizable

■ **Note**   Please note that we remarked in the above table that we highly recommend to customize some pages. Please customize these pages to adapt them to the customer look and feel and logo.

System Pages cannot be created.

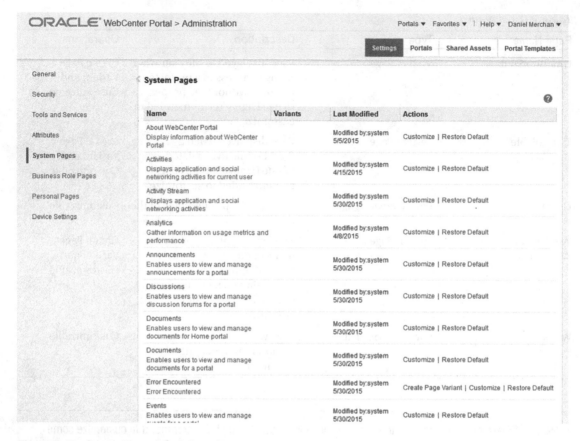

Figure 5-12. *System Pages Administration*

Working with Business Role Pages

A Portal Administrator can access the *Business Role Pages* table by navigating to Administration ➤ Settings ➤ Business Role Pages (Figure 5-13).

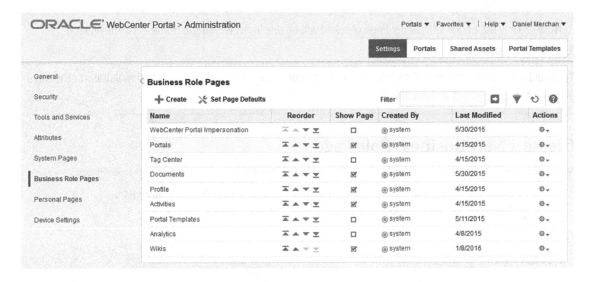

Figure 5-13. *Business Role Pages Administration*

The Out-of-the-box Business Role Pages offered in WebCenter Portal are described in the following table:

Table 5-2. *Business Role Pages*

Page Name	Description	Comments
WebCenter Portal Impersonation	Displays a page where the Portal Administrator can assign impersonation rights to a selected group of users ("impersonators") so that they can perform operations as other users ("impersonatees").	It requires Oracle Access Manager properly configured for using this service. This book will not cover this functionality; but this can be found in Oracle Documentation. Target: Administrators
Activities	Shows the activity stream of the current logged user. In addition, it displays activities from other Portals (not only Home Portal) the user has access to.	Same as the System Page. Target: authenticated-users
Analytics	Displays the metrics related to the portal, documents, pages, etc.	Same as the System Page. Hidden by default. Target: Administrators
Documents	Display the personal folder and documents of the current logged user.	Same as the System Page. Target: authenticated-users
Profile	Display the logged user Profile Gallery including the most important information of the user, connections, activities, etc.	Same as the System Page. Target: authenticated-users
Portal Templates	Displays a list of portal templates and provides a means of creating custom portal templates and filtering the template list.	Same as the System Page. Target: authenticated-users
Portals	Shows the list of portals that can be accessed by the current logged user.	Same as the System Page. Target: authenticated-users

■ **Note**   Only the pages with Show Page checked will be displayed within the Home Portal navigation (Excepting Wikis).

The real Business Role Page in the above list is Impersonation as it is focused only for Administrators. The other pages are coming from the System Pages.

Create a New Business Role Page

New Business Role Pages can be created using the administration interface of Business Role Pages.

- Click ➕ **Create** for starting the creation wizard for a new Business Role Page (Figure 5-14). Set a Page Name and select one of the available Page Styles.

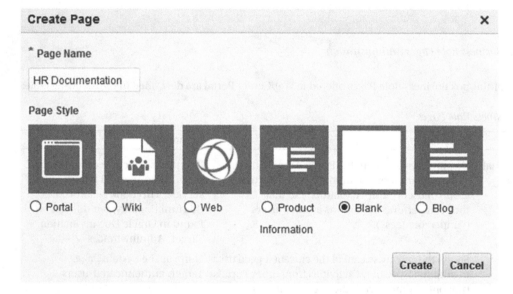

Figure 5-14. *Create new Business Role Dialog*

- Now the new Business Role Page will appear into the list of Business Role Pages. See Figure 5-15.

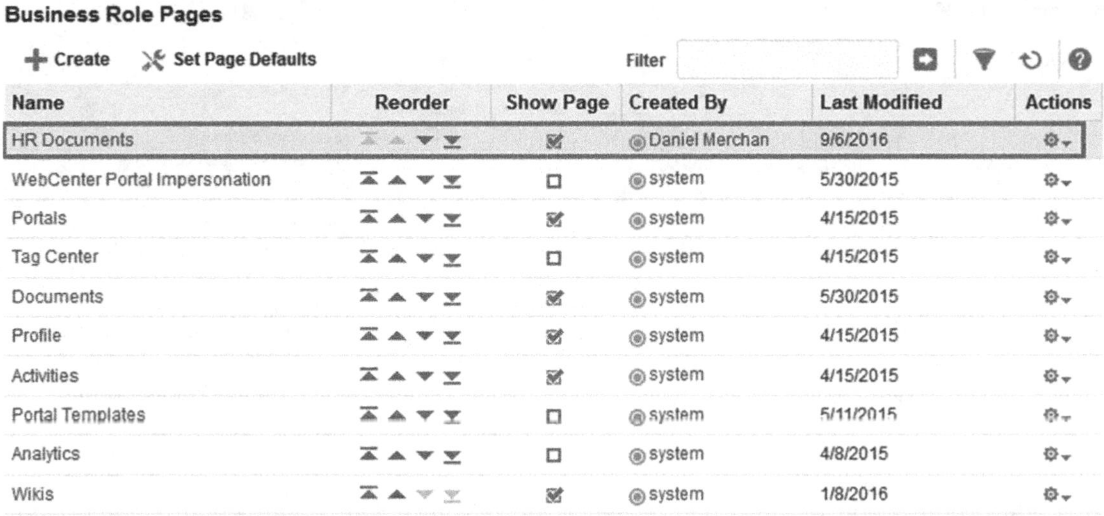

Business Role Pages

➕ Create   ✂ Set Page Defaults   Filter [   ]   ▣ | ▼ ↻ | ❓

Name	Reorder	Show Page	Created By	Last Modified	Actions
HR Documents	⊼ ▲ ▼ ⊻	☑	⊚ Daniel Merchan	9/6/2016	⚙▾
WebCenter Portal Impersonation	⊼ ▲ ▼ ⊻	☐	⊚ system	5/30/2015	⚙▾
Portals	⊼ ▲ ▼ ⊻	☑	⊚ system	4/15/2015	⚙▾
Tag Center	⊼ ▲ ▼ ⊻	☐	⊚ system	4/15/2015	⚙▾
Documents	⊼ ▲ ▼ ⊻	☑	⊚ system	5/30/2015	⚙▾
Profile	⊼ ▲ ▼ ⊻	☑	⊚ system	4/15/2015	⚙▾
Activities	⊼ ▲ ▼ ⊻	☑	⊚ system	4/15/2015	⚙▾
Portal Templates	⊼ ▲ ▼ ⊻	☐	⊚ system	5/11/2015	⚙▾
Analytics	⊼ ▲ ▼ ⊻	☐	⊚ system	4/8/2015	⚙▾
Wikis	⊼ ▲ ▼ ⊻	☑	⊚ system	1/8/2016	⚙▾

Figure 5-15. *New Business Role Page added*

■ **Note**   By default, the page is marked as Show Page. However, do not be scared of it. It will not be displayed as there is no security setting assigned to the Page yet. Therefore, it is not accessible.

- Before setting up the security. Click ⚙▾ and select Edit Page to set up the Page adding some components (Figure 5-16).

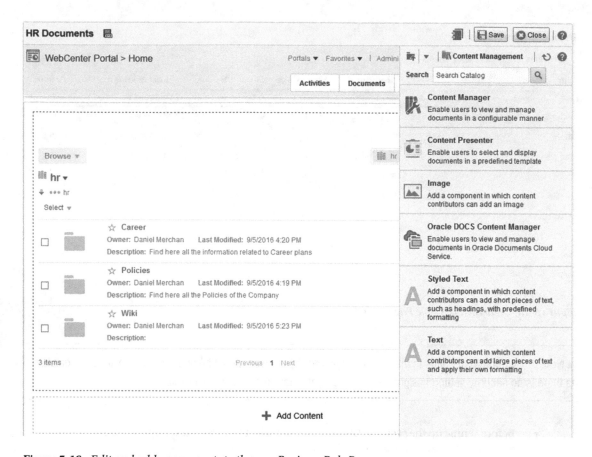

Figure 5-16. *Edit and add components to the new Business Role Page*

- After finishing editing the page, go back to the administration of Business Role Pages and then Click ⚙ ▾ ➤ **Set Page Access** and choose the Roles that can access the newly created page.

■ **Note**   Portal Security is explained later on in this book.

- Now the new Business Role Page will be displayed in the Home Portal for all the users who have the right Roles (Figure 5-17).

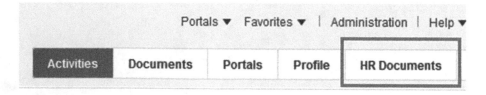

Figure 5-17. *The new Business Role Page now is part of the Home Portal*

■ **Tip**   Use Business Role Pages to display information focused to specific audiences via Home Portal.

Use Business Role Pages for Pages that will be shown across multiple Portals.

Working with Personal Pages

Users can create Personal Pages to create their own dashboards or pages with information to be displayed in the Home Portal or shared with other users (Figure 5-18).

■ **Tip**   A good example is a personal blog.

Figure 5-18.   *Personal Page in the Home Portal*

Create a Personal Page

Personal Pages can be created from the Home Portal by clicking ⚙️ ▼ and then selecting *Create Page*.

The dialog displayed is the same as the Business Role Page where the user can choose a base Page Style in order to create the page.

■ **Caution**   The action menu ⚙️ ▼ is displayed Out-of-the-box in the Home Portal because by default it uses Alta Top Navigation Page Template.

The default Page Templates of Oracle WebCenter Portal display the ⚙ ▼ (action menu). It can be included in a *Custom Page Template* by adding the following snippet of code:

Page:

```
<af:panelGroupLayout id="pglbl" inlineStyle="position:absolute;top:0px;right:0px;margin-
top:3px;" layout="vertical">
        <af:button clientComponent="true" disabled="#{portalToolbarContext.portalToolbar.editMode}"
                        icon="#{requestContext.rightToLeft ? '/adf/webcenter/
                            agentdropdown_rtl_sm_ena.png' : '/adf/webcenter/
                            agentdropdown_sm_ena.png'}"
                        id="actionsMenuLink"
                        rendered="#{!serviceCtx.scope.spaceTemplate and
                            (WCAppContext.currentScope.default ? ((!AdminConfig.
                            fusionAppsMode and security.homeSpaceEnabled) or
                            security.webCenterAdministrator): empty pageFlowScope.
                            contextActionsTaskFlow)}" shortDesc="#{uib_o_w_w_r_
                            WebCenter['NAV_TOOLS_ACTIONS_FOLDER.DESCRIPTION']}"
                        styleClass="WCActionsButton">
                <af:showPopupBehavior align="afterStart" alignId="actionsMenuLink" popupId="
                    actnRegion:actionsDropdownPopup"/>
        </af:button>
        <af:region id="actnRegion" rendered="#{!serviceCtx.scope.spaceTemplate and
            (WCAppContext.currentScope.default ? ((!AdminConfig.fusionAppsMode and security.
            homeSpaceEnabled) or security.webCenterAdministrator): true)}" value="#{bindings.
            spacesActionSubmenu.regionModel}"/>
</af:panelGroupLayout>
```

PageDef (binding to the actions Task Flow):

```
<taskFlow activation="deferred" id="spacesActionSubmenu" taskFlowId="#{not empty
pageFlowScope.contextActionsTaskFlow ? pageFlowScope.contextActionsTaskFlow : '/oracle/
webcenter/webcenterapp/view/taskflows/navigation/SpacesNavigationComponents.xml#SpacesNaviga
tionComponents'}" xmlns="http://xmlns.oracle.com/adf/controller/binding">
        <parameters/>
    </taskFlow>
```

What to Know about Administering Personal Pages

All Personal Pages created by users with rights to do it can be administered by accessing the WebCenter Portal Administration ➤ Settings ➤ Personal Pages (Figure 5-19).

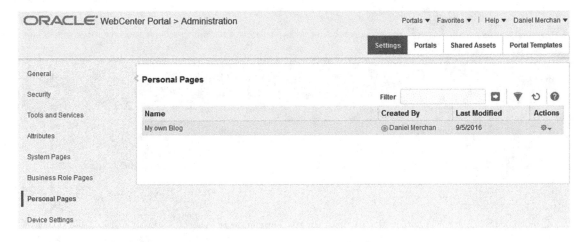

Figure 5-19. *Administration Page for Personal Pages*

Administrators can do the following tasks on the Personal Pages:

- **Edit Page**. They can help the users by adding components and setting up their pages.

- **Delete Personalization.** If any Task Flow has been customized, they can then revert it to the original without customizations.

- **Copy Page.** Administrators can copy the Page into a new Personal Page or a new Business Role Page if they consider that the page contains useful information for a specific target audience (Figure 5-20).

- **Rename the Page.**

- **Set Page Access.** To modify the security for allowing / disabling specific audiences to access the page.

- **Edit Source.** In case a developer needs to analyze or change the Page in case of bugs.

- **Delete Page.**

- **Make Public.** All the users can access to the Personal Page of the author.

- **Send via Mail.** Share the new Personal Page via E-Mail.

- **About this Page.** Basic information including the URL for directly accessing the Page.

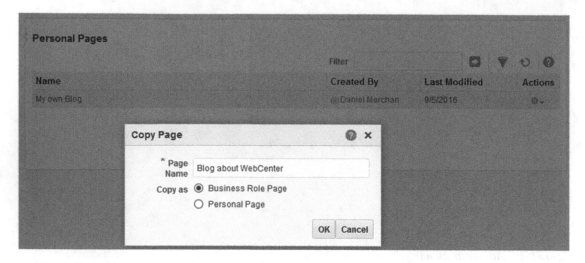

Figure 5-20. *Copy a Personal Page onto a Business Role Page*

■ **Note**   The users will require administrator assistance for changing the Page Access or to make them public.

■ **Caution**   If an employee leaves the company, ask your Portal administrator to remove the Personal Pages created by that user. Or just hide them.

Working with Portal Pages

Business Role Pages and Personal Pages are displayed mainly in the Home Portal.

The **Portal Pages** are the key to the newly created Portals. They represent the **Portal Hierarchy and Structure** about how the information and components will be displayed.

Portal Pages Administration Interface is can be accessed by clicking ▉ in the Portal Administration Toolbar displayed in the left side when Administering / Editing a specific Portal (Figure 5-21).

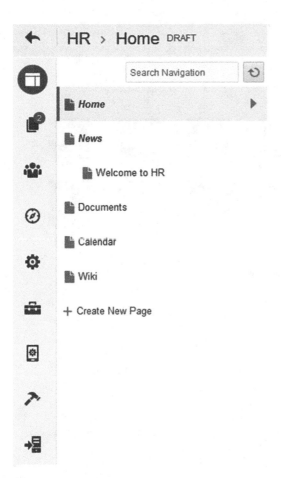

Figure 5-21. *Portal Pages Administration*

By default, a Portal is created with a Home page and the pages that you added during the Creation Wizard (Figure 5-22).

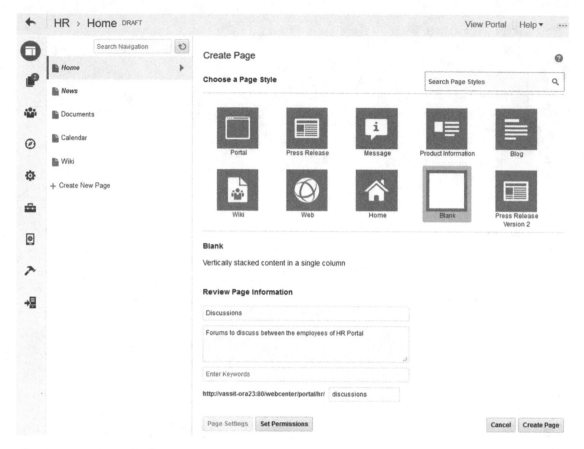

Figure 5-22. *Create Page Dialog*

Click the Quick Link + *Create New Page* to access directly to the creation of a New Page within the Portal. In this dialog the following information has to be provided:

- **Select a Page Style:** The base Layout and components preconfigured for the new Page.

- **Page Name:** Provide a unique name to the page (it cannot be duplicated).

- **Keywords:** It is very important to provide a set of Keywords. It will be used by the Tag Center for searching Pages and Documents with the same Tags.

- **URL:** It generates the end of the URL based on the Page Name. Change it if necessary.

■ **Tip**   Always change the URL to lowercase to unify the URL.

■ **Note**   The prefix **/webcenter/portal** of the WebCenter Portal URLs such /webcenter/portal/[portalname]/ [subportalname]/[page]/[subpage1] cannot be changed or removed. It is a limitation of the product.

More information about Oracle WebCenter Portal Pretty URLs in Oracle Documentation: https://docs.oracle. com/middleware/12211/wcp/build/GUID-4CB4CDFD-8F89-4C0C-A66A-E5C1789F9D5A.htm#WCPAA2454

In addition, there is another way for creating pages and not only pages. In addition, links to other items or parts to the portal can be created.

Click 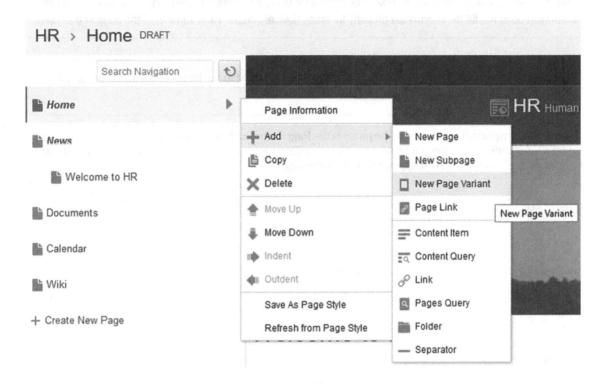 and then click *Add* to show all the options that a Portal Administrator can create (Figure 5-23):

Figure 5-23. *Administration options for a Portal Page*

- **Add New Page**: It is the same functionality as + Create New Page. It will create the page and put the page after the selected one in the hierarchy.

- **Add Sub Page**: Same as the creation of a Page. In this case it will indent the page as a child of the selected one.

- **Add Page Variant**: Use this option for creation a variant of the selected page. A Page Variant is another version of the current page that will be rendered only for a specific set of Devices configured for that Page Variant. For example, if you have a page with lot of information and components, then maybe this page is not properly readable for mobile devices. Creating a Page Variant in this case allows you to reduce the number of components or use a different layout more suitable for these specific devices.

- **Page Link**: It expose links to pages in Subportals or in the Home Portal.

- **Content Item**: Use it for adding links to direct documents of the Content Repository.

- **Content Query**: Add a collection of links to specific documents based on a CMIS Query.

- **Pages Query**: List of pages based on a query.

- **Folder**: Used for structuring the Portal Hierarchy.

- **Separator**: Used for adding separators between items of the Portal Hierarchy.

■ **Note**   Page Template and Layouts should be developed using a responsive design. However, sometimes the information does not fill the information properly for small devices. Create Page Variants of the page in that case.

■ **Caution**   The usage of Folder and Separator items are very linked to the Page Template and the way that the developer used it for rendering the navigation.

Another important option about the pages is the **Page Information**. Here the Portal Administrators can set up a lot of different options and attributes for a specific page (Figure 5-24). Some of the most important options of the Advanced Tab are explained in the following tables.

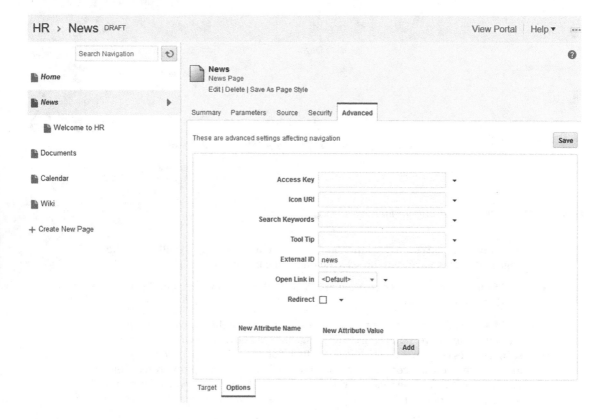

Figure 5-24. *Attributes of a Navigation Item*

(Some of the information displayed in the following tables comes directly from Oracle Documentation.)

Table 5-3. *Target Tab*

Property	Applies to (not all type of navigation items)	Description
ID	All items types	Unique ID for the navigation item. It is used when using Navigation API for rendering a navigation. Change it if necessary to something more descriptive.
Name	All items types	The name to be displayed in the Portal Navigation.
Description	All items types	Just a descriptive text for the navigation item.
Visible	All items types	Use this Boolean property to hide / show an item link based on an EL Expression.
Path	Content Item Content Query Page Link	Here is where you provide the URL or set up via the helper wizard the link to a specific page, item, or items.
Content Presenter Template	Content Item	Select the Template to use to display the content coming from the Content Repository.
Hide Top-Level Folder	Content Query Pages Query	Select to display the results of the query or reference directly rather than displaying them under a folder.
Page Template	Content Item Link Page Link Pages Query	Select a different Page Template in case you do not want to use the default establish for the Portal.
Query String	Content Query	To enter the CMIS Query Criteria for selecting the proper documents to display. For example: **SELECT * from cmis:document where IN_ TREE('/Enterprise Libraries/hr').**
Find Pages in	Page Query	Here you can select: • Home Portal: to include the pages of the Home Portal. • Portal: to add the Home page of a specific portal and all its other pages to the portal navigation. • Path: to add a specific page and all its subpages to the portal navigation.
Page Style	Pages Query	Used for filtering pages based on a specific Page Style.

(*continued*)

Table 5-3. (*continued*)

Property	Applies to (not all type of navigation items)	Description
Excluded Page Styles	Pages Query	Enter the paths of one or more page styles, separated by commas or spaces, to exclude from the page query. For example: /oracle/webcenter/siteresources/scopedMD/ s8bba98ff_4cbb_40b8_beee_296c916a23ed/ pageStyle/gsr1b60e8a7_2e23_48ff_9571_31ed e592de1a/TemplateWiki.jspx, /oracle/webcenter/siteresources/scopedMD/ s8bba98ff_4cbb_40b8_beee_296c916a23ed/ pageStyle/gsr1b60e8a7_2e23_48ff_9571_31ed e592de1b/TemplateBlog.jspx
Visibility	Pages Query	Select from the below list: • Show all items: To expose every page in the results of the query regardless of the *Visible* property. • Show only visible items: to show every page that also is *Visible*. • Show all but visible items: to show every page with the *Visible* property *false*.

■ **Tip**   The Paths location to specific items such as Page Styles, Page Templates, or other items of WebCenter Portal can always be checked from the Show Properties option in the Shared Assets Administration Interface.

■ **Note**   Content Presenter Templates are explained later on in the Chapter on Content Integration.

Table 5-4. *Options Tab*

Property	Description
Access Key	Key mnemonic (single character) that can be used to access the navigation item without using the mouse.
	It is used when using Navigation API for rendering a navigation.
	Change it if necessary to something more descriptive.
Icon URI	Path to an image that can represent the navigation item.
Search Keywords	Tags that facilitate the search for a specific navigation item. It can help by using the Tag Center for searching for tagged items.
Tool Tip	Brief description that will be shown in a mouse hover of the item.
External ID	ID to enable a direct reference to the item from a static link in the page.
	It is used for referencing statically to a page from external links.
	Why is External ID useful? Because the Pretty URL to a specific page can change. For example, if the Portal Administrator movers the Page to be a Subpage it will change.
	Usage:
	• /faces/wcnav_externalId/externalId from af:link in a Page
	• /wcnav_externalId/externalId in an External Link
	To directly access to a particular node of a specific Portal you can use:
	• /faces/wcnav_externalId/myNavigationItem?wc.contextURL=/spaces/myProjectSpace
	Use the parameter wc.contextURL as /spaces/[portal]/[subportal] to setup the Portal context
Open Link in	Depending on the type of navigation item you can set up how to open the link.
	For example, if it is an External Link you can open in the Same Window. In case of a Page you can use this attribute for setting if navigate using PPR navigation (Partial Refresh within the Page Template) or just a link to the specific PrettyUrl of the page.
Redirect	*For External Link navigation items only*
	This option is very important as it will render within the Page Template or redirect to the specific link.

Publishing Portal Pages

This is one of the new Features included in the 12c version that was missing in the 11g version of WebCenter Portal.

When a Contributor / Editor / Portal Administration changes or edits a Portal Page then this page will be marked as *Draft*.

In case a contributor changes text or other contents of a Page then the Portal Contribution Toolbar

will mark the icon with a blue background that indicated that the Published page and the latest saved page are different.

By Clicking ![Switch icon] (Switch) icon, then a Contributor User or Administrator can switch and see the differences between the published version and the new version of the page.

A Portal Administrator or Reviewer can publish the page by accessing to the Portal Administration toolbar and clicking ![Drafts icon] (Drafts) icon. This icon indicates how many pages are pending to Publish.

The Publish Administration interfaces is very Simple (Figure 5-25). It contains a table indicating the latest version published by who and when was the latest modification was done and by whom.

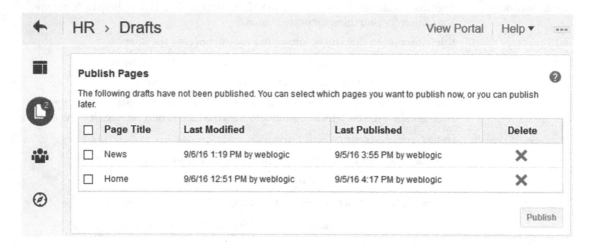

Figure 5-25. *Pages Publishing Interface*

An Administrator has to select what pages to publish and then click *Publish*. After publishing, the page will disappear from the table and users will access the newest version.

Rendering a Portal Navigation

The Portal Navigation is usually rendered within the Portal Page Template asset.

Out-of-the-box, WebCenter Portal offers two Runtime Task Flows that render the Portal Navigation that can be used as a base to understand how to render Navigation (Figure 5-26).

- Portal Side Navigation: Displays a Side navigation.

- Portal Top Navigation: Displays a Top Navigation.

Figure 5-26. *Out-of-the-box Navigation Task Flows*

These Task Flow are used by the default Alta UI Page Templates used by the product. You can find an `<af:region>` inside of these Page Templates that are linked to the Task Flows commented above.

■ **Tip**   Create a copy of the Top and Side Navigation Task Flows to access the source code in the Shared Assets Administration Console. It will give you an idea about how Alta Template renders its navigation.

There are millions of different of ways to render a Portal Navigation based on how the Portal Hierarchy is built.

For rendering the navigation of a Portal, Developers use the following EL Expression to access to the current context of the navigation.

`#{navigationContext}`

This EL Expression allows the developer to access, iterate, and operate over the Navigation of the current Portal.

Some of the APIs offered can be found in the following table (not all have been included, please check Oracle Documentation to refer the complete list).

Table 5-5. *Useful Navigation EL Expressions*

EL Expression	Usage
#{navigationContext. defaultNavigationModel}	Returns default navigation model. It gets the value from the preference bean.
#{navigationContext. currentNavigationModel}	Returns the current navigation model for the current view / current portal.

#{navigationContext. processAction}	Returns the default navigation method for binding to UI component's actionListener attribute. It is used for PPR (Partial Refresh Navigations) within the Page Template. For example:
	
	`<af:forEach var="node" varStatus="vs"`
	`  items="#{navigationContext.defaultNavigationModel.rootNode.`
	`children}">`
	`    <af:subform id="pt_sfm1">`
	`      <af:commandLink id="pt_cl1"`
	`        text="#{node.title}"`
	`        inlineStyle="font-size:small;color:White;"`
	`        actionListener="#{navigationContext.processAction}"`
	`        action="pprnav">`
	`      <f:attribute name="node" value="#{node}"/>`
	`        <af:showPopupBehavior popupId="menuPopup"`
	`          align="afterStart"`
	`          triggerType="mouseOver"/>`
	`    </af:commandLink>`

#{navigationContext. defaultNavigationModel. defaultTreeModel} #{navigationContext. defaultNavigationModel. defaultMenuModel} #{navigationContext. defaultNavigationModel. defaultListModel} #{navigationContext. defaultNavigationModel. defaultSiteMap}	Returns different representations of the Navigation Model (full Portal Hierarchy) that can be used with different ADF Components: • TreeModel: for using a <af:tree> component • MenuModel: for <af:breadcrumbs> or <af:menu> • ListModel: for iterate over it using <af:iterator> or <af:forEach> • SiteMap: Returns an XML representing the SiteMap.
#{navigationContext. defaultNavigationModel. treeModel['parameters']} #{navigationContext. defaultNavigationModel. menuModel['parameters']} #{navigationContext. defaultNavigationModel. listModel['parameters']} #{navigationContext. defaultNavigationModel. siteMap['parameters']}	Returns the representation of the navigation model, but filtered by the given parameters: • startNode=/—specify the starting node of the model (do not need "/" prefix unless requesting the root node, for example, home). • includeStartNode=true—specify true if you want to include the starting node (for example, the root node above) or false to start from its children. • depth=0—defines the initial depth of fetching. "0" means fetch the entire tree, which may take a long time. In which case, use "1" to fetch on demand (when users click the Expand icon). • prefetchOnly=false—by default (true), it returns nodes up to the depth level requested initially; deeper level nodes are returned on demand. Use false if you want only the initial sets of nodes. In which case, it does not return deeper nodes later on when requested, even when there are deeper nodes.

As a minimal example, the following code just iterates over the current navigation and prints it using ADF Faces + HTML 5 + CSS 3 Bootstrap.

```
<div class="header-menu hidden-xs">
        <af:iterator id="i1" rows="0" value="#{navigationContext.currentNavigationModel.
            listModel['startNode=/, includeStartNode=false']}" var="item">
                <div class="menu-item #{item.selected ? 'active' : ''}">
                        <a alt="#{item.attributes['ToolTip']}" href="/webcenter#{item.goLink
                                PrettyUrl}">#{WCTruncator[item.title]['25']}</a>
                </div>
        </af:iterator>
</div>
```

The code shown above just iterates and renders the first level of the navigation. In addition, it uses CSS style classes offered by Bootstrap. Font-Awesome and Bootstrap CSS are part of WebCenter Portal and can be added to the Page Template by including the following snippet of code:

```
<link href="/webcenter/uilibs/fontawesome/4.1.0/css/font-awesome.min.css" rel="stylesheet"
type="text/css"/>
        <link href="/webcenter/uilibs/bootstrap/3.2.0/css/bootstrap.min.css"
                rel="stylesheet" type="text/css"/>
```

The navigation rendering code usually is embedded in a Page Template by using one of the following techniques:

- **Embedding** the code directly in the Page Template Source Code. Recommended option if the **code is short and will not be reused** in other Page Templates.

- By wrapping it in a **Portal Asset - Runtime Task Flow**. There are two navigation Runtime Task Flows that Oracle WebCenter Portal offers by default (They can be found on Portal Administration ➤ Shared Assets ➤ Task Flows):

  - **Portal Side Navigation**: It renders a side navigation.

  - **Portal Top Navigation**: It renders a top navigation.

For example, the Alta Top Navigation Template uses the Portal Top Navigation Task Flow for rendering the Portal Navigation.

If you want to try the code shown above or your own code, then we suggest you create a copy of an existing Page Template, assign it to the Portal (by changing the General Settings in the specific Portal Administration interface), and then replace the navigation part code with your code.

In addition, there are lots of attributes and properties that can be accessed from a node. This table only represents some of them.

(*Check Oracle Documentation for a complete list.*)

Table 5-6. *Some of the useful Navigation Item EL Expressions*

EL Expression	Usage
#{node.title}	Title of the resource node.
#{node.externalURL}	The URL configured when the node is an External Link.
#{node.goLinkPrettyUrl}	Returns the friendly URL to the node to be used in an af:link or <a href> tag.
#{node.navigable}	Returns a Boolean to know if the node is navigable or not. For example, folders and separators are not navigable items.
#{node.separator}	Returns a Boolean to check if the current item is a separator. It is used to print some HTML on between the navigation nodes.
#{node.leaf}	To know if the current node is a leaf.
#{node.parent}	For accessing to the parent node in case of a Subpage.
#{node.selected}	Returns a Boolean if the current node is the selected in the current navigation model.

Another complex example is the following one extracted from the **Unicorns Page Template included by default in Oracle WebCenter Portal**:

```
<af:iterator id="i1" value="#{boilerBean.navigationModelPath == null ? navigationContext.
defaultNavigationModel.listModel['startNode=/, includeStartNode=false'] : navigationContext.
navigationModel[modelPath=boilerBean.navigationModelPath].listModel['startNode=/,
includeStartNode=false']}" var="side_menu_item">
                <af:switcher facetName="#{( side_menu_item.separator ?
                    'separatorFacet' : (boilerBean.navigationModelPath == null ?
                    (o_w_w_sc_i_v_b_spacesPageTemplate.excludedPage[navigationContext.
                    defaultNavigationModel.node['/'].parametersRaw['excludedPages']]
                    [side_menu_item.path] ? 'null' : (!empty side_menu_item.children
                    or side_menu_item.navigable ? 'menuItemFacet' : 'null')) : (o_w_w_
                    sc_i_v_b_spacesPageTemplate.excludedPage[navigationContext.navig
                    ationModel[modelPath=boilerBean.navigationModelPath].node['/'].
                    parametersRaw['excludedPages']][side_menu_item.path] ? 'null' :
                    (!empty side_menu_item.children or side_menu_item.navigable ?
                    'menuItemFacet' : 'null')) ) )}" id="s1">
                <f:facet name="separatorFacet"/>
                <f:facet name="menuItemFacet">
                    <af:switcher facetName="#{!(!empty side_menu_item.parametersRaw['
                        visibilityCondition'] and !o_w_w_sc_i_v_b_spacesPageTemplate.
                        check[side_menu_item.parametersRaw['visibilityCondition']]) ?
                        ( empty side_menu_item.children ? 'navigationItemFacet' :
                        'navigationMenuFacet') : 'null'}" id="s3">
                    <f:facet name="navigationItemFacet">
                        <li class="#{side_menu_item.selected == 'true' ? 'active' : ''}">
                            <a href="#{facesContext.externalContext.
                                requestContextPath}#{side_menu_item.goLinkPrettyUrl}">
                                <i class="fa #{!empty side_menu_item.attributes
                                        ['fa-icon'] ? side_menu_item.attributes
                                        ['fa-icon'] : 'fa-home'}"/>
                                <span id="menuitem">#{side_menu_item.title}</span>
```

```
                    </a>
                  </li>
                </f:facet>
                <f:facet name="navigationMenuFacet">
                  <li class="submenu #{boilerBean.navigationModelPath ==
                      null ? (side_menu_item.id == navigationContext.
                      defaultNavigationModel.currentSelection.parent.id ? 'active
                      open' : '') : (side_menu_item.id == navigationContext.na
                      vigationModel[modelPath=boilerBean.navigationModelPath].
                      currentSelection.parent.id ? 'active open' : '')}">
                    <a href="#">
                      <i class="fa #{!empty side_menu_item.attributes
                              ['fa-icon'] ? side_menu_item.attributes
                              ['fa-icon'] : 'fa-home'}"/>
                      <span id="submenu">#{side_menu_item.title}</span>
                      <i class="arrow fa fa-chevron-right"/>
                    </a>
                    <ul>
                      <af:iterator id="i2" value="#{side_menu_item.
                          children}" var="side_submenu_item">
                        <af:switcher facetName="#{!side_submenu_item.
                            separator and side_submenu_item.navigable and
                            !(!empty side_submenu_item.parametersRaw['visi
                            bilityCondition']
                                and !o_w_w_sc_i_v_b_spacesPageTemplate.
                                    check[side_submenu_item.parameters
                                    Raw['visibilityCondition']]) ?
                                    'navMenuChildFacet' : 'null'}" id="s4">
                          <f:facet name="navMenuChildFacet">
                            <li class="#{side_submenu_item.selected ==
                                'true' ? 'active' : ''}">
                              <a href="#{facesContext.externalContext.
                                  requestContextPath}#{side_
                                  submenu_item.goLinkPrettyUrl}">
                                <i class="fa #{!empty side_submenu_
                                    item.attributes['fa-icon'] ?
                                    side_submenu_item.attributes
                                    ['fa-icon'] : 'fa-home'}"/>
                                <span id="subitem">#{side_submenu_
                                    item.title}</span>
                              </a>
                            </li>
                          </f:facet>
                        </af:switcher>
                      </af:iterator>
                    </ul>
                  </li>
                </f:facet>
              </af:switcher>
            </f:facet>
          </af:switcher>
        </af:iterator>
```

Here it shows a navigation of two levels using some of the useful EL Expressions and mixes ADF Faces with HTML 5, which will help you to achieve your navigation look & feel easier.

In order to understand better the above code let's explain it by parts:

- The first iterator: just set the Navigation Context in the root of the Page Hierarchy.

- The first switcher is checking if the current item node is a Separator or a Menu Item.

- In case of a Separator then it does not render anything.

- In case of a Menu Item, then it checks if the current item is visible. If it is visible, then it checks if it has children or not for rendering a multilevel menu or just a link.

Some of the important EL Expressions shown in the above example are:

- #{facesContext.externalContext.requestContextPath}: This EL Expression calculates the first part of the URL (http(s)://[host]:[port]/webcenter).

- #{side_submenu_item.goLinkPrettyUrl}: The goLinkPrettyUrl property helps for building a link to a node.

- side_menu_item.attributes['fa-icon']: Custom Attributes can be contributed for a specific Portal Page by accessing to Page Options ➤ Page Information ➤ Advanced Tab ➤ Options Tab. Here a Portal Manager can set up custom attributes that can be used when rendering the navigation. In this example, it is used for choosing the icon to be displayed within the navigation link.

- We strongly recommend that you create a Copy of the Unicorn or Mosaic Page Templates and change the navigation source code in order to understand how the navigation rendering works.

■ **Caution**   boilerBean is an advanced managed bean that holds advanced information. It is used by WebCenter Product Development. Avoid using undocumented code and just focus on navigationContext EL API.

■ **Tip**   Build the navigation using Bootstrap CSS in order to render the navigation properly depending on the device that is accessing the Portal. For example, Mosaic and Unicorn Out-of-the-box Templates use it for rendering the menu depending on the device width.

■ **Caution**   How the Page Template is developed affects how the Page Hierarchy has to be.

For example: Sometimes you split the links shown in the Header in a Header Folder and the links to be shown in the Footer in a Footer Folder. In this case the Page Template will use the following EL Expression in each part for retrieving the proper links:

```
#{navigationContext.defaultNavigationModel.listModel['startNode=/pages_header,
includeStartNode=false']}
```

This means that all the links that you want to display have to be added under the header folder. If you want to use this Page Template for other Portal, then you have to have to take this into consideration when building the Portal Pages Hierarchy.

CHAPTER 6

■ ■ ■

Extend Portal with Shared Libraries

Out-of-the-box, **Oracle WebCenter Portal** offers tools for creating Portals and Pages consuming data from REST, Web Services, or Database. However, sometimes you are required to develop complex components, which are difficult to achieve using only the Runtime tools.

Using **JDeveloper IDE**, developers can extend Oracle WebCenter Portal deploying **custom Oracle ADF assets** such **ADF Task Flows**, **Managed Beans**, and **Data Controls** such as Shared Libraries into the Application Server.

What Are Shared Libraries?

Shared Java EE libraries in **WebLogic Application Server** provides a mechanism for sharing Java EE Modules among Enterprise Applications.

■ **Note**   The Shared Libraries are commonly packaged in WAR or EAR files.

Using this mechanism, applications will reference external libraries instead of packaging them internally in the J2EE libraries folders such as WEB-INF/lib or APP-INF/lib.

For a better understanding about the shared-libraries mechanism, Figure 6-1 shows how **J2EE Application B** and the **J2EE Application C** share the same libraries deployed in the **shared-library2.war**. In addition, the **shared-library2.war** depends on other two Shared Libraries called **shared-library3.war** and **shared-library4.war.**

■ **Note**   Shared Libraries is a WebLogic Application Server mechanism and not a J2EE standard. J2EE Applications need a WebLogic Descriptor File (such **weblogic.xml**) for referencing them.

© Vinay Kumar and Daniel Merchán García 2017
V. Kumar and D. M. García, *Beginning Oracle WebCenter Portal 12c*, DOI 10.1007/978-1-4842-2532-5_6

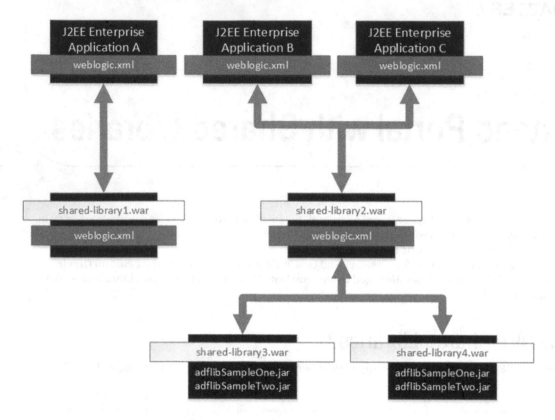

Figure 6-1. *This is an example of Shared Libraries in WebLogic Application Server*

Understanding WebCenter Portal Shared Library

Oracle WebCenter Portal is a **pre-packaged** J2EE Enterprise Application (EAR) build on top of Oracle ADF Framework. Developers cannot directly modify a WebCenter Portal EAR file. Then how can developers add extra functionality to Oracle WebCenter Portal? The answer is easy, using **Shared Libraries**.

By default, Oracle WebCenter Portal references a Shared Library called **extend.spaces.webapp.war**. This Shared Library is used for extending WebCenter Portal for including custom Oracle ADF assets (ADF Bounded Task Flows, Managed Beans, Data Controls, etc.).

■ **Note**   **Portlets** are not developed and deployed within **extend.spaces.webapp.war** Shared Library. Portlets are deployed separately and consumed remotely in WebCenter Portal via WSRP 2.0 standard.

There are two ways for working with Portal Shared Library (Figure 6-2):

- Adding the ADF Assets directly into the Portal Shared Library extend.spaces.webapp.war

- Referencing external Shared Libraries from the extend.spaces.webapp.war

■ **Tip**   We strongly recommend that you develop your extensions in different Shared Libraries referenced from the Portal Shared Library.

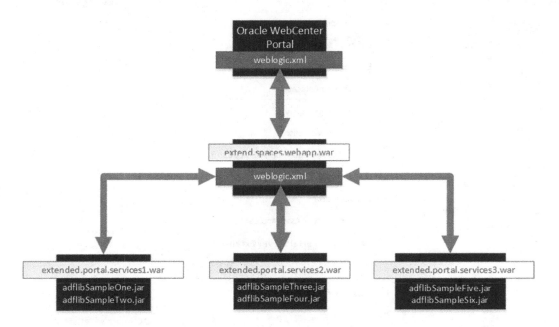

Figure 6-2. *Portal Shared Library referencing external Shared Libraries*

WebCenter Portal Server Extension

Developers uses **JDeveloper** Application Template: **WebCenter Portal Server Extension** (Figure 6-3) for deploying new versions of **extend.spaces.webapp.war shared library.**

■ **Note**   JDeveloper requires the following extensions installed: **WebCenter Core Design Time** and **WebCenter Framework and Services Design Time.**

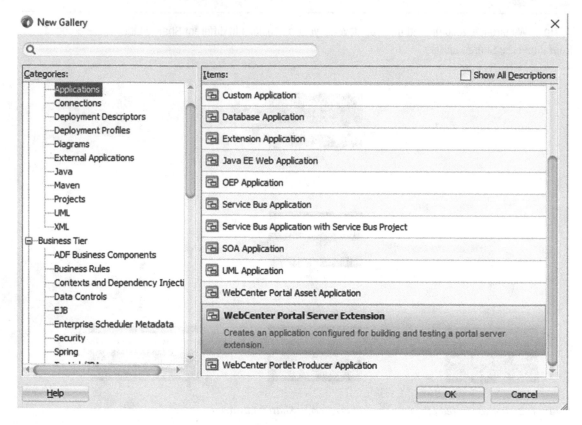

Figure 6-3. JDeveloper WebCenter Portal Server Extension Template

This Application template creates an Application Workspace that contains the following two projects (Figure 6-4):

- **PortalExtension**: Used for developing and coding custom ADF Assets.

- **PortalSharedLibrary**: Used for redeploying new versions of the **extend.spaces.webapp.war** shared library.

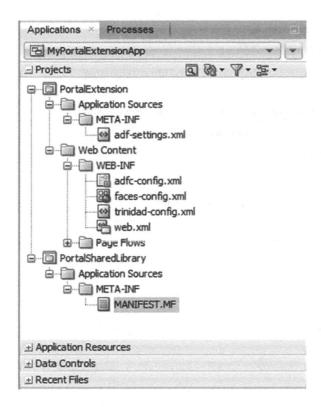

Figure 6-4. *JDeveloper WebCenter Portal Server Extension Application Workspace*

By default, the PortalExtension project generates an ADF JAR Library called **adflibPortalExtension.jar** that is part of the extend.spaces.webapp.war shared library deployed using PortalSharedLibrary project (Figure 6-5).

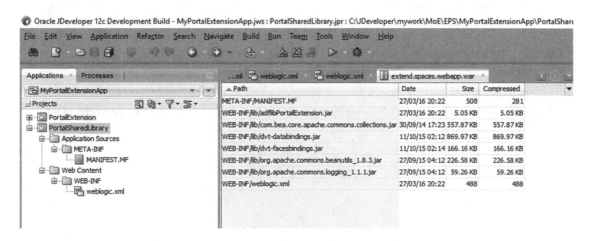

Figure 6-5. *Default content of extend.spaces.webapp.war*

Configuring PortalSharedLibrary Project

The PortalSharedLibrary project should be used only for the following:

- Redeploying new versions of the extend.spaces.webapp.war shared library changing the version in the **MANIFEST.MF** file.

- Reference external shared libraries using the WebLogic Descriptor file **weblogic.xml**

- Overriding ADF context parameters in the descriptor file **web.xml**

As shown in the above list, this project should only contain three files.

■ **Tip**   Avoid including custom code or ADF Assets in this project for maintainability.

The **MANIFEST.MF** file contains the information of the shared library:

```
Manifest-Version: 1.0
Ant-Version: Apache Ant 1.9.2
Created-By: 1.8.0_40-b25 (Oracle Corporation)
Extension-List: bpmSpaces
bpmSpaces-Extension-Name: oracle.bpm.spaces
Package:
Specification-Version: 2.0
Implementation-Version: 12.2.1.0.1
Implementation-Label: 12.2.1.0.1
Implementation-Vendor: Oracle
Implementation-Patch-Number:
Implementation-Patch-List:
Implementation-Title: Oracle WebCenter Spaces App Extension View V2
Extension-Name: extend.spaces.webapp
```

The most important property of the MANIFEST.MF file is the **Implementation-Version.** This property indicates the version of the library.

■ **Caution**   Do not delete any property of the MANIFEST.MF or it can prevent WebCenter Portal from running properly.

By default, the installation of WebCenter Portal deploys a base library with 12.2.1 version (Figure 6-6).

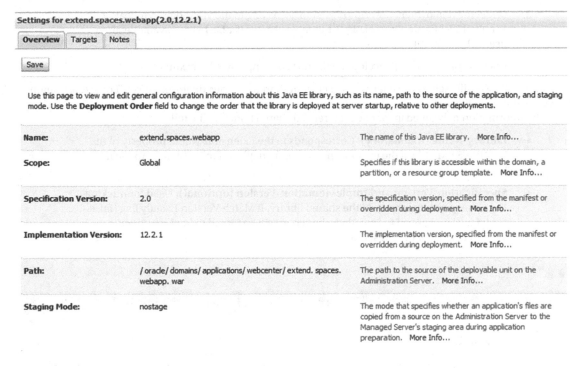

Figure 6-6. *Default version of extend.spaces.webapp*

Each redeployment of the extend.spaces.webapp.war shared library is required to increase the **Implementation-Version** number of the MANIFEST.MF file. WebCenter Portal will use always the higher Implementation-Version of the deployed shared library.

■ **Caution**   Never remove the base version of the extend.spaces.webapp.war shared library deployed by the WebCenter Portal installer.

What about the descriptor files **web.xml** and **weblogic.xml**?
As you may notice, JDeveloper does not create these files automatically using WebCenter Portal Server Application Template. These files need to be created manually.

How to Create WebLogic Descriptor File

As commented on before, weblogic.xml descriptor file is used for referencing external shared libraries. Follow the next steps for creating one in your PortalSharedLibrary project.

1. Right-click PortalSharedLibrary project and then click New/From Gallery/ Deployment Descriptors/WebLogic Deployment Descriptor.

2. Select **weblogic.xml** from the list of descriptors.

3. Select the deployment descriptor version according to the WebLogic Application Server. If WebCenter Portal is 12.2.1 then use 12.2.1. If 12.2.1 is not available, then use 12.1.3 as it will work also.

4. Click *Finish* and then JDeveloper will create an empty weblogic.xml file.

In this file we will register the references to custom shared libraries deployed in WebLogic Application Server as shown in Figure 6-7.

The information to be filled in for each referenced shared library is the following:

- **Library-Name (mandatory)**: Corresponds to the Extension-Name property of the MANIFEST.MF file of the custom shared library deployed in WebLogic Application Server.

- **Specification-Version and Implementation-Version (optional):** Used for tracking the corresponding version of the shared library. If Match Version Exactly flag (false by default) is changed to true, then the server will be forced to load the specific version instead of the latest one.

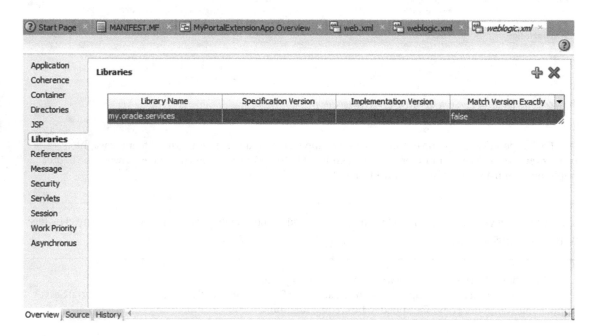

Figure 6-7. *weblogic.xml with a custom shared library registered*

■ **Tip**   We recommend leaving the Specification-Version and Implementation-Version properties empty during the development. In addition, set the Match Version Flag to false so it always references the latest version of the shared library.

How to Create J2EE Descriptor File

As commented on before, web.xml is used for overriding some ADF Context-Parameters. By default, JDeveloper does not create this descriptor file. Follow the next steps for creating this file in the PortalSharedLibrary project.

1. Right-click PortalSharedLibrary project and then click New/From Gallery/ Deployment Descriptors/J2EE Deployment Descriptor.

2. Choose **web.xml** from the J2EE Descriptors list.

3. Select 3.0 as deployment version.

4. Click *Finish*.

It creates an empty web.xml file for adding context-params.

■ **Caution** JDeveloper sometimes adds extra information into the web.xml when adding new dependencies into the project. Keep the file clean with only the Context-Params overridden. Servlets, Filters, and Listeners can make WebCenter Portal fail to run.

Summary

The Application Workspaces has to look like Figure 6-8.

Figure 6-8. *Overview of the Portal Server Extension Application*

Configuring PortalExtension Project

The Portal Extension project is an ADF Project configured for developing Oracle ADF Assets on it.

We strongly recommend using this project **only** for **ADF Bounded Task Flows**, **Data Controls** or **Managed Beans,** which only consume **Oracle WebCenter Portal API**.

All other Task Flows or components that integrate with third-party systems should be developed in separate Application Workspaces and deployed as shared libraries.

Development Life Cycle

In order to consolidate the concepts shown previously, we are going to make a summary about the development of a life cycle that a developer should follow when developing ADF Assets for WebCenter Portal.

The following diagram (Figure 6-9) shows a summary of the main steps.

1. Develop your custom ADF Components into separate ADF Applications.

2. Prepare your custom ADF Projects for generating ADF JAR Libraries.

3. Package the ADF JAR Libraries into a shared library and deploy it into WebLogic Application Server.

4. Register the shared libraries in the weblogic.xml file of the PortalSharedLibrary Project.

5. Increase the version of the MANIFEST.MF file of the PortalSharedLibrary and deploy the new extend.spaces.webapp.war shared library.

6. Restart the Managed Server where WebCenter Portal is running.

7. Add your Custom ADF Component into the Portal Resource Catalog.

8. Drag and Drop the component into a WebCenter Portal Page.

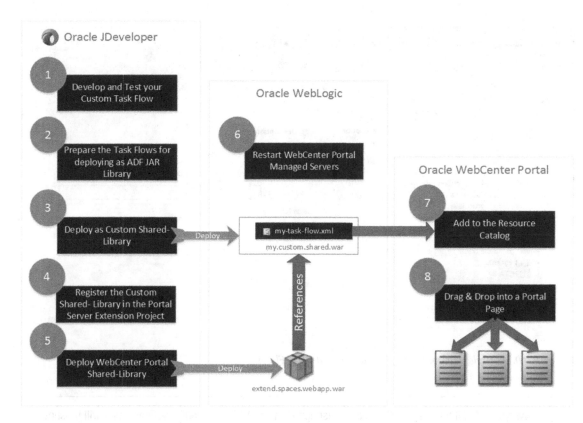

Figure 6-9. *Development Life Cycle of ADF Assets*

Example

ADDING A CUSTOM ADF TASK FLOW TO WEBCENTER PORTAL

This example shows how to add a custom ADF Task Flow into WebCenter Portal following the steps described above.

1. In JDeveloper 12.2.1 create an ADF Fusion Web Application for developing an ADF Task Flow. This template will create two projects (Figure 6-10):

    a. **Model**: This project is used for creating Business Services and Data Control for accessing the data. In this example, create a Java Data Control that generates a mocked list of Oracle Products.

    b. **ViewController**: Create an ADF Bounded Task Flow to consume the Business Service. In this case of the example we just Drag and Drop a List View of the Oracle Products into the fragment.

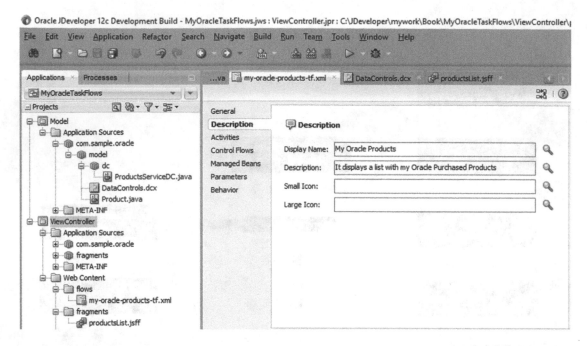

Figure 6-10. *Sample workspace for developing ADF Task Flows*

■ **Tip** Always try to fill the Display Name and Description of the ADF Bounded Task Flows as it will be shown to be more friendly in the Portal Resource Catalog.

Test your components locally before deploying them to WebCenter Portal Server. It will save time.

■ **Note** This book is focused on Portal Concepts. It assumes basic experience with Oracle ADF Framework.

---

    c.   Prepare the Model and ViewController projects to generate ADF JAR Library of each one:

         i.   **Model**: Create a new Deployment Profile as ADF JAR Library (Figure 6-11).

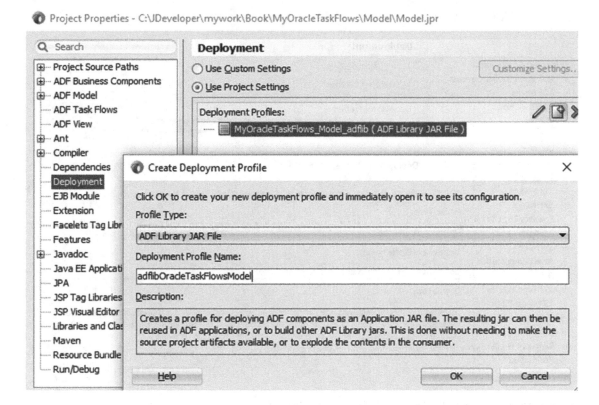

Figure 6-11. *Generate ADF Library for Model project*

ii. **ViewController**: Create a new Deployment Profile as ADF JAR Library (Figure 6-12).

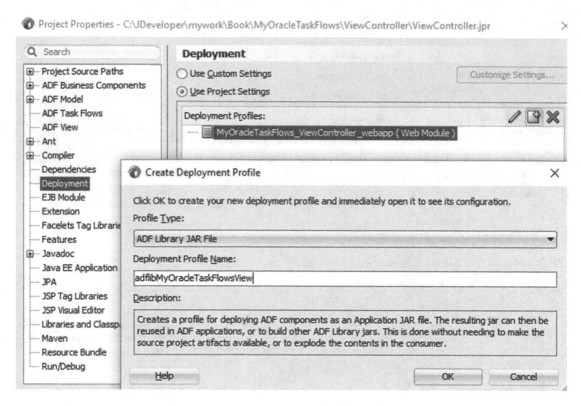

Figure 6-12. *Generate ADF Library for ViewController Project*

■ **Tip** Use adflib as the prefix for your ADF JAR Libraries as they are different from normal JAR Libraries.

---

2. Create a Generic Project in the same Application Workspace of ViewController and Model. We are going to use this project for deploying the ADF JAR Libraries together into the same Shared Library.

   a. Create a MANIFEST.MF file in the source folder of the Generic Project (Figure 6-13).

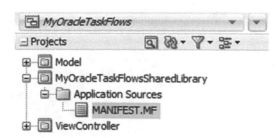

Figure 6-13. *ADF Workspace with Shared Library deployer project*

b. Use the following snippet to fill the MANIFEST.MF file.

```
Manifest-Version: 1.0
Created-By: Daniel and Vinay
Extension-Name: my.oracle.taskflows
Implementation-Label: WORKPLACE_12.2.1_GENERIC_151013.2001
Implementation-Title: my.oracle.taskflows
Implementation-Vendor: Oracle
Implementation-Version: 12.2.1.0.1
Specification-Title: my.oracle.taskflows
Specification-Vendor: Oracle
Specification-Version: 1.0
```

■ **Note Extension-Name** is the name that will be used for referencing this Shared Library via wcblogic.xml descriptor file. **Implementation-Version** is the current version of the library.

c. Configure a Deployment Profile for the Generic Project:

i. Select WAR File as type (Figure 6-14).

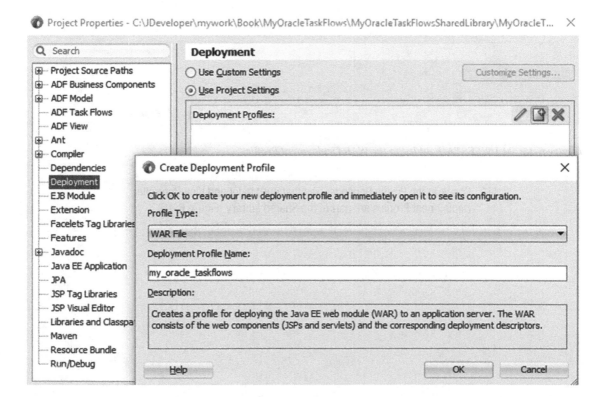

Figure 6-14. Shared Library Deployment Profile as WAR type

ii.   Edit the Deployment Profile and add the MANIFEST.MF file as part of the WAR (Figure 6-15).

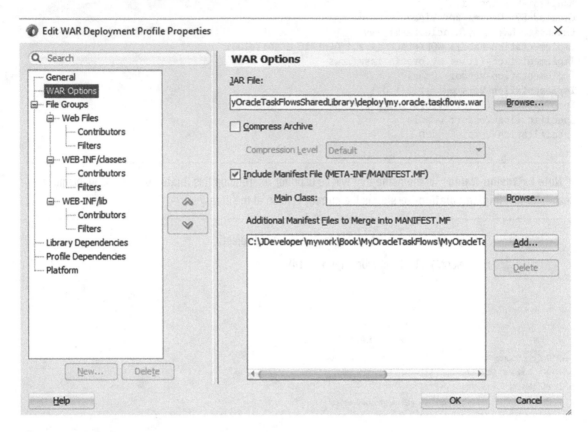

Figure 6-15. MANIFEST.MF added to the WAR Deployment Profile

iii.   Check in the Profile Dependencies that our Model and ViewController Deployment Profiles are part of the Shared Library (Figure 6-16).

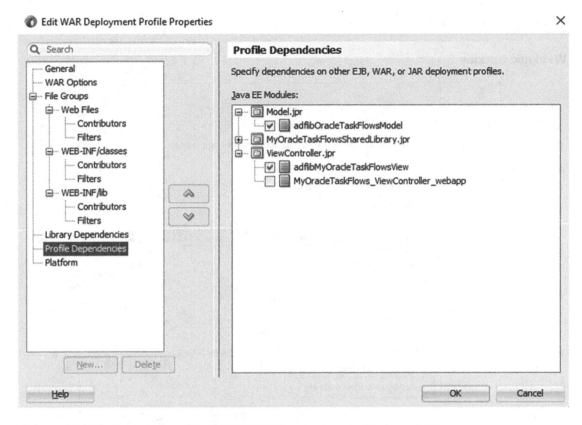

Figure 6-16. *ViewController and Model ADF JAR Libraries as part of the Shared Library*

3. Deploy the Shared Library in WebLogic Application Server. Right-click the recently created SharedLibrary project and click Deploy.

   a. Select to Deploy to an Application Server. (You need to register a previous Application Server with a WebCenter Portal Installation; however, this is not covered in this book).

   b. Make sure that you deploy a Shared Library in the WebCenter Portal Managed Server (Figure 6-17).

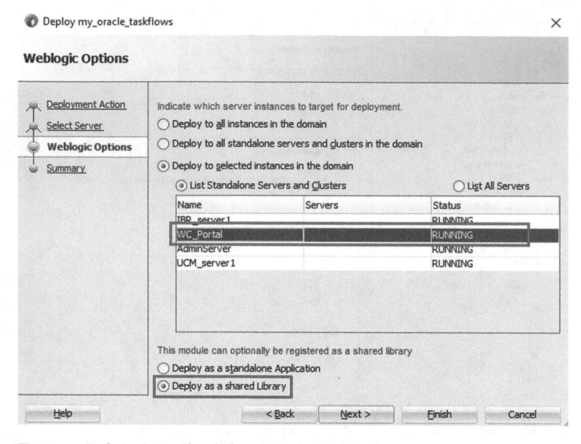

Figure 6-17. *Deploying Custom Shared Library into WebCenter Portal Server*

■ **Note** In JDeveloper Deployment Tab it will show messages that include the LibSpecVersion and the LibImplVersion of the Shared Library. If these messages do not appear, it means that it was marked to be deployed as an Application instead of a Shared Library.

---

4. Open the WebCenter Portal Server Extension Application and register the shared library in the weblogic.xml descriptor file of PortalSharedLibrary project. The Library Name must be the same as the **Extension-Name** used in the MANIFEST.MF of the deployed Shared Library (Figure 6-18).

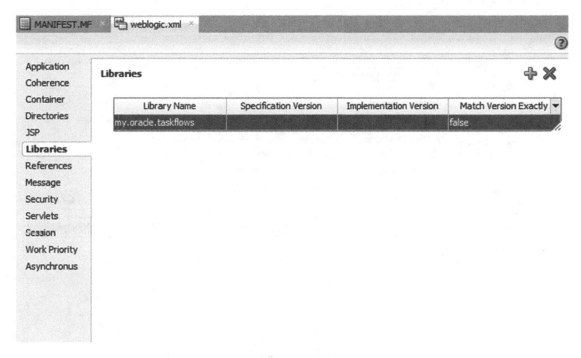

Figure 6-18. *Registering in PortalSharedLibrary the deployed Shared Library*

5. Increase, if necessary, the Implementation-Version of the MANIFEST.MF file of the PortalSharedLibrary Project. Right-Click in PortalSharedLibrary and deploy as a Shared Library in WebCenter Portal Managed Server (Figure 6-19). Make sure that the new Shared Library is deployed correctly (Figure 6-20).

___

■ **Note**   It is not necessary to redeploy new versions of the **extend.spaces.webapp.war** every time that we deploy a new version of the other referenced shared libraries. We only need to redeploy the **extend.spaces. webapp.war** only in the case that it has changes. It means changes in the web.xml, weblogic.xml files of the PortalSharedLibrary Project, or added code into PortalExtension project.

___

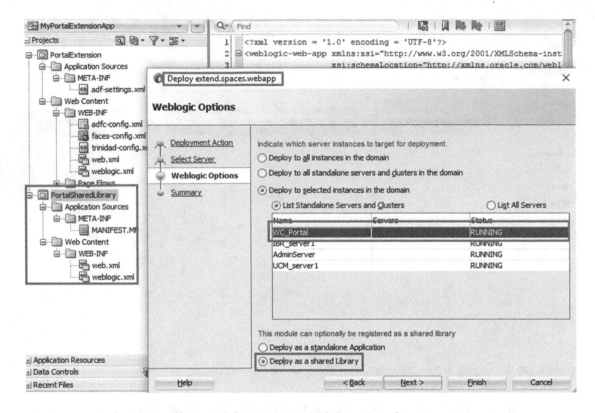

Figure 6-19. *Deploying extend.spaces.webapp.war into WebCenter Portal*

Deployments

	Name △	State	Health	Type	Targets	Scope	Domain Partitions	Deployment Order
☐	emcoresdkimpl_jar(11.2.0.1.0,12.1.0.0.0)	Active		Library	AdminServer	Global		100
☐	emcoresdk_jar(11.2.0.1.0,12.1.0.0.0)	Active		Library	AdminServer	Global		100
☐	emcore_jar	Active		Library	AdminServer	Global		100
☐	em_common(12.4,12.1.0.4.0)	Active		Library	AdminServer	Global		100
☐	em_core_ppc_pojo_jar	Active		Library	AdminServer	Global		100
☐	em_error(12.4,12.1.0.4.0)	Active		Library	AdminServer	Global		100
☐	em_sdkcore_ppc_public_pojo_jar	Active		Library	AdminServer	Global		100
☐	extend.spaces.webapp(2.0,12.2.1)	Active		Library	AdminServer, WC_Portal	Global		300
☐	extend.spaces.webapp(2.0,12.2.1.0.1)	Active		Library	WC_Portal	Global		300
☐	jsf(2.0,1.0.0.0_2-2-8)	Active		Library	AdminServer, IBR_server1, UCM_server1, WC_Portal	Global		100

Install   Update   Delete   Showing 21 to 30 of 85   Previous | Next

Figure 6-20. *New version of the extend.spaces.webapp.war shared library*

6. Restart all WebCenter Portal Managed Servers to make Portal take the latest changes (Figure 6-21).

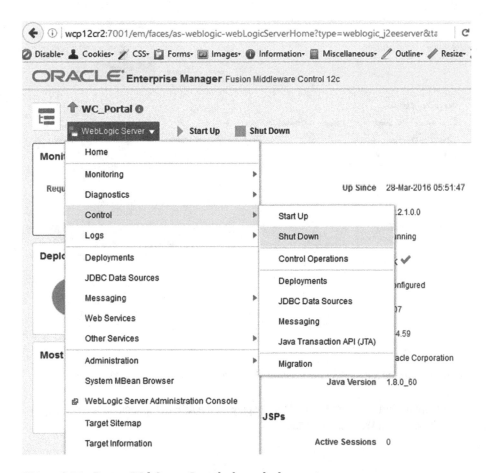

Figure 6-21. *Restart WebCenter Portal after redeployment*

■ **Tip** For clustered environments, restart one by one so that you do not lose availability.

---

7. Add the deployed Custom Task Flow to the Resource Catalog used by your Portal.

   a. As a Portal Administrator, go to Shared Assets Administration / Resource Catalogs.

   b. Edit the Resource Catalog being used by your Portal Pages (Figure 6-22). In case you do not have a Custom Resource Catalog, then follow the next steps for configuring one:

      i. Go to your Portal Administration Console ➤ Assets.

      ii. Select the Default Portal Catalog and then create a Copy of it (Actions ➤ Copy). Make sure you have the Available check marked.

      iii. Go to General Settings and then set the new created Resource Catalog as the Resource Catalog for the Pages.

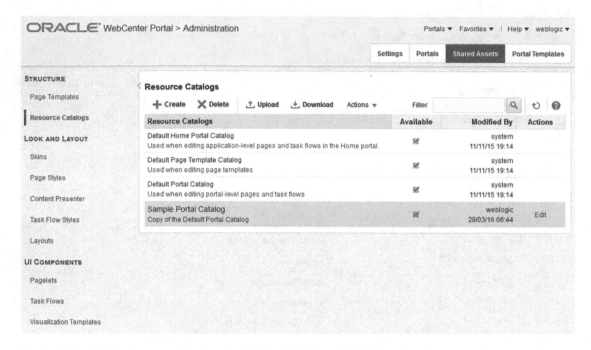

Figure 6-22. *Edit the Resource Catalog for Adding the Custom Task Flow*

      c. Click on Add from Library (Figure 6-23). It will display all the ADF Components within the Class path of WebCenter Portal.

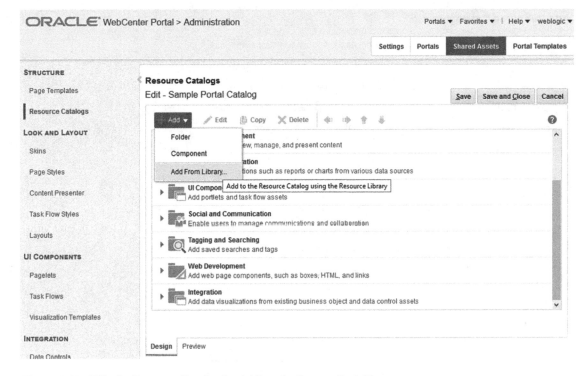

Figure 6-23. *Edit the Resource Catalog for Adding the Custom Task Flow*

    d.   Search and add your Custom Task Flow (Figure 6-24).

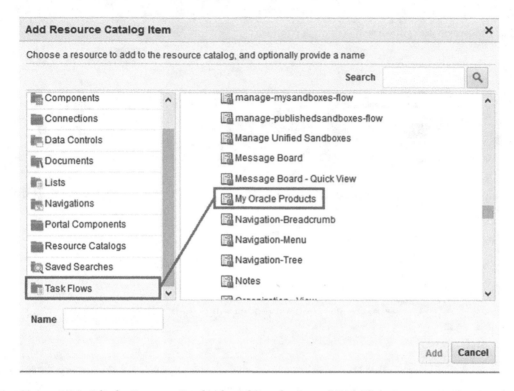

Figure 6-24. *Edit the Resource Catalog for Adding the Custom Task Flow*

    e.   Now, when editing a Portal Page, add your custom component (Figure 6-25),

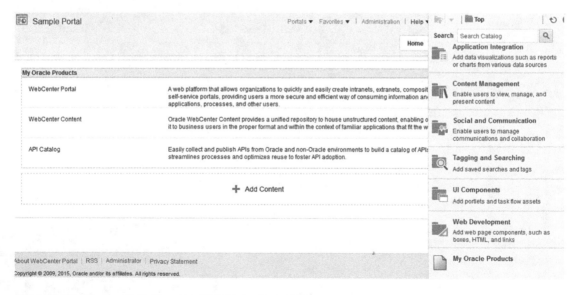

Figure 6-25. *Custom Task Flow in a WebCenter Portal Page*

CHAPTER 7

■■■

WebCenter Portal Task Flow Customization

Overview

WebCenter Portal provides multiple Out-of-box task flows for multiple functionalities. For example, content manager (Document explorer task flow in 11g) task flow, search task flow, discussion task flow, etc. WebCenter Portal provides lot of features by wrapping it in ADF Task Flows. Quite often Out-of-box task flows don't fit the project's business requirements. Either the user interface needs changes or some functionalities are not required, or there is a need to add additional information. In such circumstances, task flow customization can be done to meet the requirements.

There is a slight change in the Task Flow customization process in WebCenter Portal 12c compared to the process in the previous versions. Earlier, there was a task flow customization application template for customization. In WebCenter Portal 12c, there is no application template to achieve that. Customization can be stored in the MDS layer and deployed over WebCenter Portal. With default JDeveloper customization roles, task flows can be customized to extend the feature or alter the look and feel. Customization with JDeveloper is an easy process and does not require much coding.

Mostly task flow customization can be done to change user interface or to remove or add some features. Customizations beyond 30% to 40% will not work effectively. If a change to a standard task flow is more than 40%, then building a new custom Task Flow is recommended.

For achieving WebCenter Portal task flow customizations, create seeded customizations for task flows in an ADF Fusion technology application and package the task flow customizations in a JAR archive using JDeveloper. Import the webcenter jar into JDeveloper project. Make the customization and import the seeded customizations later to the MDS repository attached to the WebCenter Portal instance.

Task Flow customization can be done in two ways:

- Runtime Customization
- Design Time Customization with JDeveloper

Process of Design Time Customization

The following diagram (Figure 7-1) shows the process of making design time customization.

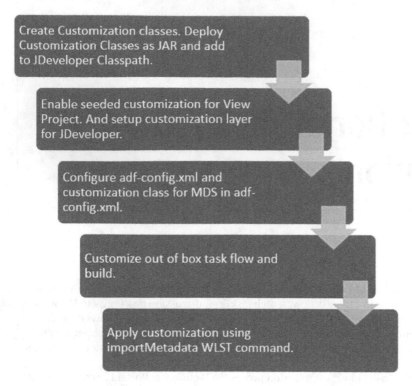

Figure 7-1. *Process of Task Flow Customization*

Setting Up a Customizable WebCenter Portal Application

1. Create an "ADF Fusion Web Application" as shown in Figure 7-2.

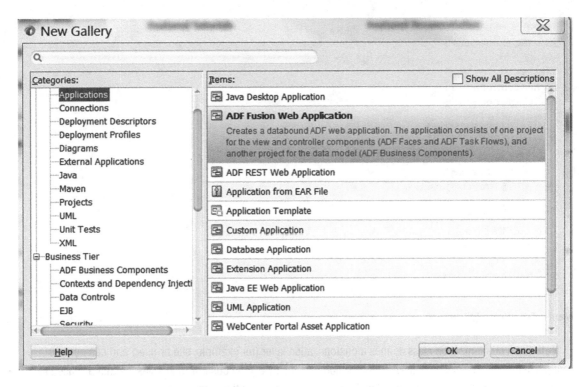

Figure 7-2. *Create Fusion ADF Application*

2. Create customization classes in project. These classes are the interface that MDS uses to define which customization applies to the base definition metadata.

   These classes are packaged in JAR and later used in the classpath of JDeveloper (Figure 7-3).

Figure 7-3. Project Structure

Note Each customization class defines a customization layer (for example, site or user) and can contain multiple layer values. For a task flow customization, use the layer. The customization classes that are used in the application should be available in JDeveloper when customizing the application.

3. In ViewController project, right-click and create new java class "**WCPSiteCC**" extending "**oracle.mds.cust.CustomizationClass**" (Figure 7-4).

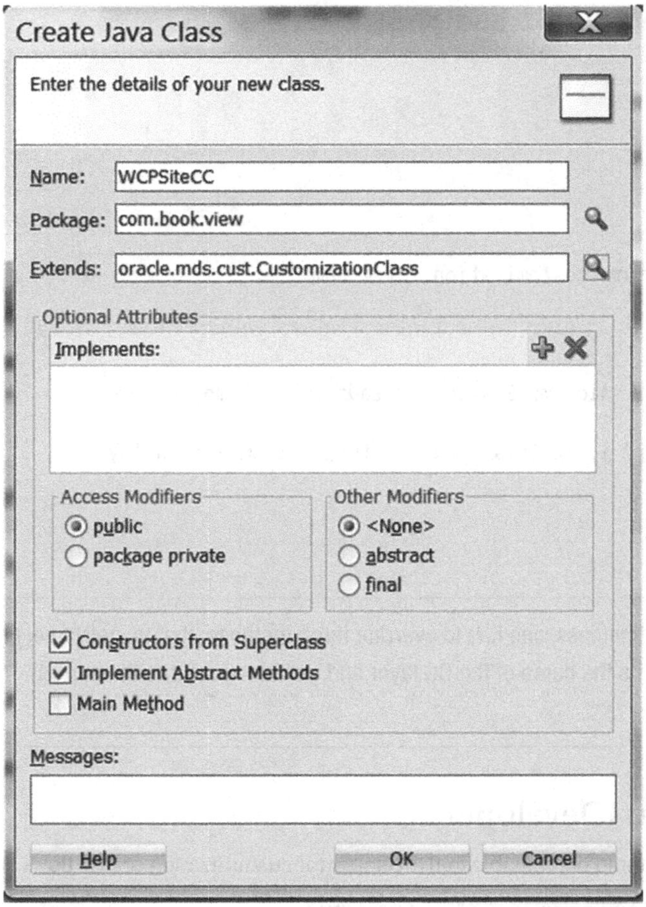

Figure 7-4. *Create Customization Class*

4. In WCPSiteCC.java class, add the following code and rebuild the ViewController project.

```
package com.book.view;

import oracle.mds.cust.CacheHint;
import oracle.mds.cust.CustomizationClass;
import java.io.IOException;
import java.io.InputStream;
import java.util.Properties;
import oracle.mds.core.MetadataObject;
import oracle.mds.core.RestrictedSession;

public class WCPSiteCC extends CustomizationClass {
    public WCPSiteCC() {
        super();
    }
```

```java
    @Override
    public CacheHint getCacheHint() {
        // TODO Implement this method
        return null;
    }

    @Override
    public String getName() {
        // Add your logic.
        return "site"; //this should return customization layer name.
    }

    @Override
    public String[] getValue(RestrictedSession mdsSession, MetadataObject mo) {
        // TODO Implement this method
        return new String[] { "webcenter" }; // This should return customization layer
value.
    }
}
```

■ **Note**   Now when extending from CustomizationClass, one has to override three methods: that is, getName(), getValue(), and getCacheHint(). getName() returns the name of the CC layer and getValue() returns the current layer value.

Adding Customization Class in JDeveloper

As mentioned above, the customization class should be available to JDeveloper for customization of task flows.

1. Right-click ViewController project and navigate to project properties.

2. In Project Properties window, select **Deployment** tab, click on new deployment profile (Figure 7-5).

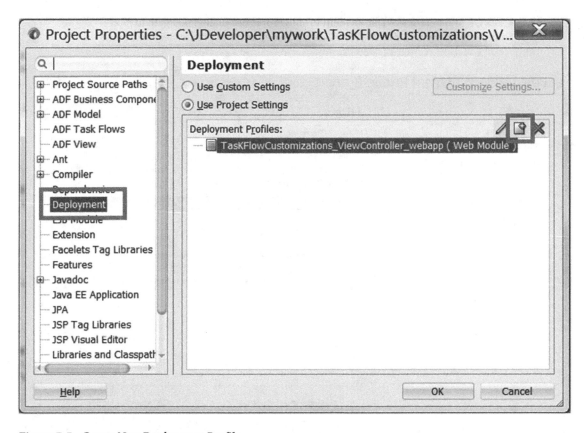

Figure 7-5. *Create New Deployment Profile*

3. Provide Deployment Profile Name and Profile Type should be JAR File (Figure 7-6).

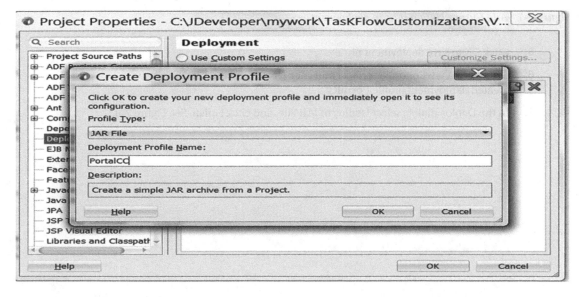

Figure 7-6. *JAR Deployment Profile*

4. Click OK and in Edit JAR Deployment Profile Properties dialog, navigate to filters in Project Output and add WCPSiteCC.class in deployment profile. See Figure 7-7.

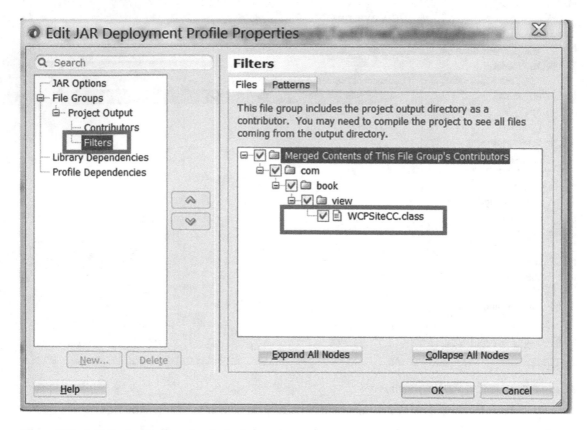

Figure 7-7. *Add Customization class in deployment*

5. Click OK to save deployment profile.

6. Right-click ViewController project and click Deploy option. Choose newly created deployment profile **PortalCC.**

7. In the Deploy dialog, select Deploy to JAR File, and click Finish. See Figure 7-8.

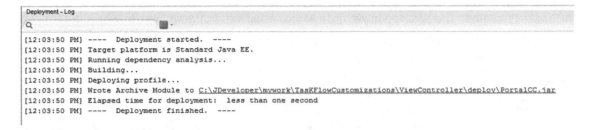

Figure 7-8. *Deployment – Log*

8. Select project properties of ViewController project. Select **Libraries and Classpath** and click Add JAR/Directory option to add **PortalCC.jar** to view Controller's classpath (Figure 7-9).

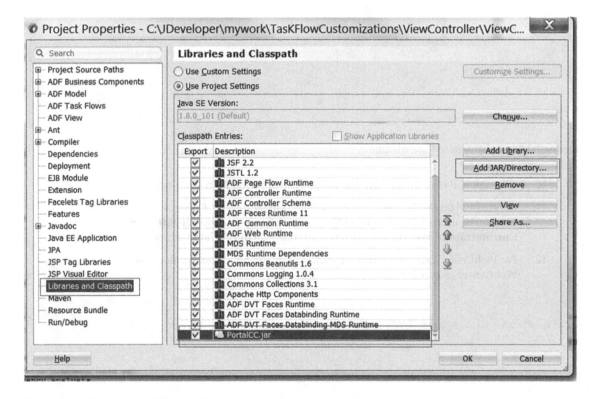

Figure 7-9. *Libraries and Classpath*

9. Select project properties and click on **ADF View**. Select the **Enable Seeded Customizations** check box (Figure 7-10).

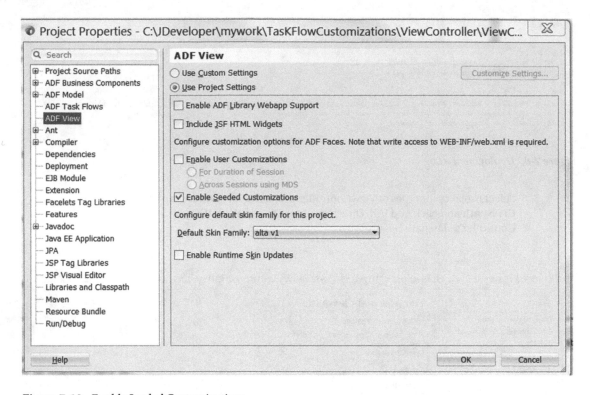

Figure 7-10. Enable Seeded Customizations

10. Click OK and save all. We enabled seeded customization for the project.

11. For customizing WebCenter Portal task flows, configure the CC layer values that can be used in the JDeveloper Customization role. In **JDEV_HOME/jdev/ CustomizationLayerValues.xml**, you can configure the CC layer values.

12. For WebCenter Task Flow customization, we will use **Site** layer as value with **WebCenter** (Figure 7-11).

```
<cust-layers  xmlns="http://xmlns.oracle.com/mds/dt">
  <cust-layer name="site" id-prefix="s">

    <!-- ADF SiteCC always returns the value as "site" -->
    <cust-layer-value value="webcenter" display-name="WebCenter"/>
  </cust-layer>
</cust-layers>
```

Figure 7-11. WebCenter Task Flow customization Site Layer

This configuration will set **WebCenter** as the layer value for **Site** layer.

13. The **adf-config.xml** file of the application must have **cust-config** element in the mds section. The cust-config allows clients to define an ordered and named list of customization classes. You can use the overview editor for the file to add customization classes.

14. Open the adf-config.xml file of the application in the Overview editor. Select **MDS.**

15. Add **WCPSiteCC** class as a Customization Class and save all (Figure 7-12).

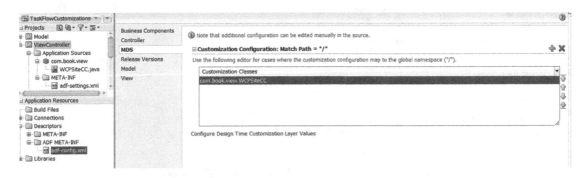

Figure 7-12. *Add Customization class*

Customizing WebCenter Portal Task Flows of Design Time Customization

Once the above setup of JDeveloper is complete, Out-of-box task flows in WebCenter Portal can be customized and altered/extended.

1. For customization WebCenter JAR should to be added to the classpath of JDeveloper in default role.

2. Open project properties and select Libraries and Classpath and click on add JAR option.

3. WebCenter JARs can be found at this path:**JDEV_HOME/jdeveloper/webcenter/ modules/oracle.webcenter.framework**

4. Click select and ok for project properties. See Figure 7-13.

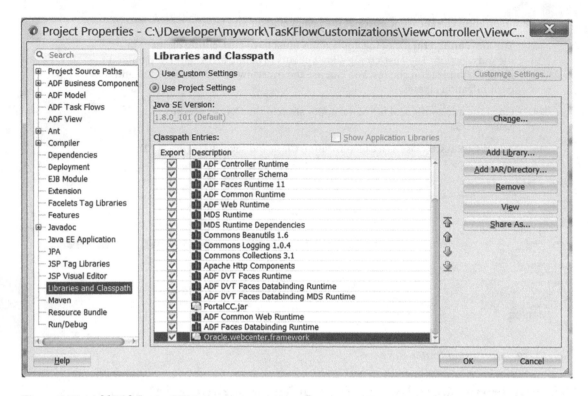

Figure 7-13. *Add WebCenter JARs*

5. Click save all and open JDeveloper Customization Developer role from Tools ➤ Switch Roles ➤ Customization Developer.

6. JDeveloper will restart and open in customization role. Make sure to verify customization layer name as "**site**" and value as "**webcenter**" (Figure 7-14).

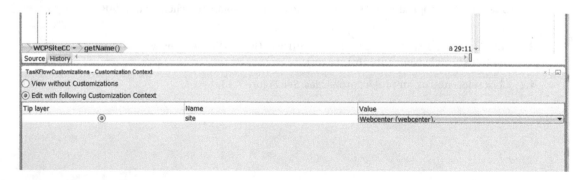

Figure 7-14. *Site as Customization layer*

7. Now customization can be done in the task flow or fragments. Open doclib-service-view.jar and then make changes in any of jsff page (Figure 7-15).

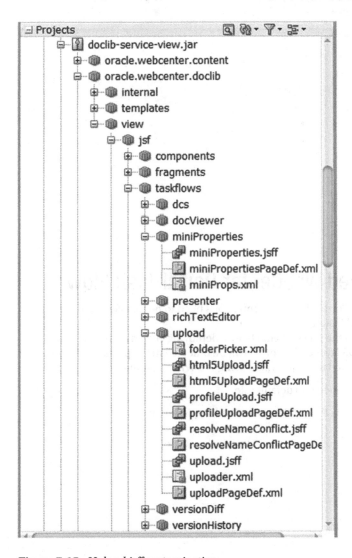

Figure 7-15. *Upload.jsff customization*

8. All Customization made will be stored in Application Directory/ViewController/libraryCustomizations (Figure 7-16).

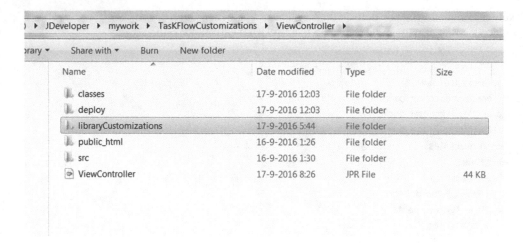

Figure 7-16. Library Customization folder

Deployment of Customized WebCenter Portal Task Flow

To view these customizations in WebCenter Portal, these customizations need to be transferred to the MDS repository of the deployed WebCenter Portal instance.

It is recommended to make a back-up of the MDS schema before deploying customizations. This customization will be overwritten in the MDS layer and changes will be reflected in the portal environment. Customizations can also be removed or restored to default value using the WLST command.

1. Rebuild the application in JDeveloper with default role.

2. Create a JAR deployment profile via Project Properties and Deployment (Figure 7-17).

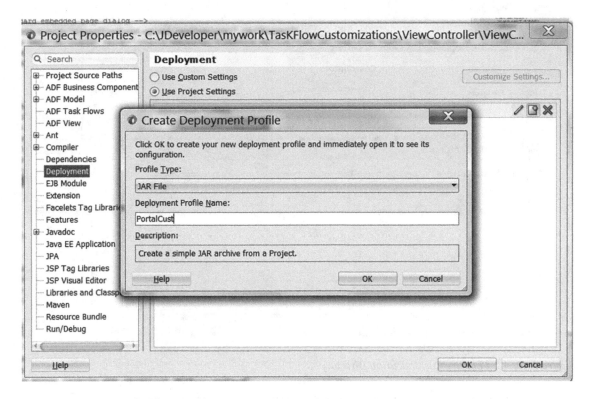

Figure 7-17. *JAR Deployment Profile*

3. In Edit JAR Deployment Profile Properties, add libraryCustomizations directory in Contributors pane. See Figure 7-18.

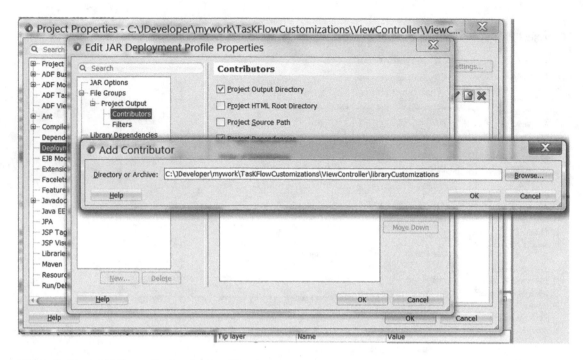

Figure 7-18. *Add Library Customization Directory*

4. Deploy project in new deployment profile and build the jar. Select **Deploy to JAR File** as deployment action (Figure 7-19).

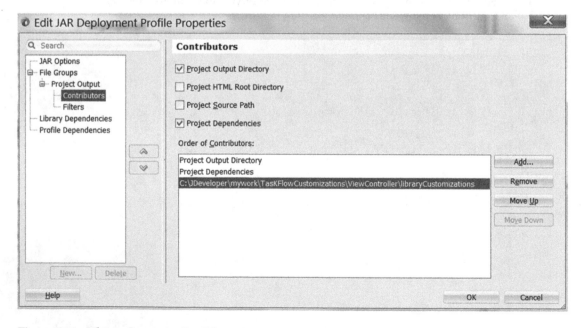

Figure 7-19. *Library Customization Directory*

5. Extract newly generated JAR and put it at a different location. This location will be used while using WLST command to import in MDS (Figure 7-20).

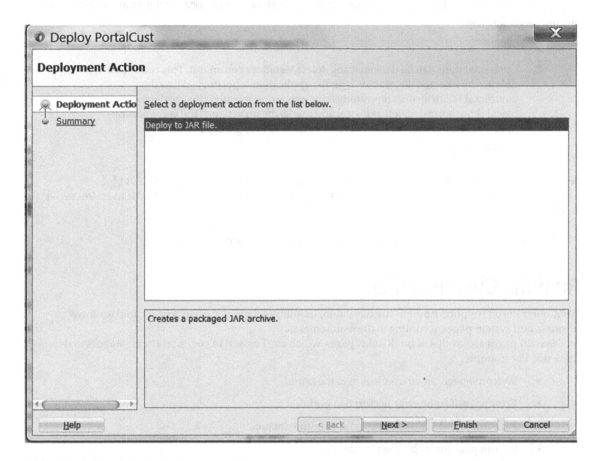

Figure 7-20. Deploy to JAR File

6. Use the WLST command to import these task flow customizations into the WebCenter Portal application's MDS repository. The following is the example command to import customization:

```
wls:/weblogic/serverConfig>importMetadata(application='webcenter', server='WC_Portal',
fromLocation='/tmp/webcentercust, docs="/**")
```

■ **Note** Open wlst windows from Middleware home/WebCenter Installation directory/common/bin and run wlst.sh (unix) or wlst.cmd(windows). Connect by providing weblogic crendentials.

---

7. Now after successful execution of **importMetadata** command, customizations are deployed on application's MDS repository. Customizations can be verified by viewing the particular task flow.

■ **Note** ImportMetadata This command imports application metadata. Use the exportMetadata command and importMetadata command to transfer application metadata from one server location (for example, testing) to another server location.

---

8. Customizations can be deleted using **deleteMetadata** command. This command deletes the selected documents from the application repository. When this command is run against repositories that support versioning (that is, database-based repositories), delete is logical and marks the tip version (the latest version) of the selected documents as "deleted" in the MDS repository partition.

Syntax for command

```
deleteMetadata(application, server, docs [, restrictCustTo] [, excludeAllCust] [,
excludeBaseDocs] [, excludeExtendedMetadata] [, cancelOnException] [, applicationVersion] [,
tenantName])
```

The steps discussed above can be used in design time customization.

Runtime Customization

WebCenter Portal supports runtime customization. In Administration console, a user can customize business and system pages according to the requirements.

System pages are groups of small utility pages, which can be used in common circumstances in day-to-day work. For example,

- Welcome page, when user logs in to the portal.

- Error page, if some error occurred in portal.

- Page not found, if invalid URL is hit in portal domain.

- Sign-in page for WebCenter Portal, etc.

All pages have common functionality, which will be required in every portal. The user can customize in portal console, without any coding.

The system page Task Flow Editor provides an environment for customizing all instances of a seeded task flow in a given scope in one operation. Administrators or users with specified roles can add a seeded task flow to this page and then customize it to apply the customizations to all instances of the task flow (Figure 7-21).

No Pages Accessible Displays when no pages are accessible	Modified by:fmwadmin 5/13/2015	Create Page Variant	Customize | Restore Default
Page Not Found Page Not Found	Modified by:system 5/30/2015	Create Page Variant	Customize | Restore Default
Page Viewer Displays a page	Modified by:system 4/15/2015	Customize | Restore Default	
Portal Not Found Portal Not Found	Modified by:system 5/30/2015	Create Page Variant | Customize | Restore Default	
Portals			

Figure 7-21. *Create Page Variant*

The Administrator can customize built-in system pages to make a required user interface according to project needs. Customization can delete existing components or add new components and change the layout. However, it is not possible to edit or delete system page input fields and buttons.

To customize a variant of a system page for a device group, expand the system page variant icon, then click Edit for the device group you want to customize. Here different page variants can be created for different mobile devices (Figure 7-22).

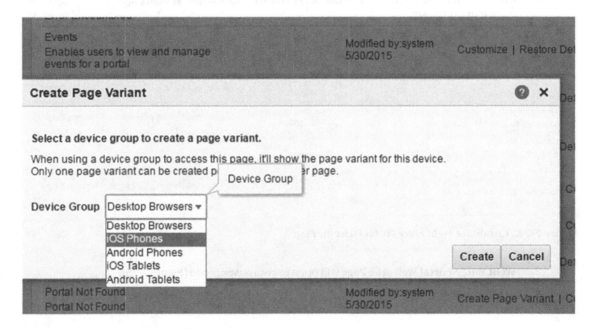

Figure 7-22. *Create Page Variant for Device*

Customizing System Pages

1. Navigate to "**host:port/webcenter/portal/admin/settings**" and click on System Pages. See Figures 7-23 and 7-24.

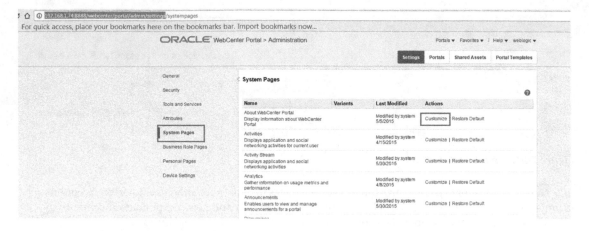

Figure 7-23. *Customizing System Pages*

2. Click the **Customize** link for *"WebCenter Portal Welcome Page"* system page to open it in Composer.

Task Flow Viewer Displays task flows	Modified by:system 4/15/2015	Customize | Restore Default
Unauthorized Reports unauthorized access	Modified by:system 5/30/2015	Create Page Variant | Customize | Restore Default
Unavailable Displays when a portal is unavailable	Modified by:system 5/30/2015	Create Page Variant | Customize | Restore Default
User Profile Displays the profile gallery for users other than current user	Modified by:system 4/15/2015	Customize | Restore Default
WebCenter Portal Welcome Page WebCenter Portal Welcome Page	Modified by:system 5/30/2015	Create Page Variant | Customize | Restore Default

Figure 7-24. *Customize WebCenter Portal Welcome Page*

3. **WebCenter Portal Welcome Page** will open in **composer** mode (Figure 7-25).

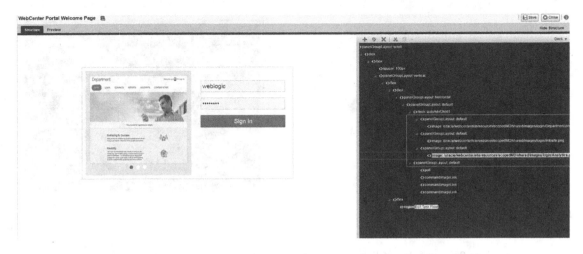

Figure 7-25. *Composer edit mode*

4. Change the images as selected in composer mode. Select image of right-hand side and click edit (Figure 7-26).

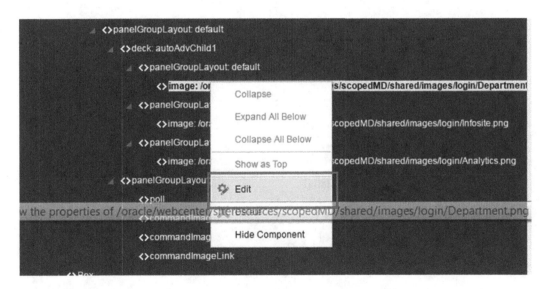

Figure 7-26. *Edit image*

5. In display options, change the source and add image URL from the Web. Edit source for all images by clicking edit and change source in display option (Figure 7-27).

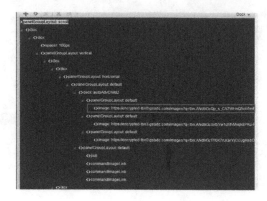

Figure 7-27. *Change image URL*

6. Click on Save and close. Click on WebCenter Portal Welcome page. Now images on the page have been changed. Customization has been applied using MDS (Figure 7-28).

Figure 7-28. *WebCenter Portal Welcome page*

Removing System Page Customization

Removing or setting the default state of system pages is also possible from the System pages section in **Settings** page.

1. Navigate to settings page in Administration and select **System Pages.**

2. Click Restore Default next to WebCenter Portal Welcome page (Figure 7-29).

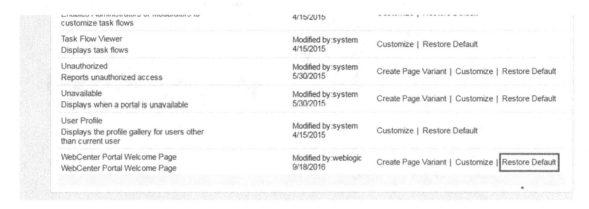

Figure 7-29. *Restore Default*

3. Restore Default pop-up message is displayed for confirmation. Click Restore (Figure 7-30).

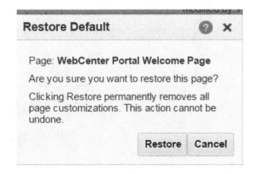

Figure 7-30. *Restore default pop-up*

4. Now click again to verify that welcome page is restored to its default state (Figure 7-31).

Figure 7-31. *Restore default state of Portal Welcome page*

CHAPTER 8

■ ■ ■

Portlets Integration Using JSR 286

WebCenter Portal offers different development strategies for transactional features, portlets and Task Flows being the most common. The challenge of developing a web portal is to bring all distinct applications/data into one place. Different applications or technologies fulfill different features. Choice of technology can also come into play depending on expertise and ease of development.

Portlet technology in Java not only helps to build a web portal but also provides service orchestration, in which distinct services can be integrated seamlessly at the user interface layer, allowing businesses to quickly adapt to changes.

JSR 286 is a specification that consists of a set of APIs to enable interoperability between portlets and portals, addressing the areas of aggregation, personalization, presentation, and security. JSR 286 supports WSRP (Web Services for Remote Portlets) in comparison with JSR 168, which doesn't.

A JSR 286 enabled portlet allows a plug and play user interface within the portal. It supports a repository of services that users can reference to surface applications in their portlets.

In this chapter, you will learn basics of portlets and how they simplify the development of a portal. We will talk in details about portlet development with respect to JDeveloper and WebCenter. Following are some of the characteristics of portlets:

- Portlets are developed with industry standards. Task Flows are an Oracle standard.

- Portlets are deployed as WAR applications to a managed server.

- A portlet runs on a remote server so it can be consumed by several portals.

- Portlets have a static look and feel (they do not share the CSS of the portal page).

- Because portlets run on separate servers, they usually have a slower performance than Task Flows. See Figure 8-1.

© Vinay Kumar and Daniel Merchán García 2017
V. Kumar and D. M. García, *Beginning Oracle WebCenter Portal 12c*, DOI 10.1007/978-1-4842-2532-5_8

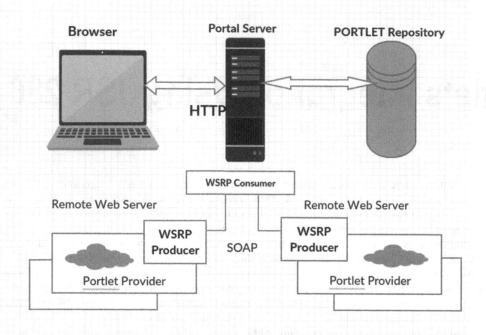

Figure 8-1. *WSRP Architecture*

Why Portlet?

Portlets are reusable components in the Web, which can bring content from different sources. Portlets can display static content to highly complex business logic. It runs on separate containers and exposes in portal technologies. Portlets help to reduce the complexity of organization eco system by bringing CRM, ERP, and the supply chain together. For example: PeopleSoft, JDEdwards, Oracle E-Business Suite, Siebel, etc.

In Oracle stack, these are very useful. Various components can be brought together using portlets. Supported applications include:

- **PeopleSoft**— PeopleSoft applications can be easily exposed as WSRP portlets.

- **JD Edwards**— JD Edwards stand-alone regions can be easily exposed as portlets.

- **Oracle E-Business Suite**—Oracle E-Business Suite provides several prebuilt portlets, such as Applications Navigator, Favorites, and Worklist that can be added to WebCenter Portal. Custom portlets can be created using the EBS R12 Portlet Generator. These portlets are JSR-168 and WSRP-compliant and can be used with third-party web development tools.

- Other prebuilt portlets are available through Oracle's partnership with leading system integrators, software vendors, and content providers. For example .net application can be integrated with WebCenter Portal using Oracle WebCenter WSRP Producer for .NET.It allows any .NET application to act as a WSRP producer.

- ADF application, task flow, or JSF pages can be converted to portlet and integrated in a portlet environment using Oracle JSF Portlet Bridge.

Portlet vs. Task Flow

A common confusion for an ADF developer is deciding when to use portlet and when to use task flow.

Portlets are pluggable components on the Web that can be edited and customized by the user. Portlets run on separate containers; hence security is managed separately and doesn't impact consumer application resources. Response times might be high. Portlets deployed in portlet servers act as portlet producers. JSR 286-based portlet supports inter portlet communication using event. WS security with OWSM (Oracle Web Services Manager) is used for authentication.

Task flows are also reusable components that support customization. It runs on the same container, supports security, skinning, etc. Response times will be better and fast. Task flows can build rich user interfaces. It is tightly coupled and can impact resources of consumed applications. Task flow communicates via contextual events.

When to use Portlet-

- While using legacy applications.

- Multiple pluggable applications in the architecture.

- Doesn't impact consumer application performance.

- Personalization features required in the application.

- Bringing multiple heterogeneous applications under one user interface.

- Technology learning curve for existing developer team.

When to Use Task Flow-

- Building rich user interface.

- Run in same container, response time will be fast.

- No additional security management needed. Full support of ADF and webcenter security.

- Skinning will be easy and support for ADF application.

- No requirement for integration with heterogeneous environment. You can still convert ADF task flow into portlet.

- No technology curve for ADF developer.

■ **Note**   Performance of ADF converted task flow is not very good because of a JSF Portlet Bridge overhead layer.

Creation of Portlet

To create a portal in a portal browser, make sure the portlet server is up and running.

1. In JDeveloper 12.2.1.1.0, create a new application. Select the Oracle WebCenter PortletProducer Application template (Figure 8-2).

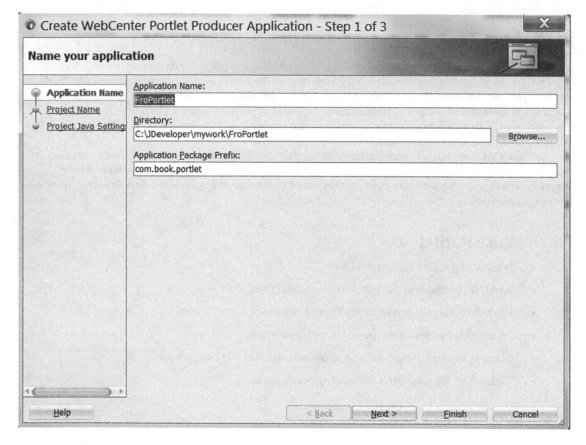

Figure 8-2. *Create portlet in Jdeveloper*

2. Set the Application Name as FroPortlet.

3. Select Project Name and see project features (Figure 8-3).

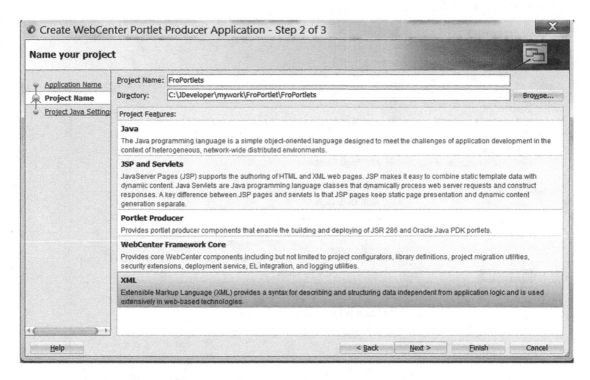

Figure 8-3. *Project Features*

4. You can create a portlet using multiple technologies, but we will be covering ADF technology to make portlets as most readers will be familiar with this technology. We can deploy this portlet to portlet server using the deployment wizard.

5. Right-click on the application and navigate to new from Gallery and click on ADF task flow from Web Tier (Figure 8-4).

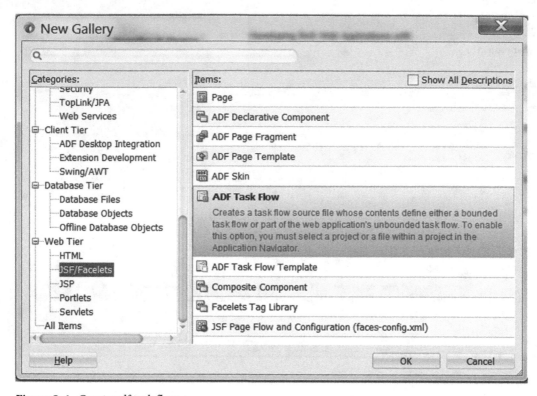

Figure 8-4. *Create adf task flow*

6. Provide name of task flow. Select check box named Create as Bounded Task Flow with page fragments as shown in Figure 8-5.

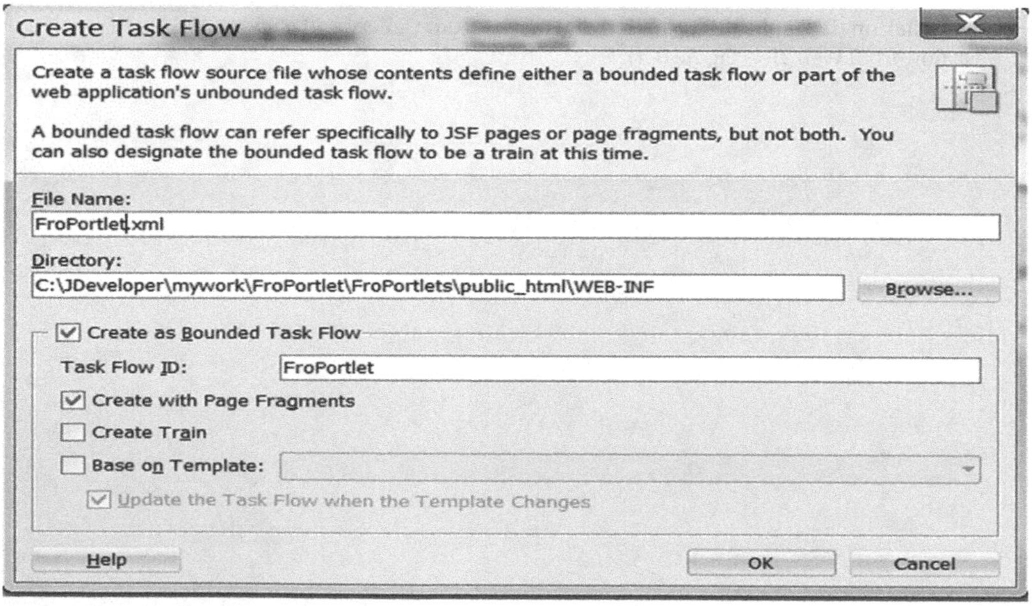

Figure 8-5. *Create adf task flow*

7. Now the project structure is as shown in Figure 8-6.

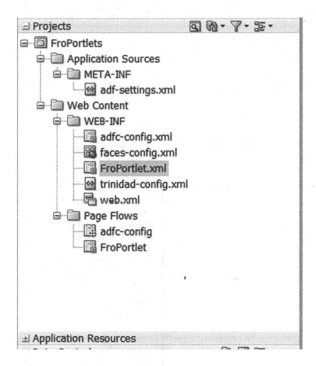

Figure 8-6. *Project structure*

8. Drag and drop a view activity in task flow FroPortlet.xml as below in Figure 8-7.

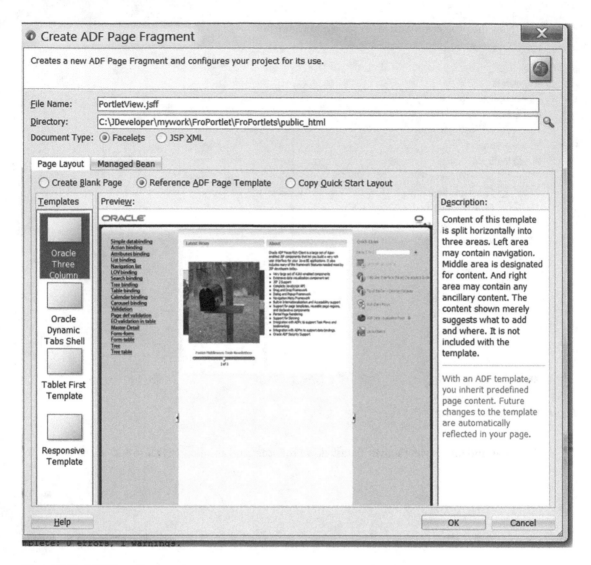

Figure 8-7. *ADF Page Fragment*

9. Add content to page, or drag drop component from data control. For a sample, add some images and text (Figure 8-8).

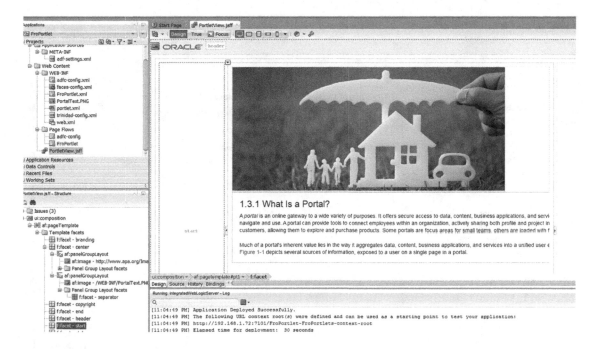

Figure 8-8. *ADF Page Fragment with data*

10. Task flow is now complete and ready to be deployed as portlet.

11. Right-click on project ➤ new ➤ From Gallery ➤ Web Tier ➤ Portlet ➤ Manage Portlet Entries of Task Flow.

12. Same portlet conversion can be done by right-clicking on task flow and selecting Create Portlet Entry (Figure 8-9).

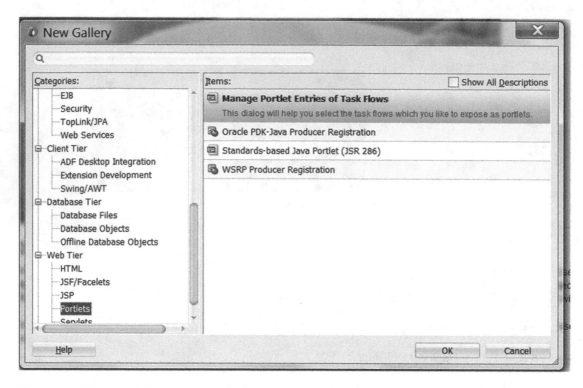

Figure 8-9. Manage Portlet Entries of Task Flow

13.   Select right task flow to convert to convert into portlet (Figure 8-10).

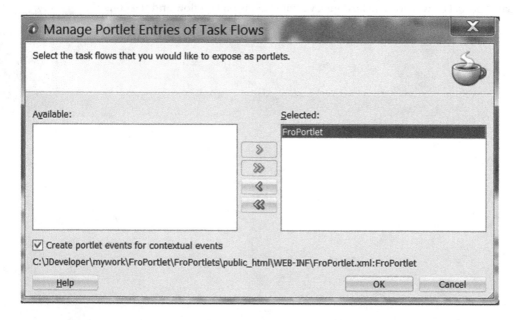

Figure 8-10. Task Flow selection in Manage Portlet Entries of Task Flow

14. Select **Create portlet events for contextual events** to create portlet events in the portlet.xml file for any contextual events exposed by the task flows. This option is selected by default.

15. Portlet events enable a portlet to communicate with the page on which it resides and with other portlets on that page.

16. Click OK to create portlets for the selected task flows.

17. When portlets have been created, you should receive message like "New portlet has been successfully created."

18. New portlet.xml will be created in project structure (Figure 8-11).

Figure 8-11. *Portlet mode in Portlet.xml*

19. This portlet.xml can run on integrated WebLogic server or deployed on WebLogic managed server. Click portlet.xml and run.

20. After Portlet deployment on integrated WebLogic server, URL with following address "localhost:port/contextroot/portlets/info" will open.

21. Click on **WSRP v2 WSDL**link to view wsdl, which can be registered in WebCenter Portal and portlet producer (Figure 8-12).

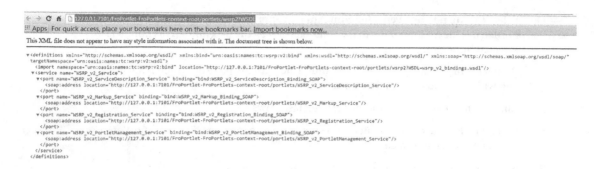

Figure 8-12. Portlet WSDL

22. After testing locally, application can be deployed on weblogic managed server. While deploying, pop-up will be displayed as shown in Figure 8-13

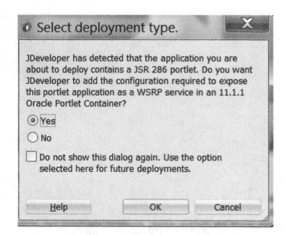

Figure 8-13. Portlet Deployment Type

23. After successful deployment, go to WebCenter Portal console.

24. Navigate to Administration ➤ Tools and Services-Portlet producers.

25. Provide producer name. This name will be displayed under portlet, while adding this portlet into page. Select Producer Type as WSRP Producer (Figure 8-14).

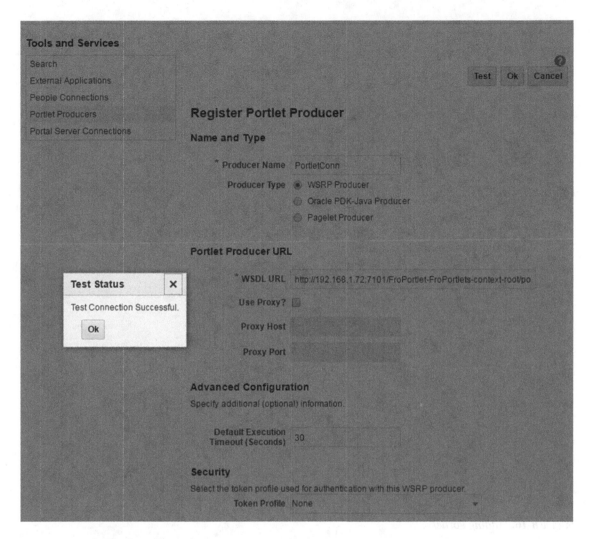

Figure 8-14. Register Portlet Producer

26. Add WSDL URL and other information and click test. Click OK on successful Test Status Pop-Up.

27. Now create a new portal with a page. Edit page and add content from resource catalog (Figure 8-15).

Figure 8-15. *Edit page*

28. Click on UI Component ➤ Portlet ➤ PortletConn (Name of portlet producer) ➤ Portlet Name and add (Figure 8-16).

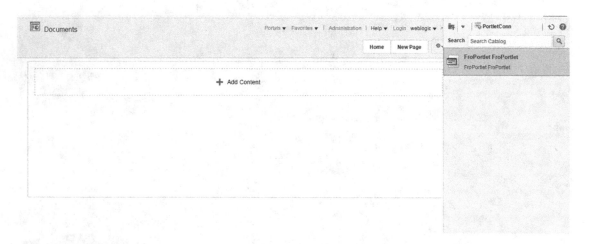

Figure 8-16. *Adding Portlet*

29. Portlet added in page. Click save and view portal. See Figure 8-17.

Figure 8-17. *Portlet in portal*

Portlet from a JSF Application

Oracle JSF Portlet Bridge provides features to expose a JSF application or task flow as portlets. JSF application can convert to portlet using the Create Portlet Entry dialog; no coding is required.

To create a JSF portlet from an existing application page:

1. In JDeveloper, open the application that contains the JSF page that you want to portletize.

2. In the project structure right-click JSF page and choose Create Portlet Entry.

■ **Note** Page containing portlet can't be converted to portlet.

---

3. In the Create Portlet Entry dialog, in the Portlet Name field, enter a name for the portlet.

4. Provide Display name and title.

5. In the Short Title field, enter a short title for your portlet.

6. In the Description field, enter a description for your portlet.

7. Select Create portlet events for contextual events to create portlet events in the portlet.xml file for any contextual events exposed by the page. This option is selected by default.

8. Click OK.

When you create a JSF portlet based on a page, a portlet.xml file is created (or updated if it already exists) to contain the portlet entry for the page. The file is open for viewing or editing.

After that you can follow the same process as discussed in the previous section to deploy on a weblogic managed server and register into portal environment using portlet producer and add-in portal pages.

Create JSR 286 Portlet

1. Open Portlet producer application and right-click New ➤ From Gallery ➤ Web Tier ➤ Portlets ➤ **Standards-based Java Portlet (JSR 286).** See Figure 8-18.

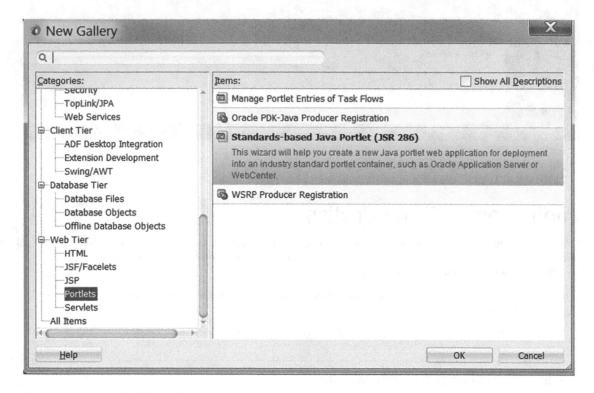

Figure 8-18. *Standards-based Java Portlet option in new Gallery*

■ **Tip** If application contains JSR 286 portlet already, then new portlet can be added by right-clicking portlet. xml and choosing **Add portlet** or editing portlet.xml by going to design tab and clicking **Add icon** on portlets tab.

---

2. Provide name, class, package and other information in General Portlet Information (Figure 8-19).

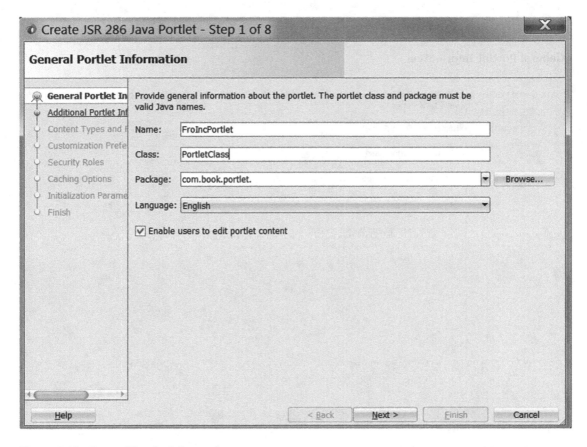

Figure 8-19. *General Portlet information*

3. Provide all other information in various tabs like display name, title, description, etc. (Figure 8-20).

■ **Note** Display Name, Title, Description, and keyword will not be used in WebCenter Portal. This is useful if the portlet will be consumed in a third-party application.

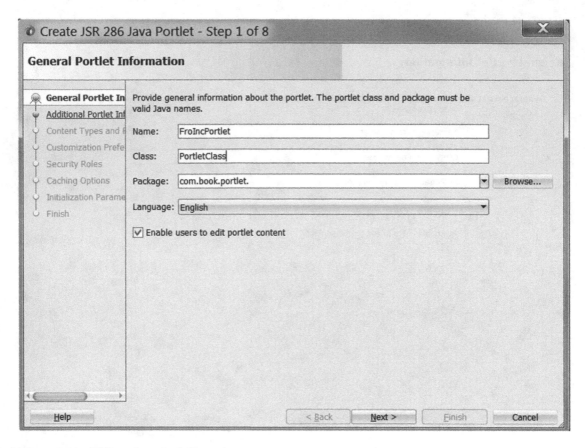

Figure 8-20. *Additonal portlet information*

4. In **Content Types and Portlet Modes**, you can select the implementation method of portlet modes. Either you can use ADF –Faces JSPX or standard JSPs (Figure 8-21).

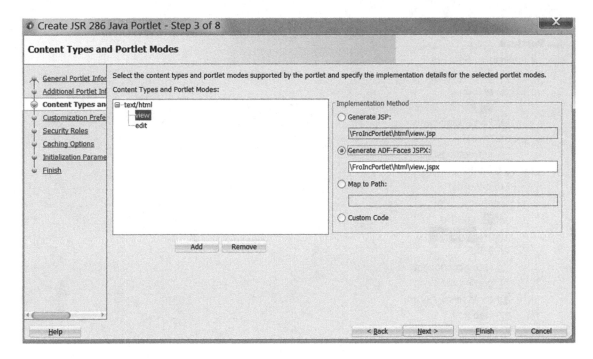

Figure 8-21. *Generate Portlet mode view*

5.   Select Generate ADF-Faces JSPX options to generate a page in which ADF-Faces components can be used. Provide name of ADF-based view. Similarly, edit mode view can also be selected.

6.   Select all other tabs information like customization preference, security roles, caching option and initialization parameters and click finish. Project structure will be as shown in Figure 8-22.

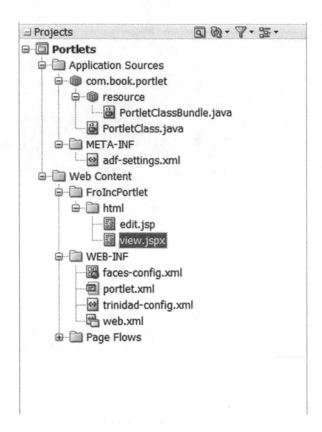

Figure 8-22. *JSR 286 Portlet project structure*

7. Add business logic in portlet and deploy portlets as discussed earlier in a previous section. Register wsdl in portlet producer and add portlets in portal pages as before.

CHAPTER 9

■ ■ ■

Creating Pagelet Producer

Overview

Portal technology is used to aggregate information from multiple sources. These aggregations can be done using service-orientated architecture, portlet-based, or direct from information source. In some situations, the above-mentioned solutions don't meet the requirements. For example, no direct connection is available to a source application or third-party application separated by different domains, organizations, etc. To serve these types of challenges, WebCenter Portal gives Pagelet technology.

Pagelet Technology is a feature of consuming existing third-party web user interfaces and using it as a reusable component in a page, called a **Pagelet.** Pagelet Producer is a key solution inside WebCenter Portal. Earlier this technology was called as Ensemble and it served as a gateway between legacy web content and the Portal. The idea is to use Pagelet Producer to bring content from remote servers, manipulate this content (with HTML injection), and present it to the user in the Portal page. This will bring any html to serve in portal page. HTML by Pagelet can be parameterized, configurable, and can communicate with each other. It will manipulate a URL from a remote server. It is good for making pages more modern and adding new interfaces in a portal just by clipping a page from a different URL.

When to use Pagelet

- Adding User Interface from web applications that don't expose any medium of integration, either through APIs.

- Applications that support portlets can be easily integrated as Pagelet, that is, portlets as WSRP, Oracle PDK-Java, CSP, and WebParts.

It can provide a web UI to almost all Oracle web-based products, that is, Oracle WebCenter Portal, Oracle WebCenter Sites, or any product that uses HTML. This is quite useful for clipping, injecting, parsing, and event handling.

Pagelet Producer Architecture

Pagelet Producer is designed with multiple modules and scripts. Pagelet architecture, as mentioned in Oracle documentation is described in Figure 9-1 and shows all internal components in detail. Security is managed using Oracle Platform Security Services (OPSS). Various modules are defined using a combination of HTML and JS. All clipping content is stored in an MDS schema. HTTP client is used to access remote URLs. JavaScript plays a key role in rendering the content. HTTP client does URL rewriting internally.

© Vinay Kumar and Daniel Merchán García 2017

V. Kumar and D. M. García, *Beginning Oracle WebCenter Portal 12c*, DOI 10.1007/978-1-4842-2532-5_9

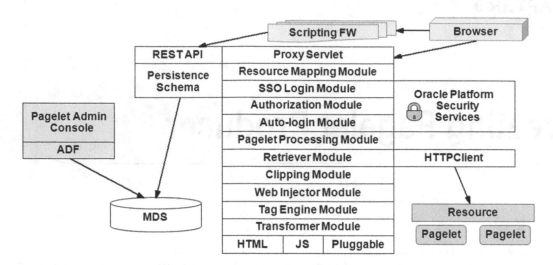

Figure 9-1. *Pagelet Producer internal architecture*

Figure 9-2 discusses more about how Pagelet Producer works with WebCenter Portal.

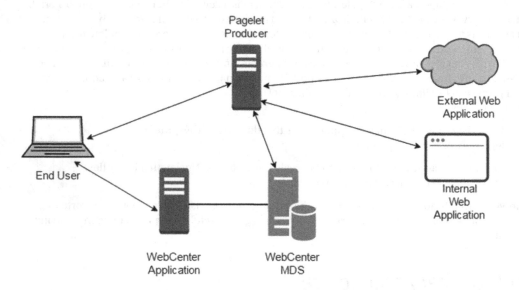

Figure 9-2. *Pagelet Producer interaction flow*

Pagelet Producer is a Java application that runs on a J2EE application server. It runs on an MDS database schema. When a user requests a WebCenter Portal page that contains Pagelet, the portal returns the response as a page consisting of JavaScript that invokes Pagelet Producer resources to render the pagelet in the page. JavaScript is responsible for rendering **Pagelet Producer.**

Pagelet Producer calls internal or external web application as wrappers of HTML content. It transforms the HTML content (rewriting URL) and returns content to the browser for rendering process. All external/internal applications are registered in Pagelet Producer as **resources.** When creating a resource in Pagelet Producer, it will make a proxy to map an internal application to remote URLs. Resources also transform content and manage authentication. Pagelet Producer has dynamic registration.

Pagelet Producer acts as a proxy server and manages transactions between a portal and external resources. HTTP client is a medium of communication between Services on external resources and the Pagelet Producer. For example, when an end user requests a portal page, Pagelet Producer makes an asynchronous call to external resources to bring HTML content for the page.

Creating Pagelet Producer Resource

1. Make sure WC_Portlet managed server is running. Navigate to WebCenter Pagelet Producer Admin (`http://host:port/pagelets/admin`) and login as WebLogic. See Figure 9-3.

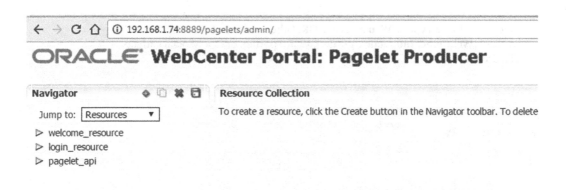

Figure 9-3. *WebCenter Portal Pagelet Producer console*

2. In the home page, select existing resources and click on create button (Figure 9-4).

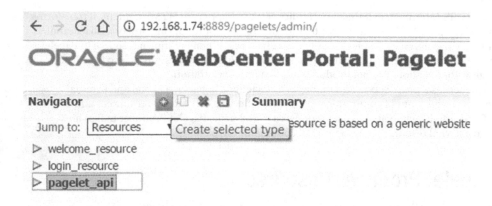

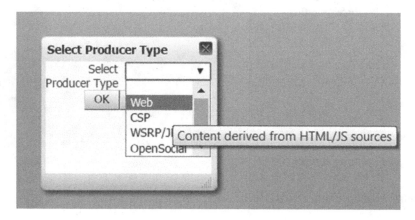

Figure 9-4. Create new resource

3. Select **Producer Type** as **Web** and click OK. Other options of Producer Type are CSP (WebCenter Interaction portlet), WSRP portlet, or OpenSocial gadgets (Figure 9-5).

Figure 9-5. Select Producer Type

4. Provide Name of resource, source, and destination URL. Also enable check boxes for **DHTML Rewriting** and **Asynchronous Rewriting**. In the example below, a weather website named "accuweather" is used to display weather information of a city in portal using Pagelet Producer. Source and destination URL is as follows.

Source URL : http://www.accuweather.com/

Destination URL : en/nl/amsterdam/249758/weather-forecast/249758/

5. Click on **save** icon. Select Pagelets inside "accuweather" and click on **create** icon (Figure 9-6).

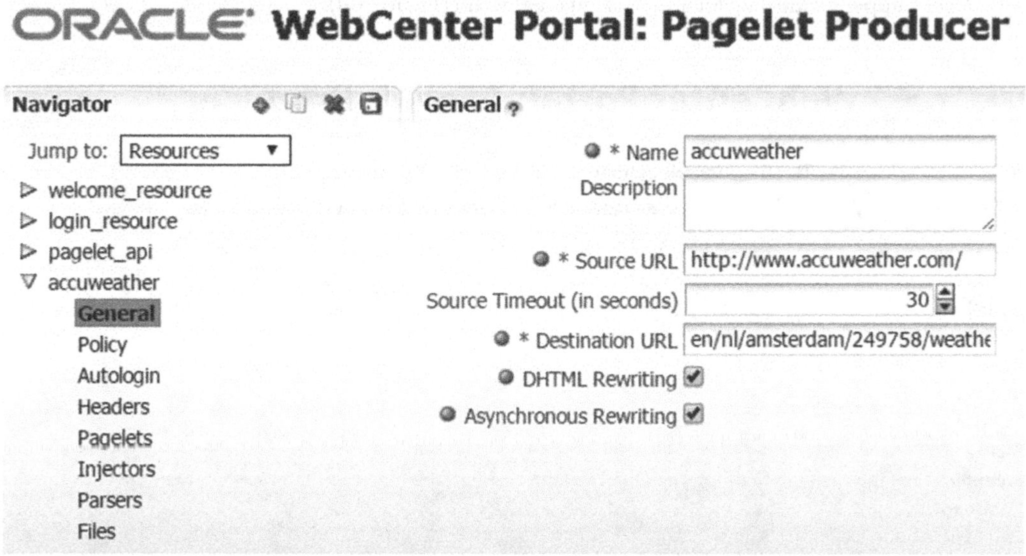

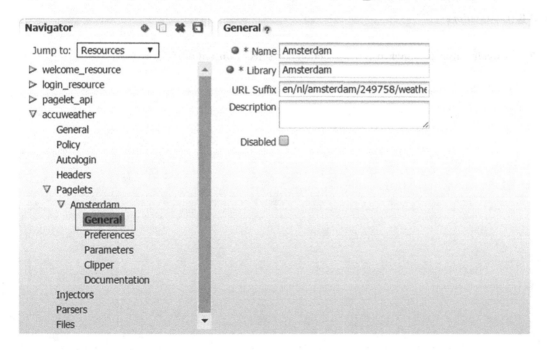

Figure 9-6. *Create resource*

6. Select general tab and provide name and URL suffix as in Figure 9-7 and **Save** all.

Figure 9-7. *Provide Pagelets name*

7. Select Clipper inside pagelet and click on create icon (Figure 9-8).

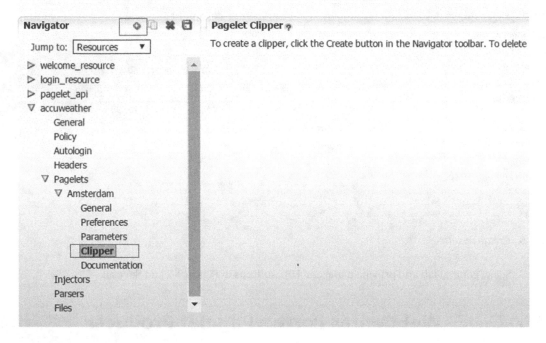

Figure 9-8. *Create clipper*

8. Provide name of clipper in general section and select **Content** tab (Figure 9-9).

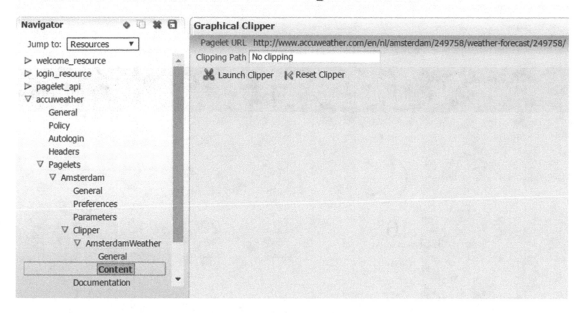

Figure 9-9. *Clipper content*

9. Click on **Launch Clipper.** New page opens in pagelets with content of accuweather website (Figure 9-10).

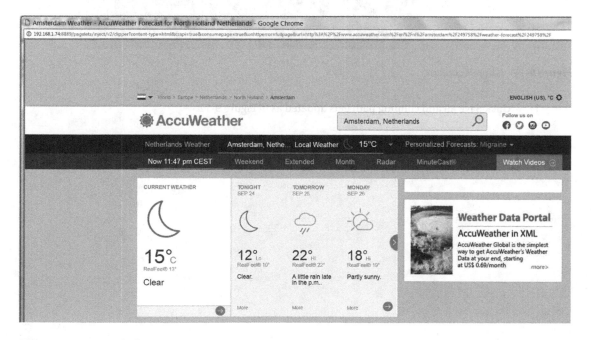

Figure 9-10. *Launch clipper*

10. Select selected part of page using a clipper of Pagelets (Figure 9-11).

Figure 9-11. *Clipper content*

11. Click Save all and clipping path gets updated as in Figure 9-12.

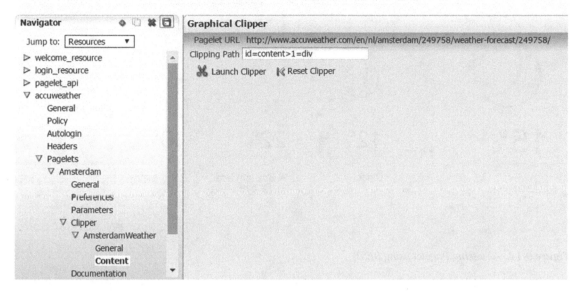

Figure 9-12. Graphical clipper

12. Test the clipper content from Documentation section. Select **Documentation** (Figure 9-13) and test by clicking **Access Pagelet using REST.** Pagelet can be accessed using REST and JavaScript. Inserting the following JavaScript will add pagelets into portal page (Figure 9-14).

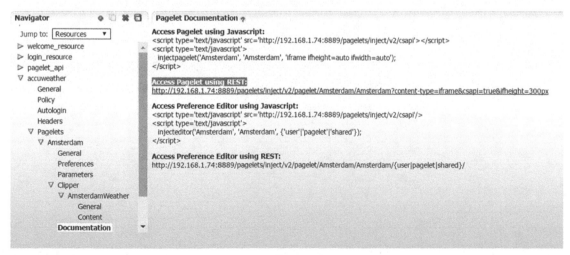

Figure 9-13. Documentation

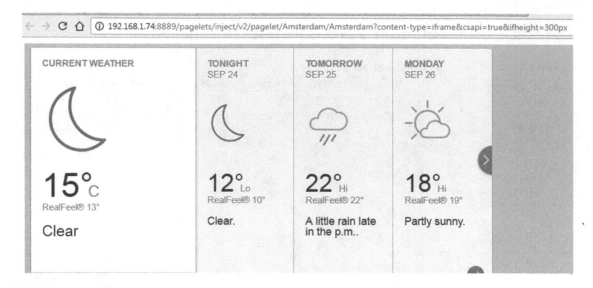

Figure 9-14. *Accessing Pagelet using REST*

Pagelets in WebCenter Portal

Pagelets created can be consumed in WebCenter Portal. Before consuming in page, it should be registered using Portlet Producer.

1. Navigate to portal setting page in Administration console.

2. Click on **Tools and Services** (Figure 9-15).

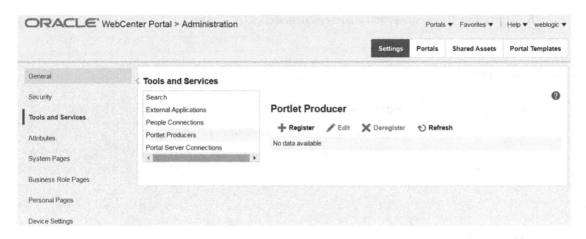

Figure 9-15. Tools and Services

3. Select Portlet Producer and click on **Register** icon.

4. Select **Producer Type** as Pagelet Producer. Provide pagelets console URL in **Server URL** (Figure 9-16).

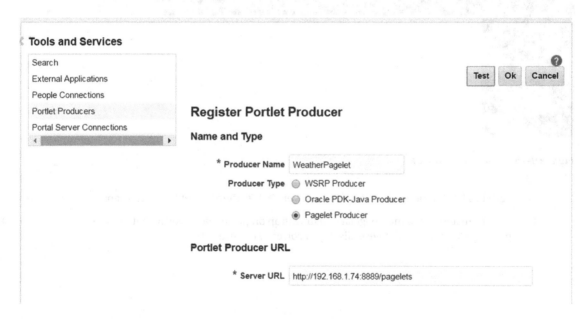

Figure 9-16. Register Portlet Producer

5.   Click Test. If test connection is successful then click OK (Figure 9-17).

Figure 9-17.   *Portlet Producer lists*

6.   Open any new or existing portal in edit mode. In page edit mode, click on Add content (Figure 9-18).

Figure 9-18.   *Add content in page*

7.   Select as UI Components ➤ Pagelet Producers ➤ WeatherPagelet ➤ Amsterdam.

8.   Select Amsterdam named pagelet and drag drop on portal page. Verify that pagelet added in portal page is displayed correctly (Figure 9-19).

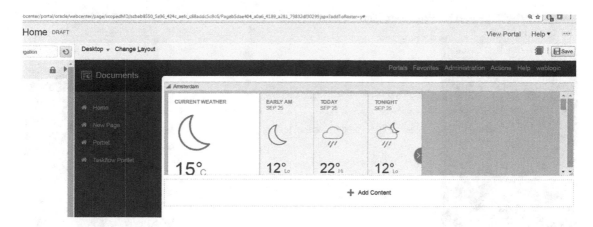

Figure 9-19. *Pagelets in page*

9. Click on configure icon and select **Parameters** (Figure 9-20).

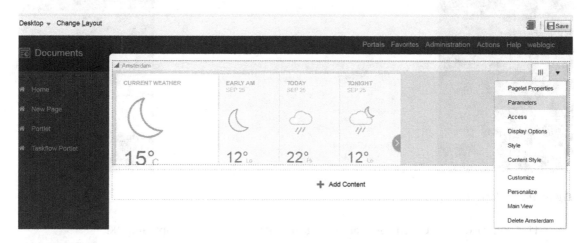

Figure 9-20. *Pagelets in page*

10. Pagelet parameters can be changed. By default, it is displayed in Iframe. Change Iframe height to 900px. Click Apply and OK (Figure 9-21).

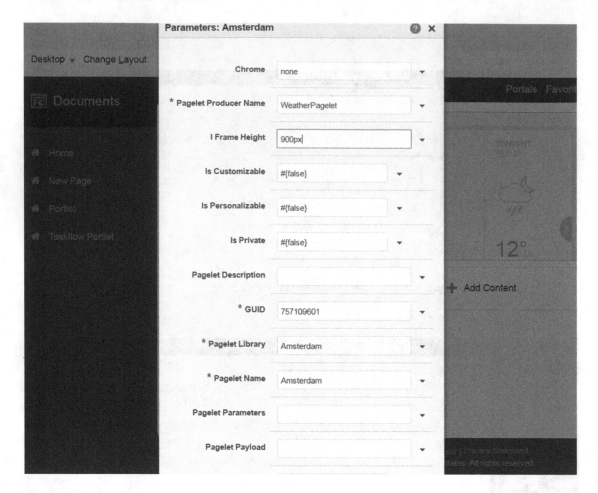

Figure 9-21. *Pagelets parameters*

11. Similarly select Content Style and change height as 1000px. Click apply and OK.

12. In configure section properties, parameters, display options, content style can be managed (Figure 9-22).

Figure 9-22. *Pagelets parameters*

13. Edit page looks as what is shown in Figure 9-23.

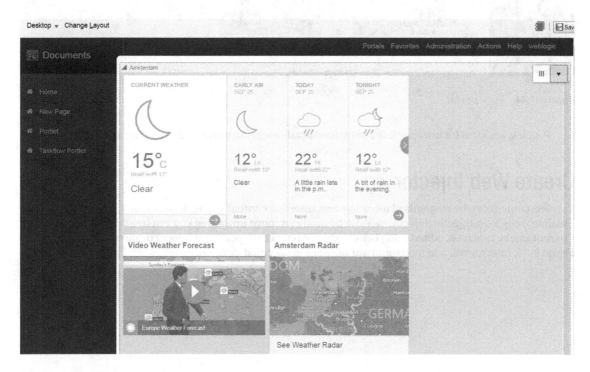

Figure 9-23. *Edit page*

14. Click Save and view portal (Figure 9-24).

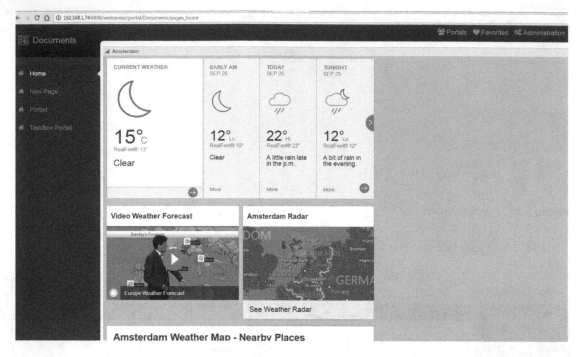

Figure 9-24. *View portal*

Pagelets are ideal for bringing third-party functionalities in the portal without doing any development.

Create Web Injector

Pagelets content can be customized using Injector. Inserting content in pagelet at a specified location is possible using Web Injector. Injector can also be used to remove unwanted content by adding blank injector. Content can be replaced, edited using before, after, or replace properties at Inject Location. As pointed out in Figure 9-25, Injector will add image and text message in specified location.

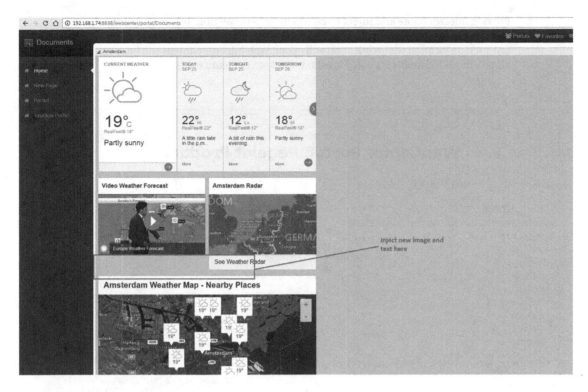

Figure 9-25. *Inject image and text*

1. For creating Web Injector, select **Injectors** section in accuweather resource. Click on create icon (Figure 9-26).

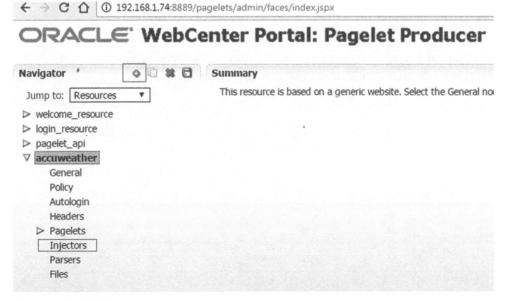

Figure 9-26. *Web Injectors*

2. Provide injector name and **Inject Location** in General section. **Inject Location** can be Before, After, or Replace in resource's HTML Content. This text will point out specific location where injection will occur. Web injector content will be added/modified in this specified location. Click save (Figure 9-27).

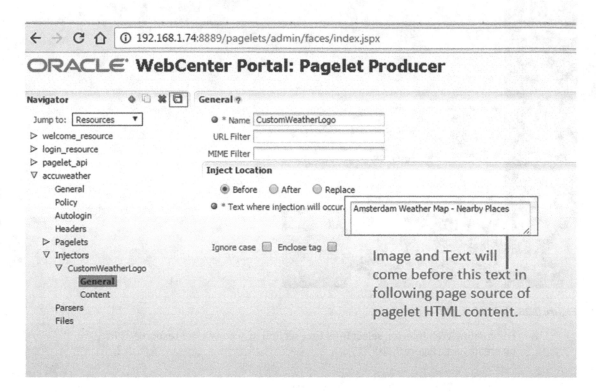

Figure 9-27. *Web Injector information*

3. Select **Content** section. Add image HTML tag with image source followed by custom text message in Content section as shown in Figure 9-28.

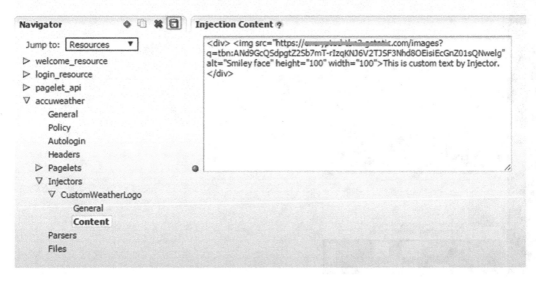

Figure 9-28. Web Injector content information

4. Click Save.

■ **Note**   Web Injector is ideal for adding and replacing content in Pagelet Resource HTML content. Simple Text message can be used to point out specified location in page for modifying content. Following are important Inject Location. – Before. – After - Replace.

---

5. Open portal in which we added Pagelet Producer earlier and verify the pagelet content (Figure 9-29).

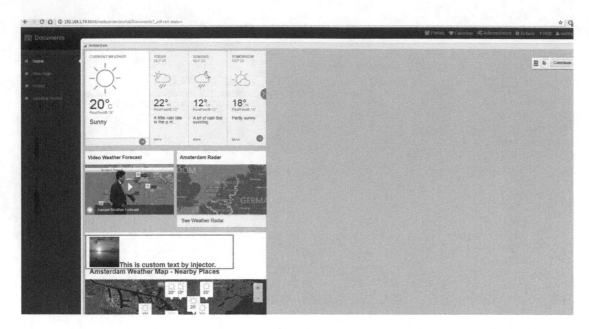

Figure 9-29. *View Portal with Injector*

Similar to adding a content, removing the content is also possible using custom JavaScript. In General section, HTML header can be added for example. **</head>** (Figure 9-30).

ORACLE° WebCenter Portal: Pagelet Producer

Navigator	◆ ▢ ✖ 🗗	General ?
Jump to: Resources ▼		● * Name RemoveHeaderFooter
▷ welcome_resource		URL Filter
▷ login_resource		MIME Filter
▷ pagelet_api		**Inject Location**
▽ accuweather		
General		● Before ○ After ○ Replace
Policy		● * Text where injection will occur. </head>
Autologin		
Headers		
▷ Pagelets		Ignore case ▢ Enclose tag ▢
▽ Injectors		
▽ RemoveHeaderFooter		
General		
Content		
Parsers		
Files		

Figure 9-30. *Remove Header Footer*

The following JavaScript tag will get handle of header and footer tag (Figure 9-31).

```
<script type="text/javascript">
if (window.addEventListener) {
window.addEventListener('load', removeContent, false);
} else if (document.attachEvent) {
window.attachEvent('onload', removeContent);
}
function removeContent() {
var header = null;
// find the header table by class
if (document.getElementsByClassName) {
head = document.getElementsByClassName('headTagName')[0];
footer = document.getElementsByClassName('footerTagName')[0];
}
if (header != null) {
head.style.display = 'none';
footer.style.display = 'none';
}
}
</script>
```

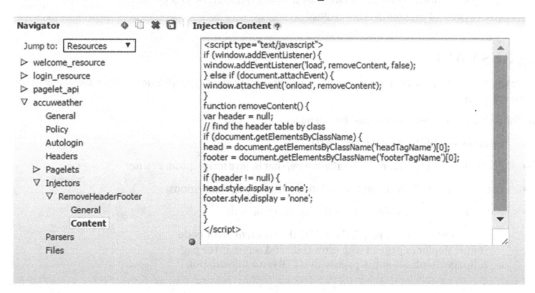

Figure 9-31. *Remove Header Footer with JavaScript*

Adding a Pagelet to a Page

Once pagelet is created and deployed , it can be inserted in proxied or non-proxied web applications page by:

- JavaScript
- REST

Using JavaScript

function injectpagelet(library, name, iframe_options, payload, params, context_id, element_id, is_in_community)

The inject pagelet method has the following attributes :

- iframe_options: This attribute is optional and tells whether to use Iframe or not.
- payload: This is optional and sends with request as parameters.
- params: These are query string format parameters for pagelets..
- context_id: It should be Integer value. This is an identifier for external party.
- element_id: HTML id of component, in which pagelet content should be inserted.
- is_in_community: This decides whether the pagelet is part of a community (WebCenter Interaction) or group page.

Using REST API

http://proxy:port/inject/v2/pagelet/libraryname/pageletname? content-type=iframe&csapi=true&ifheight=123px&ifclass=myclass

The following parameters are defined for the pagelet inject URL:

- instanceid: This is pagelet instance ID.
- content-type: This will return content type, that is, javascript, html, iframe.
- csapi: Confirms if CSAPI will be included with the pagelet response.
- onhttperror: This decides how to display the error code:
  - comment: Replaces pagelet with HTML comment error code.
  - inline: Replaces pagelet with error code and server error page.
  - fullpage: Replaces entire page with HTTP error information.

CHAPTER 10

■ ■ ■

Portal Security Administration

The Security is one of the main key concepts to learn about Enterprise Portals as they are the Single Secure Entry point for the information.

In this chapter you will learn about the following:

- An overview about the Portal Architecture and the Security Layers for learning the basic concepts about security.

- How System Administrators can change Security Settings using Oracle Enterprise Manager Console.

- How Portal Administrators can modify security settings of services and components using the Portal Administration Console.

Security Architecture

Oracle WebCenter Portal is a pre-built J2EE Application that is built on top of Oracle ADF Framework (wrapper on top of JSF framework).

To be precise, Oracle ADF is an end-to-end Java EE framework that simplifies application development by providing Out-of-the-box infrastructure services and a visual and declarative development experience.

As it is built on top of Oracle ADF, it implements **Oracle ADF Security** Framework that is just another security framework wrapping the Java Standard JAAS (Java Authentication and Authorization Service).

■ **Tip**   This book is focused on Oracle WebCenter Portal. Check the Oracle ADF documentation for learning about the Oracle ADF Security Framework.

Overview of Security Layers

Security concepts do not finish on Oracle ADF Security. There are multiple layers that you should understand before (Figure 10-1).

© Vinay Kumar and Daniel Merchán García 2017
V. Kumar and D. M. García, *Beginning Oracle WebCenter Portal 12c*, DOI 10.1007/978-1-4842-2532-5_10

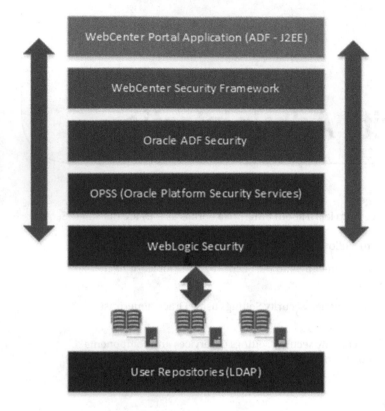

Figure 10-1. *WebCenter Portal Security Layers*

- **WebCenter Portal Application Security**: This is the Top Layer and what the Administrator or user sees. Basically, WebCenter Portal provides:

  - Administration for global security settings for mapping Application Roles with permissions.

  - Administration of specific Portal security for specific Portals. What the users, who are members to a specific, Portal have rights to.

  - Self-Registration: Allows the end users to register into the identity store.

  - External Applications: WebCenter Portal allows to you to register External Applications that are not part of the Portal Architecture. For example: With access to their Gmail account, Users can store their credentials of different accounts in a secure way.

- **WebCenter Security Framework**: All the activities and tasks that a user or administrator can do is because of the WebCenter Security Framework. This framework has the following features:

  - Implements a Security Model that enables global security and Portal-specific security.

  - Implements a Permission-based authorization.

- Implements a Role-mapping based authorization.

- Allows end users to store their credentials mappings for External Applications securely.

- **Oracle ADF Security**: As commented before, WebCenter Portal is an ADF Application that uses Oracle ADF Security for Authentication and Authorization of the users. The main key features of Oracle ADF Security are the following:

  - Page, Task Flow, and ADF Components authorization. WebCenter Portal Pages are Oracle ADF pages on behind.

  - Credential Mappings APIs.

  - Login, Logout functionalities for all kind of security configurations (using or not using Single Sign-On).

- **Oracle Platform Security Services (OPSS)**: All the Oracle Fusion Middleware applications, and then Oracle WebCenter Portal, rely on OPSS for abstracting the security API independently from the LDAP or back-end configuration that holds the user and roles information. Some of the main features of OPSS are the following:

  - It implements Out-of-the-box and assigns the Authenticated and Anonymous roles to users accessing the applications.

  - Implements the three pillars:

    - **Identity Store**: Repository of users and groups. It must be LDAP-based. Out-of-the-box, WebCenter Portal uses the DefaultAuthenticator of WebLogic (embedded LDAP of the Application Server); avoid using this for a production environment.

    - **Policy Store**: Repository where the application and system policies are stored. Basically, it stores the mapping between Roles and Permissions by application.

    - **Credential Store**: Repository of credentials used by the applications for storing them securely.

  - Implements Identity Management Services for creating and editing and deleting users in the LDAP configured as Identity Store.

  - Authorization based on permissions-role mapping stored in the Policy Store.

- **WebLogic Server Security**: The application server is where the user providers are configured. WebLogic is responsible for the following:

  - WebLogic Authenticators: It handles open user sessions within the Application Server.

  - Identity Providers: The application server can be configured with multiple LDAP providers to retrieve user / roles information.

  - Identity Asserters: For asserting users from given token (Single Sign-On).

Understanding WebCenter Portal Security

By default, WebCenter Portal configures a set of predefined Application Roles that can be assigned to a user or to a group of users (called Enterprise Groups). These roles give to the users a set of permissions over the services offered by WebCenter Portal.

Before talking about these Out-of-the-box Application Roles, default permissions, or how to administer the roles, let's first understand all the components within WebCenter Portal.

WebLogic Application Server, by default, uses an internal LDAP that is accessed via the default Identity Provider *DefaultAuthenticator*. For production environments, WebLogic Application Server must be configured with external LDAPs such OID (Oracle Internet Directory), AD (Active Director) or other LDAPs or Virtualized LDAPs such as OUD (Oracle Unified Directory).

The Identity Store is configured as WebLogic Domain Level and only can be configured against one of the LDAP repositories. It means that WebCenter Portal will only use that LDAP (through OPSS API) for Identity Management Operations such as creation of users and modification of passwords. (Figure 10-2).

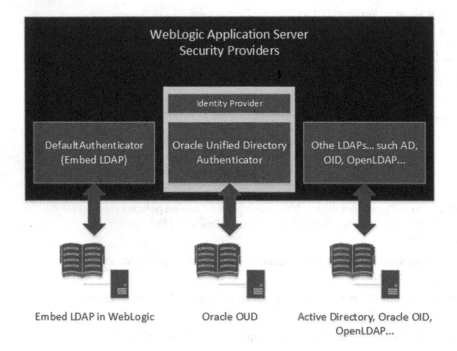

Figure 10-2. *Example of WebCenter Portal + WebLogic with Multiple LDAPs*

Basically, a user authenticating in Oracle WebCenter Portal will authenticate against the LDAP providers configured in WebLogic Application Server (if this is configured to try to authenticate against all of them). In case the authentication was successful, then it will load the User Profile Information and the Enterprise Groups from the LDAP that it is configured as Identity Store. However, if it does not find the user in the Identity Store it will be a Virtual User authenticated without information or Enterprise Groups / Roles associated (only Authenticated-Role and Anonymous-Role).

Using virtualized LDAPs that act as unique authentication providers and identity store repositories are a good solution. However, not always there is infrastructure for a virtualized LDAP. WebLogic Application Server brings other configurations to aggregate multiple LDAPs into a single LDAP (libOVD) and also to build the user Profile partially or fully from multiple user repositories.

■ **Note** Oracle WebLogic Application Server brings mechanisms to aggregate multiple Identity Store LDAPs (libOVD). However, the performance can be affected using this type of virtualization solution. The best practice is to use a virtualized LDAP such as OUD (Oracle Unified Directory).

The Policy Store and Credential Store, Out-of-the-box, are configured against the Oracle Database OPSS Schema.

■ **Note** OPSS Database Schema is created during the installation of WebCenter Portal.

Oracle WebCenter Portal makes use of the Policy Store for storing all the Mapping of the Application Roles – Permissions of the components. As commented before, it uses WebCenter Security Framework, which already implements the WebCenter Security Model that allows you to have multiple Portals secured independently.

The Credential Store is where WebCenter Portal securely stores credentials for the connection to the back-end WebCenter Services and also for all the External Applications (Figure 10-3).

■ **Note** Since 12.2.1, the Policy Store and Credential Store are installed, by default, against the Database. Remember, the policy store based on the file system is not supported for production environments due to performance.

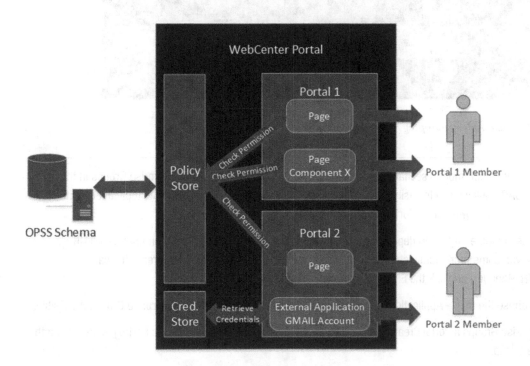

Figure 10-3. Overview about usage of Policy Store and Credential Store

Application Roles vs. Enterprise Groups

The Application Roles are the Roles that are mapped to a set of permissions within an Application and only exist in the scope of the application.

The Enterprise Groups are the logical organization of the users from an external repository.

How are the Application Roles and Enterprise Groups linked?

The Identity Store stores the User and Roles / Enterprise group information coming from the LDAP. Application Roles can be mapped to (Figure 10-4):

- **Users**: The user directly receives the Application Role and the permissions set for that Application Role.

- **Enterprise Group / Role**: All the users within the group receive the Application Role and the permissions set for that Application Role.

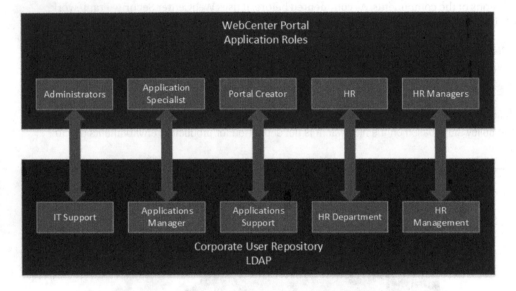

Figure 10-4. *Example of mapping Application Roles with Enterprise Groups*

■ **Tip**   It is very common to see large companies with users well structured in Enterprise Groups in the company LDAP. It allows you to easily set up Roles and Permissions to people for all the applications within the Company, not only in WebCenter Portal.

For example: Imagine for the HR department you have a group called HR and maybe another called HR Managers with some more administration permissions. In WebCenter Portal you will create the same (HR and HR Manager) and link the Enterprise Groups instead of direct users.

Try not to abuse the User - Application Role assignation; try to group the users in Enterprise Groups if possible.

With Enterprise Groups a Portal Creator can add easily all the members for the specific Portal just by adding the Enterprise Group.

Default Application Roles in WebCenter Portal

Out-of-the-box, WebCenter Portal creates a set of Application Roles that are described in the following table:

Table 10-1. *Default Application Roles in WebCenter Portal*

Application Role	Description	Type / Comments
Administrator	Administrators can set application-wide properties for WebCenter Portal, create business role pages, configure defaults for discussion forums, mail, and people connection services, register producers and external applications, as well as perform other administrative duties such as editing and customizing System Pages. In addition, they can also manage users and roles, delegate or revoke privileges to/from other users, manage portals and portal templates, and also import and export portal as well as deploy and propagate portal to between different environments. Out-of-the-box, the system administrator is the only user assigned full administrative privileges for the WebCenter Portal through the Administrator role.	Role manager via Portal Administration Console. By default, it will assign the weblogic administrator user as the main administrator, which is coming from the embedded LDAP. Change it to use administrator users from the External user repository.
AppConnectionsManager	It allows the users to create connections for Portlet Producers and External Applications. Note: This Role is created Out-of-the-box by WebCenter Portal Installer and only the Administrator users are members of this Role.	This Role cannot be administrated via Portal Administration UI. It can be administrated via WebLogic Administration Console or Enterprise Manager.
AppConnectionsViewer	Same as AppConnectionsManager, but only with view permission. Users cannot manage or administrate the connections of Portlet Producer or External Applications.	This Role cannot be administrated via Portal Administration UI. It can be administrated via WebLogic Administration Console or Enterprise Manager.

(*continued*)

Table 10-1. (*continued*)

Application Role	Description	Type / Comments
Application Specialist	Application Specialists can create portals; manage portal templates; create, edit, and delete pages, page styles, page templates, Content Presenter templates, data controls, pagelets, resource catalogs, skins, task flow styles, and task flows; update People Connections data; and connect with people. As a difference with Administrators, they cannot manage security permissions or customize System Pages.	This role is something like the "Administrator" user of a Business User with experience in WebCenter Portal to support the Portal Managers to complete their tasks.
Portal Creator	This Role only gives permissions for Create Portals and Manage Portal Templates. After creating a Portal, the user receives the Portal-Level Role called Portal Manager that gives all the Administration privileges for that Specific Portal.	A Portal Creator should be mapped to business users that will create the Portals and populate the Portals with Pages and components.
Authenticated User	This is the Role given to every user that can authenticate against WebCenter Portal. They can access the Home Portal. By default, this role gives the following rights: • Portal Server: View • Create Portals • Create Portal Templates • Create Pages • Update People Connections Data • Connect with People	This role is directly mapped to the OPSS authenticated role.
Public - User	Role given to all the users that have access via Browser to WebCenter Portal (unauthenticated or authenticated). They can see only Public Portals and Pages or Documents that are marked as Public.	Take care about giving any Administration rights to the Public - User as it will give rights to everyone.

Default Application Roles as Portal Level

As shown in the previous topic, when a Portal Creator or someone creates a Portal then WebCenter Portal gives to the creator the Portal-Level Role: **Portal Manager**.

It gives Administration rights for managing Pages, Publishing Pages, administering security for that specific Portal, etc.

Administrator vs. Administrator Portal Level?

Administrators of WebCenter Portal can administrate at all levels of WebCenter Portal: Application, Home Portal, and all created Portals (Figure 10-5).

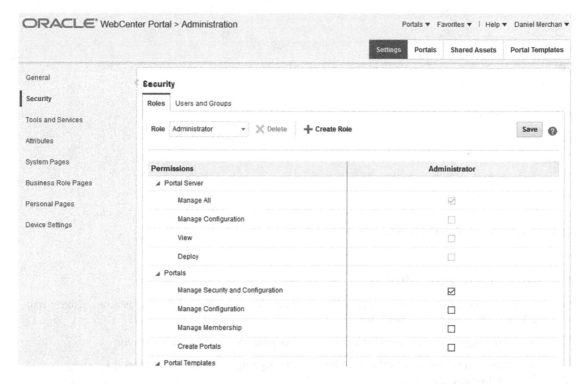

Figure 10-5. *WebCenter Portal General Administration UI*

Portal Managers (Administrator Portal Level) administrates only in Portal Level for configuring the Security, General Settings such as Page Template, Skin, etc., and the capability of Publishing Pages for that specific Portal (Figure 10-6).

■ **Note**   If you had experience with WebCenter Portal 11g version, you saw that the Portal Roles: **Participant** and **Viewer** has been **removed** in 12c version. Generate your own Custom Application Roles to give the specific permissions to the members of a Portal.

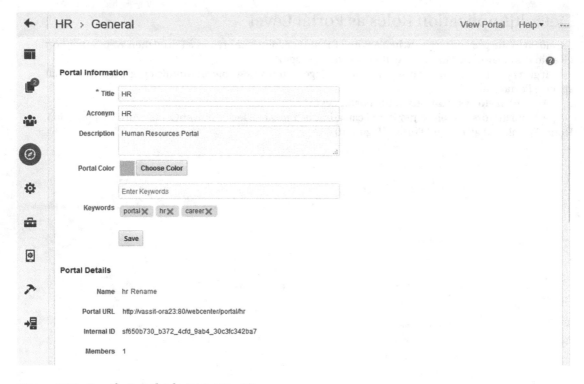

Figure 10-6. *Specific Portal Administration UI*

Custom Application Roles

Out-of-the-box, a Portal Creator receives a Portal Manager role that makes them the Administrators of the Portal. The Portal Manager is responsible for:

- Creating the specific portal roles and which permissions are assigned to them.

- Managing the membership of the Portal and assigning to the groups of users the desired application roles.

For example: People working in HR departments are members of the HR Enterprise Group in the LDAP repository. The Portal Manager is responsible for:

- Adding the HR Enterprise Group as members of the HR Portal.

- Assigning the group HR Member Application Role to set the specific permissions to the Portal Services.

■ **Note**   Users that are members of a Portal automatically inherit the Authenticated - Role permissions and they will have a basic set of permissions.

In the following topics, you are going to learn and see how to use the Administration UIs for managing security.

Using Enterprise Manager for Security Administration UI

WebCenter Portal is an Oracle ADF Application with Oracle ADF Security enabled. It means that System Administrators can manage the Application Policies using the Oracle Enterprise Manager Console that brings the Oracle Fusion Middleware Infrastructure.

This administration UI should be only used for:

- Managing the Administration role in case of externalizing the Administrator user of WebCenter Portal (usually 'weblogic' user).

- Editing any specific permission to a specific ADF component such a Task Flow or Pages deployed out of the Portal scope.

■ **Caution**   Try to avoid creating your own set of Policies and Permissions manually as WebCenter Framework Security uses a naming convention for creating the Policies based on the specific portal details.

System Administrators can access the Application Policies management following the next steps:

- Log in into the Enterprise Manager Console (Usually http://[adminserver]:[adminport]/em)

- Navigate through the farm tree until you find the WebCenter Portal Application and click it (Figure 10-7). It will open the Overview Page of WebCenter Portal.

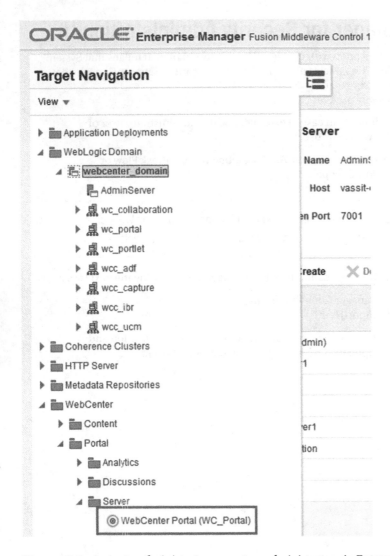

Figure 10-7. Access to administrate as a system administrator via Enterprise Manager

- Click on the Top menu and find the Security option in the menu (Figure 10-8).

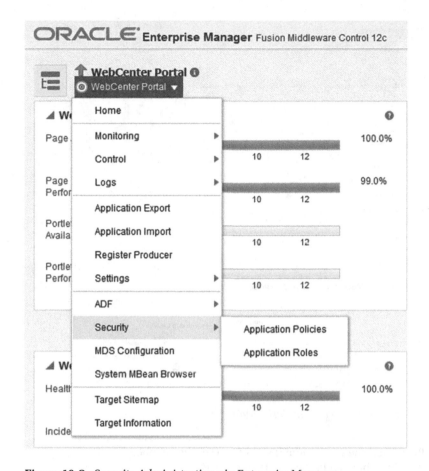

Figure 10-8. *Security Administration via Enterprise Manager*

- Here you have two options:

  - **Application Policies**: Here a system administrator can manage the permissions
    assigned to the specific roles created by WebCenter Portal (Figure 10-9).

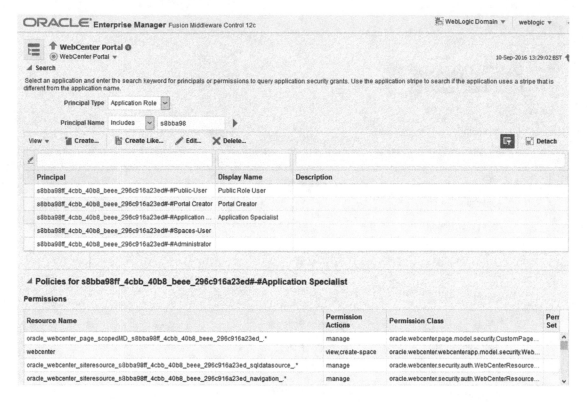

Figure 10-9. *Application Policies Administration via Enterprise Manager*

- **Application Roles**: Here the system administrator can see the membership of the user to a specific WebCenter Portal Role (Figure 10-10).

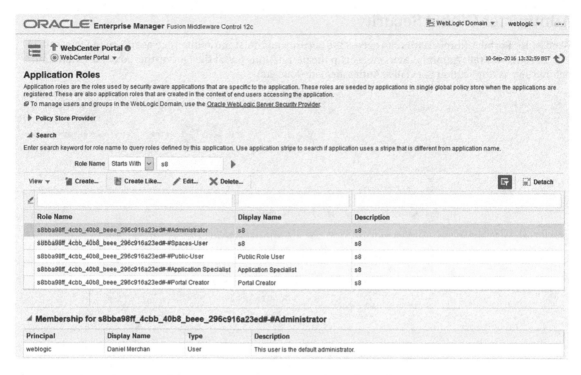

Figure 10-10. *Application Roles managed through Enterprise Manager Console*

■ **Caution**   DO NOT CREATE YOUR OWN ROLES USING THIS UI. This UI only has to be used if the Oracle Documentation says to use it or for any fix that is required by the Permissions or Roles by an expert.

■ **Note**   Roles are created by WebCenter Security Framework using the following Syntax: [PortalGUID]#-#[RoleName]

■ **Tip**   Always use the Portal Security Administration UI for managing WebCenter Portal Security.

Using of WebCenter Portal Security Administration UI

As mentioned before, there are two levels of security in WebCenter Portal: Global Security Settings and Portal-Level security.

In this part of the chapter we will take a look over the Portal Security Administration UI and how administrators can set up the security.

Administer Global Security

WebCenter Portal Administrators can access the Security administration interface as shown in Figure 10-11.

In the **Roles tab**, Administrators can set up the permissions for all the Out-of-the-box Roles mentioned before such as Application Specialist, Authenticated-Role, etc.

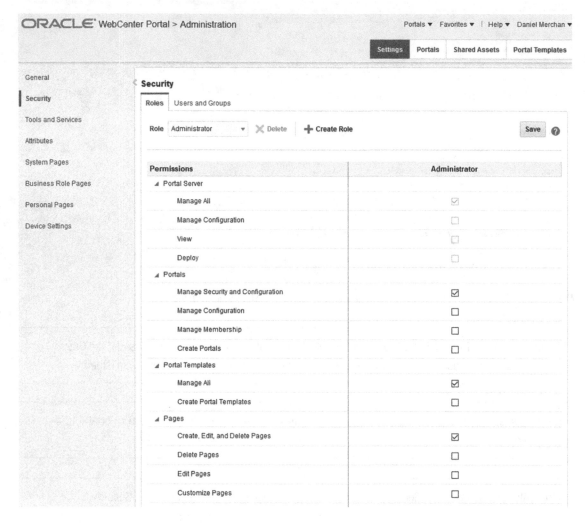

Figure 10-11. *WebCenter Portal Global Security Settings*

■ **Tip** Authenticated User and Portal Creator security permissions will be inherited by the Authenticated Users who are members of a Portal and the Portal Manager will be inherit from the Portal Creator after creating a New Portal. Please, set them up properly if you want Portal Managers of Members of a Portal to have less permissions.

In addition, new Roles can be created with some mix of permissions. For example, if you need a new Global Role that has just capabilities for Managing Memberships you can create a Membership Member with just the Portals ➤ Managed Membership permission (Figure 10-12).

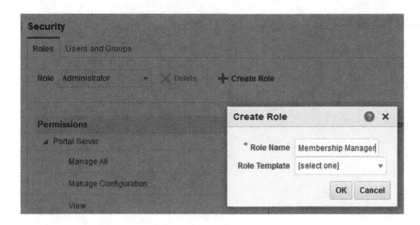

Figure 10-12. Creating a new Global Role

In the **Users and Groups tab**, Administrators can assign Global Roles to specific users or group of users (Enterprise Groups) (Figure 10-13).

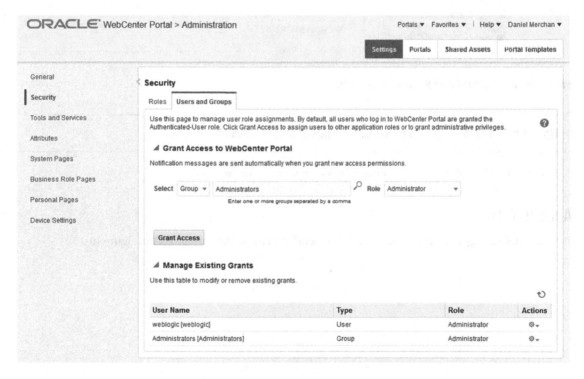

Figure 10-13. Granting Global Security to Users / Groups

Here, Administrators can search for specific users or Enterprise Groups coming from the Identity Store.

Administer Portal-Level Security

The Portal-Level security UI is accessed by clicking in when Editing / Administering a Portal (Figure 10-14).

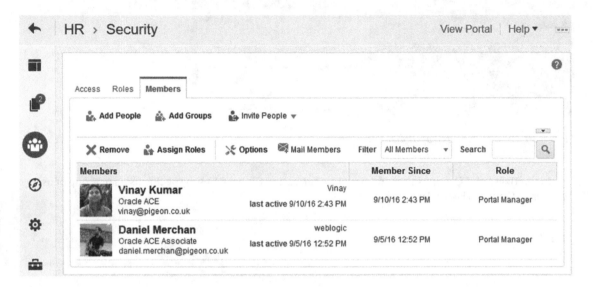

Figure 10-14. Portal-Level Security Administration

■ **Tip**   Only Portal Managers can administrate the Portal-Level Security by default.

In this interface, there are three main tabs for configuring the security.

Access Tab

Here a Portal Manager can establish a high-level security access to the current Portal (Figure 10-15):

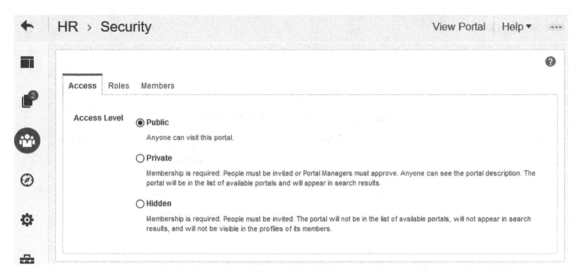

Figure 10-15. *Portal-Level Security Administration - Access Tab*

- **Public**: It is a Public Portal and then unauthenticated users can access to all the Pages and Components that are accessible for Public Access.

- **Private**: Only Members of the Portal can access.

- **Hidden**: It is private, but this portal will not be shown in the Portal Lists.

■ **Note**   By default, Oracle WebCenter Portal creates the Portal with Public Access if the Portal Creator did not change this option during the Wizard. We recommend creating the Portals privately by default.

Roles Tab

This section of the Portal-Level Security Interface allows a Portal Manager to Administrate Roles and Permissions (Figure 10-16).

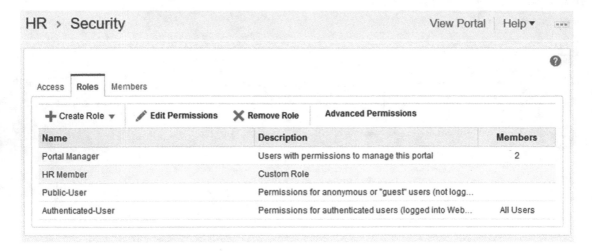

Figure 10-16. *Portal-Level Security Administration - Roles Tab*

- ➕ **Create Role** ▼ : Allows the users to Create a New Custom Role. In addition, it allows user to create three different predefined Roles with a custom setup of Permissions:

  - **Delegated Manager**: It has a complete set of administrative permissions over the Portal.

  - **Participant**: Allows the Users of this Role to use the Portal Services and Create new things such Documents, Discussions etc.

  - **Viewer**: Only allows users to consume and view the Pages and Services offered by the Portal.

- ✏️ **Edit Permissions**: Edit the Permissions for the current selected Role (Figure 5-17).

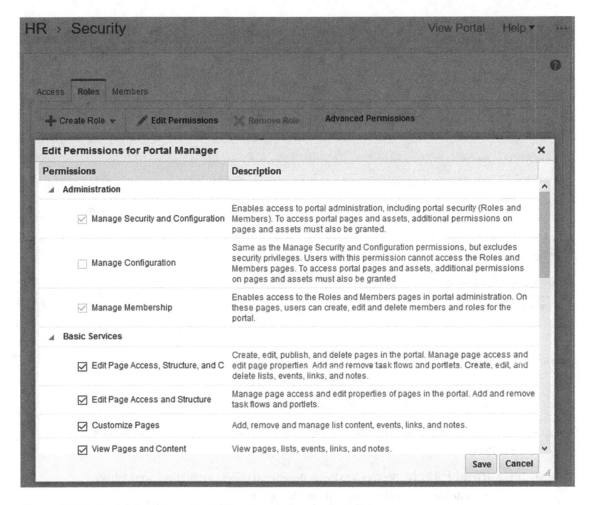

Figure 10-17. *Portal-Level Security: Edition Permissions for Portal Manager*

- ✖ **Remove Role** : Removes the selected Role from the list and then revokes the permissions to all the users that are part of this Role.

- **Advanced Permissions**: Enables showing of more specific Permissions when Granting Permissions to a specific Role. This cannot be undone. By default, it is shown a default set of Permissions.

Members Tab

In this Administration Tab, the Portal Manager or Administrator can manage the Membership to this Portal. In addition, it can assign different Portal Roles to the Users or Group of Users added to this Portal (Figure 10-18). The options available are:

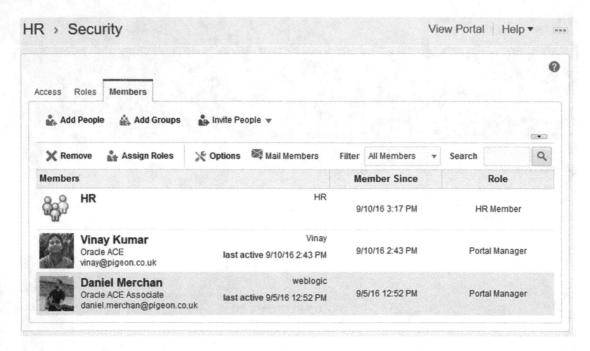

Figure 10-18. *Portal-Level Security: Members - Tab*

- 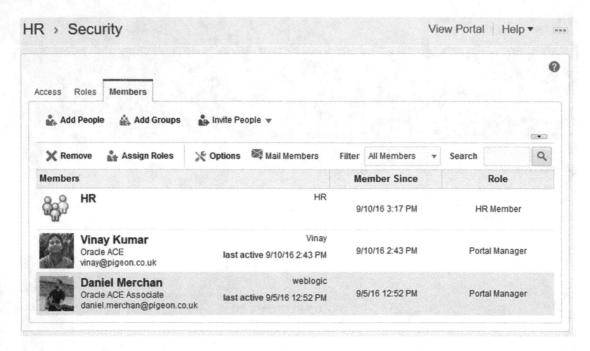 **Add People**: Use it for adding a specific user to the Portal.

- **Add Groups** : Use it for adding a specific Enterprise Group / Group of users to the Portal.

- **Invite People** ▼: Use it to invite Registered Users to join this Portal / invite Non-Registered Users to Register and join this portal.

- **Options**: Here it can be set up if the Portal allows or doesn't allow Self -Membership registration or which Roles are allowed to do it (Figure 10-19).

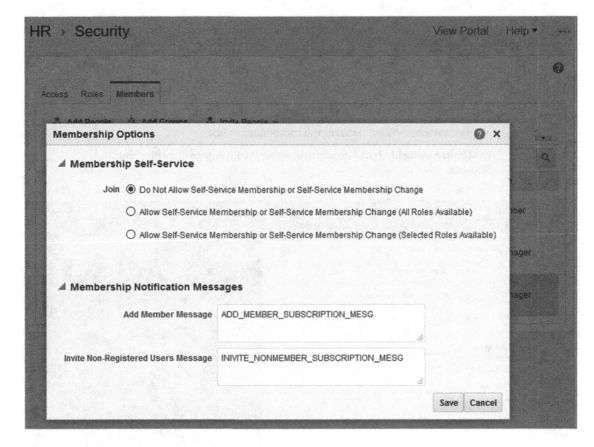

Figure 10-19. *Portal-Level Security: Membership Options*

For each member or group of members, there are the following options:

- **Remove** : Use it for revoking the Membership of the current selected User / User Group.

- **Assign Roles** : To change and assign Roles to the current selected User / User Group.

Securing Page Components

Components added to WebCenter Pages have a configuration option called *Access* (Figure 10-20). Here it can be set up the visibility of the component based depending on the configured option:

- **Show Component**: It shows the component to the Members of the Portal.

- **Hide Component**: It hide the component for everyone that access to the Page.

- **Customize by role or user**:

- It can be set up for showing the component for:

  - Specific Users

  - Specific Group of Users

  - Users with specific Roles

  - Authenticated Role: Any authenticated user can see it

  - Anonymous - Role: It makes the component *Public*

- **Customize using EL**: It can be set up to a specific EL Expression returning a Boolean.

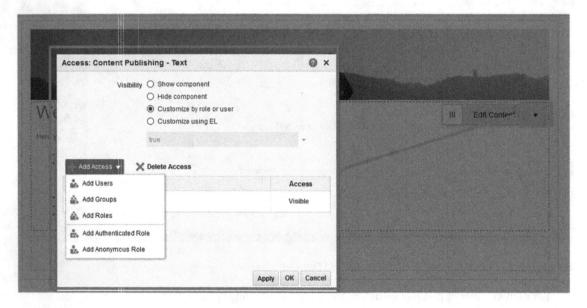

Figure 10-20. *Configuring Access in Component Level*

Usage of Security EL Expressions

There are specific scenarios where Portal Contributors want to hide components added to the pages for specific Roles or Enterprise Groups and more complex expressions than the offered by the *Access* option.

For example, the Events Task Flow in the Home Page will not be shown for a specific group of users and a specific value from other EL Expressions that are not related to security.

The EL Expressions offered Out-of-the-box are the following:

Table 10-2. *Default Application Roles in WebCenter Portal*

EL Expression	Function
#{security.authenticated}	Returns 'true' if the user is logged in. Useful to check if the user is anonymous as well.
#{securityContext.userName}	Returns the current user identification. It returns 'anonymous' if the user is not logged.
#{WCSecurityContext.currentUser['userName']}	Checks if the current user is the same as the user identifier provided as parameter. In rare cases you will use this EL Expression.
#{WCSecurityContext.userInGroup['group']}	It returns 'true' if the user is part of the Enterprise Group given by the parameter.
#{security.pageContextCommunityModerator}	Returns if the current user is a Portal Manager.
#{WCSecurityContext.userInScopedRole['role']}	Returns 'true' if the user has assigned a specific role in the current portal.

CHAPTER 11

■ ■ ■

Content Integration

Out-of-the-box, Oracle WebCenter Portal provides multiple components for displaying and manipulating content coming from different type of sources and repositories.

For example, content can be information coming from a REST API or it can be just a document file that is uploaded into the Content Repository.

In this chapter you will learn about how to work with, display, and manipulate the content within Oracle WebCenter Portal.

Overview

First of all, let's provide an overview of all the possibilities for integrating content and data offered by Oracle WebCenter Portal (Figure 11-1):

- **By using Data Presenter**, WebCenter Portal can display and manipulate data coming from REST / SOAP and Database.

- By integrating with **Oracle WebCenter Content** and **Oracle Document Cloud Service** for offering a complete **Hybric Enterprise Content Management System by using the following Out-of-the-box components:**

  - **Content Manager Task Flow** for full Hybrid ECM management life cycle over content such documents, media file, etc.

  - **Oracle Document Cloud Content Manager Task Flow** for enabling collaboration between non-Portal users and Portal users over specific documents stored in the Oracle Document Cloud.

  - **Content Presenter Task Flow** for displaying documents and files information in a custom way.

- **By using the "Web Content Management" capabilities** for displaying structured web content (For example, "News," "Articles," "Products") by selecting one of the following strategies:

  - Using WebCenter Portal **Pages** created with specific **Page Styles** with editable components: Text, Styled Text, and Image Components.

  - Building structured web content by using **Site Studio** and displaying the information by using **Content Presenter Task Flow and Custom Content Presenter Templates**.

- **By creating Blogs** and **Wikis** Pages where users can expose information. See Figure 11-1.

© Vinay Kumar and Daniel Merchán García 2017

V. Kumar and D. M. García, *Beginning Oracle WebCenter Portal 12c*, DOI 10.1007/978-1-4842-2532-5_11

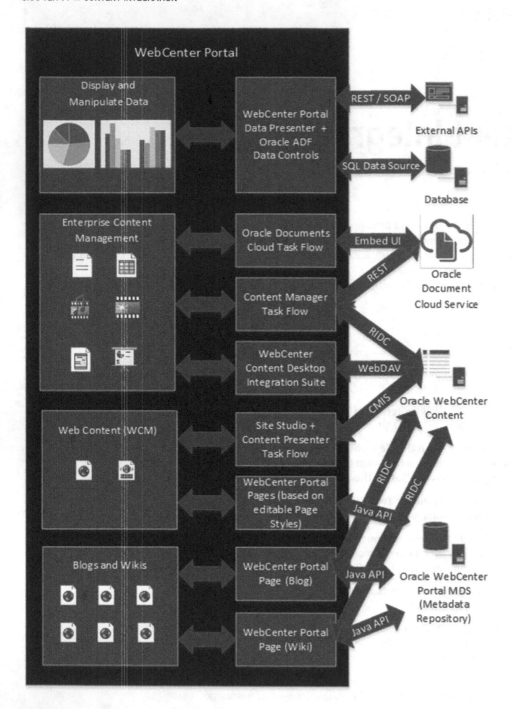

Figure 11-1. *Content and Data Integration Overview*

Publishing Content via WebCenter Content Integration

Oracle WebCenter Content is the ECM (Enterprise Content Management) solution offered by Oracle for managing documents, media files, and records.

Since the beginning releases of WebCenter Portal, WebCenter Content has been the best ally and the most powerful integration that WebCenter Portal offers (Figure 11-2).

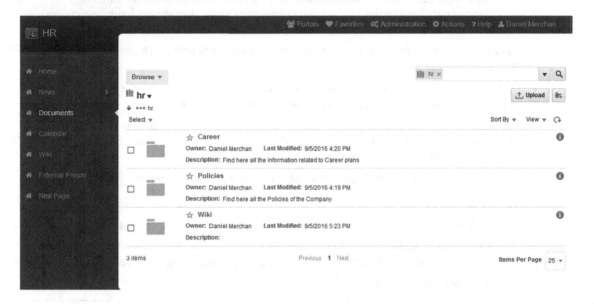

Figure 11-2. *WebCenter Portal 12c exposing WebCenter Content 12c via Content Manager Task Flow*

■ **Note** Oracle WebCenter Content has changed its name multiple times. You may find documentation of WebCenter Content by the names of Stellent or UCM (Universal Content Repository).

What's New about WebCenter Content Integration

The 12c release included multiple changes in terms of WebCenter Portal and WebCenter Content integration:

- It has **deprecated all the old Out-of-the-box components offered in WebCenter Portal 11g** (except Content Presenter Task Flow). These old components are not accessible anymore.

- WebCenter Content ADF UI and Oracle WebCenter Portal use a unique component called **Content Manager Task Flow**. This component makes the user experience seamless if he is accessing to the document repository directly WebCenter Content ADF UI or using WebCenter Portal UI as now both products use the same component for document management.

- Integration with **Oracle Document Cloud** for enabling a **Hybrid Enterprise Content Management System**:

  - By connecting WebCenter Content with Oracle Document Cloud for displaying folders and content from Oracle Document Cloud in Content Manager Task Flow.

  - By using **Oracle DOCS Content Manager Task Flow** for embedding the Oracle Document Cloud UI that enables you to integrate Oracle Document Cloud Service with WebCenter Portal.

In addition, Oracle WebCenter Content is not just a simple Content Repository; it also brings other advanced capabilities such as the following:

- File format conversion for documents, digital media (images and videos) that are uploaded into the Content Repository by using **Oracle Inbound Refinery**.

- **Imaging** capabilities such *Annotations* for enhancing collaboration over the documents uploaded into the Content Repository. WebCenter Imaging has been embedded in WebCenter Content in the 12c release.

- **Records and Retention Management** for historical and archival purposes.

■ **Note**   This book only covers WebCenter Portal - Content Integration and basic document management capabilities within WebCenter Portal. There are more capabilities and functionalities offered by a complete WebCenter Content solution that are not commented on in this book. An example of this is WebCenter Enterprise Capture for Business Processes driven by documents.

■ **Caution**   Oracle DOCS Content Manager Task Flow is available since 12.2.1.1+ (it cannot be found in the base 12c release, 12.2.1).

Overview of Oracle WebCenter Content Integration

The following diagram describes a high-level overview over the main components and the architecture of WebCenter Portal - WebCenter Content Integration (Figure 11-3).

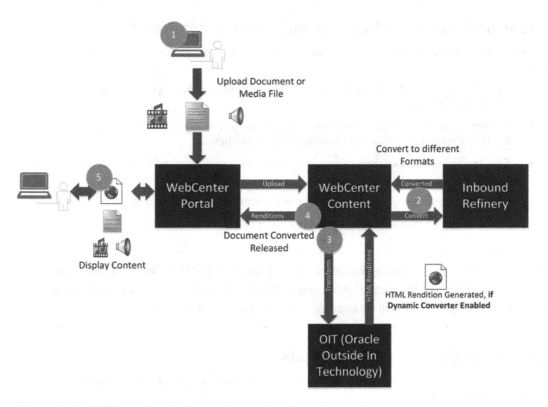

Figure 11-3. WebCenter Portal - Content Integration Overview

The integration works as follow:

1. Content can be uploaded via WebCenter Portal: Content Manager Task Flow to WebCenter Content.

2. If Inbound Refinery is properly set up with WebCenter Content and the file format is one of the configured to be converted, it is sent to Inbound Refinery for conversion and to generate new renditions. For example:

   a. In case the content is a Word Document, PPT, or Spreadsheet, Inbound Refinery can create a PDF format of these documents.

   b. In case of a video, it can be transformed to mp4 format.

   c. In case of an Image it can be transformed to multiple renditions with different sizes and formats. A good example is the Thumbnail version (small image).

3. If WebCenter Content: Dynamic Converter component is enabled, then it generates a HTML version of the document. For example: The conversion from MS-Word to HTML happens dynamically in real time when users access the document if the WebCenter Content Dynamic Converter component is enabled.

Configuring WebCenter Content with WebCenter Portal

To enable WebCenter Content as Document Management repository is mandatory to first complete the following steps:

- An Installation of WebCenter Content with Oracle Inbound Refinery (which is not covered in this book).

- Connect WebCenter Content with Inbound Refinery by creating an Inbound Refinery Provider in WebCenter Content. (Not covered here.)

- Enable some mandatory components in WebCenter Content required by WebCenter Portal.

- Configure the connection between WebCenter Portal and WebCenter Content.

- Enable the Documents Tool Service in WebCenter Portal Administration.

■ **Note**   Oracle recommends installing WebCenter Content in the same WebLogic Domain as WebCenter Portal in order to reduce LDAP and security configurations. However, you can also install separately in other domains, but you will need to configure the same Identity Store between both domains.

Prepare WebCenter Content Components

There are a number of WebCenter Content Components that need to be enabled before configuring WebCenter Portal connection.

The components can be enabled by a System Administrator by navigating through WebCenter Content Console ➤ Administration ➤ Admin Server ➤ Component Manager (Figure 11-4).

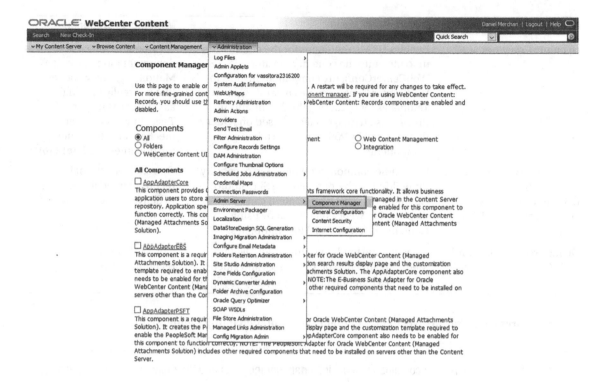

Figure 11-4. *WebCenter Content: Component Manager*

The components to be enabled are described in the following table:

Table 11-1. *WebCenter Content Components to be Enabled*

Component	Description	Mandatory / Optional
FrameworkFolders	This component provides a Hierarchical Folder Interface for the content stored in WebCenter Content file system. This component has replaced the old Folders_g as it enhances the performance and removes the limitations shown in the old foldering service.	Mandatory
WebCenterConfigure	This component makes multiple configurations to WebCenter Content to let it ready for some of the Out-of-the-box WebCenter Portal components. For example, it enables Accounts for security, creates custom metadata, create a custom set of simple content workflows, etc.	Mandatory
AutoSuggestConfig	Enables the AutoSuggest for the Search capabilities of the WebCenter Content ADF UI and Content Manager Task Flow.	Mandatory

(*continued*)

Component	Description	Mandatory / Optional
Dynamic Converter	Enables HTML renditions for the documents uploaded into the content repository. WebCenterConfigure component installs in WebCenter Content some Dynamic Converter Templates for rendering the documents in Preview as an Image Gallery based on JQuery that are used by WebCenter Portal components.	"Optional" (Official documentation marks it as Mandatory, but we believe that it is really optional as Content Manager Task Flow offers other mechanisms for rendering the documents inline) TBA
"Site Studio Components": LinkManager, SiteStudio, DBSearchContainsOp Support, and PortalVCR Helper	Site Studio components enable the capability for building Web Content using Site Studio Components. This Web Content can be displayed in WebCenter Portal by using Content Presenter Task Flow Templates.	Optional, but strongly recommended if planning to deliver structured web content.
DigitalAssetManager and DAMConverterSupport	It enables full rendition support for Digital Media documents such as images and videos. It requires Inbound Refinery properly configured.	Optional, but strongly recommended.

It requires you to restart WebCenter Content Server after enabling Components.

■ **Note**   The table above only contains the most important components and the mandatory ones required by Oracle WebCenter Portal. Follow Oracle Documentation for further details on required components of WebCenter Content.

■ **Caution**   Enabling Site Studio component requires extra steps after restarting the Content Server. An administrator has to accept the default values of Site Studio Administration ➤ Set Default Web Asset Documentation Information option.

Configure WebCenter Portal - Content Connection

The connection between WebCenter Portal and WebCenter Content is configured by using Oracle Enterprise Manager Console or WLST Scripts.

A System Administrator can find the connection details by navigating to WebCenter Portal ➤ Settings ➤ Service Configuration ➤ Content Repository through the Enterprise Manager Console (Figure 11-5).

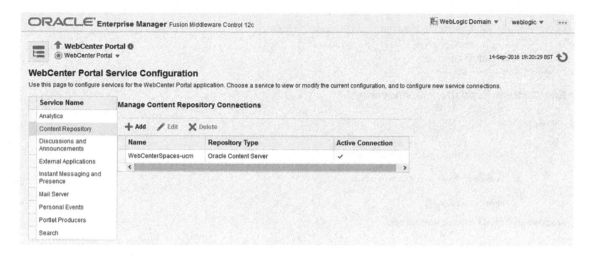

Figure 11-5. *Administration of WebCenter Portal Connections*

In this interface can be found the following scenarios:

- A connection is already configured.

- No connections are configured yet.

Out-of-the-box, a stand-alone installation of WebCenter Portal - Content will auto-configure a connection to the Content Repository the first time it starts (and it name it as WebCenterSpaces-ucm). In case the installation is in Cluster Mode, then this will not happen and the connection must be configured manually.

The following properties are required when adding or editing a connection (Figure 11-6).

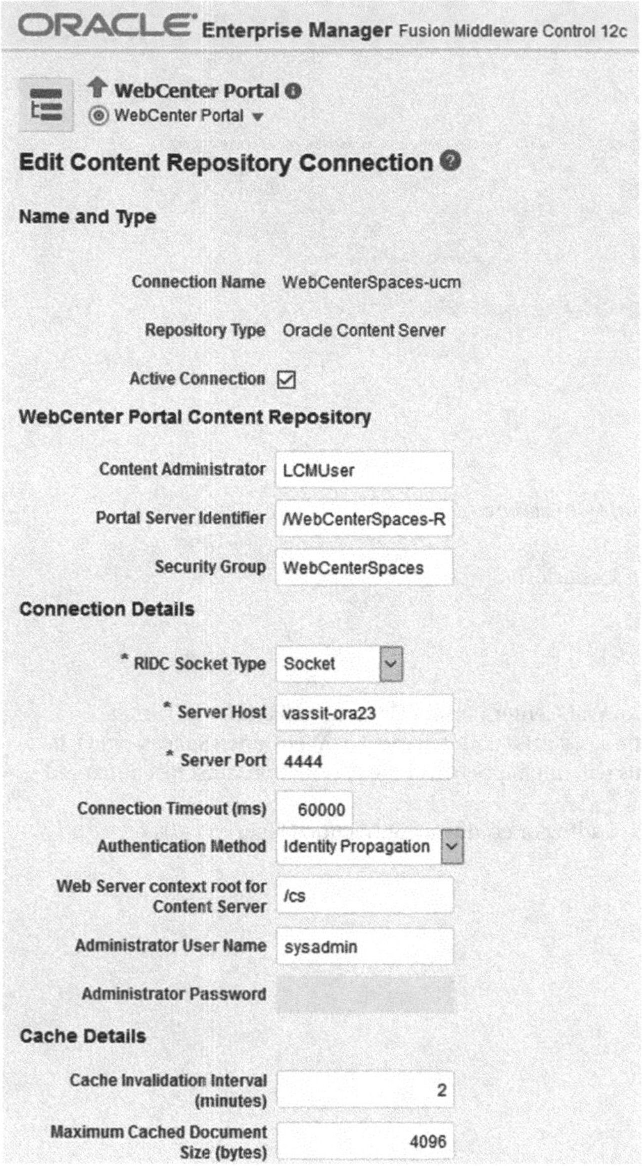

Figure 11-6. *Configuration of WebCenter Portal - Content Connection*

- **Connection Name**: Name for the connection between WebCenter Portal and Content. We recommend you use the typical name: WebCenterSpaces-ucm

- **Repository Type:** Select Oracle Content Server as we are configuring WebCenter Content connections.

- **Active Connection**: Mark as true for making this Content Repository the default one. WebCenter Portal can be connected to multiple content repositories, but just one will be the Primary.

- **Content Administrator**: User with Administration rights over the Content Server, it will be used by WebCenter Portal for creating the default content by its components. By default: LCMUser (this user is created with the default installation).

- **Portal Server Identifier**: Root folder under which WebCenter Portal application data is stored. Use, for example, the name /WebCenterSpaces-Root

- **Security Group**: WebCenter Portal will create a default Security Group and two roles based on this option and name. Name it WebCenterSpaces and then it will create two roles internally based on that name.

- See **Understanding Content Security** part of this chapter to fully understand the security model implemented in WebCenter Content by WebCenter Portal.

- **RIDC Socket Type**: Remote Intradoc is the API offered by WebCenter Content for operating with it. Select the way to connect WebCenter Portal with WebCenter Content:

  - Socket: It will use the intradoc protocol idc://

  - Socket SSL: it will use the secured intradoc protocol idcs://

  - Web: Using HTTPClient package

  - JAX-WS: Via Web Services.

- We strongly recommend that you use Intradoc Socket Type. For Web, or JAX-WS then extra authentication properties are shown.

- **Server Host (In case of Socket)**: Where WebCenter Content is located.

  - In case of stand-alone, the IP or Host where WebCenter Content is hosted.

  - In case of a Cluster, the balanced IP / reverse proxy to access to the WebCenter Content Cluster.

- **Server Port (In case of Socket)**: The Port to be used dependently of the RIDC Socket Type Selected. In case of Intradoc, the default port is 4444.

- **Connection Timeout (ms)**: Timeout in milliseconds for WebCenter Portal to consider that an open connection to WebCenter Content is taking long or it hangs. By default, 60000.

- **Authentication Method (In case of Socket)**: Use identity Propagation. It means that the authenticated user will be propagated to the content repository for checking rights.

- **Web Server context root for Content Server**: The context root used to expose the content server. By default, /cs for integration of advanced metadata and SiteStudio capabilities in WebCenter. **This must be available on the same host as WebCenter and use a single sign on**.

- **Administrator User Name**: User name with administrative rights for this WebCenter Content instance. This user will be used to fetch content type information based on profiles and track document changes for WebCenter Portal cache invalidation purposes. By default: sysadmin.

- **Cache Invalidation Interval (minutes)**: Specify the polling interval (in minutes) used by WebCenter Content to check for cache invalidations. The minimum interval is 2 minutes. The default is 0, which means that cache invalidation is disabled.

- **Maximum Cached Document Size (bytes)**: The maximum size (in bytes) for documents cached in the virtual content repository binary cache. The default is 1024 bytes (1K).

■ **Caution**   Never change the Portal Server Identifier or Security Group Name after configuring them. They are unique values used by WebCenter Portal to seed data into the repository. If you change one, then you must change the other. It will generate a new Security Base model structure and old content may not be accessible anymore.

■ **Tip**   Use Socket / Socket SSL (Intradoc) connectivity type due to performance and simplicity of configuration.

Configure the Context Root property for enabling Site Studio Contribution Capabilities and Web Content in Content Presenter. It means that WebCenter Portal and WebCenter Content must be accessed under the same host name. You can use Oracle HTTP Server or Apache HTTP server for this.

Setup for development a Cache Invalidation Interval of 0 minutes. It will help for developing Content Presenter Templates.

Maximum Cached Document Size is very useful when consuming Data Files (Web Content) that are XML files of small size. Set it up properly depending on the Java Virtual Machine memory assigned. Big sizes can make the JVM run out of memory quickly. For example: 102400 (100 Kilobytes).

Understanding Content Security Model

It is important that Portal Administrators and System Administrators understand the Security Model implemented by WebCenter Portal in WebCenter Content Repository.

By default, Oracle WebCenter Content offers three mechanisms for securing content (Figure 11-7).

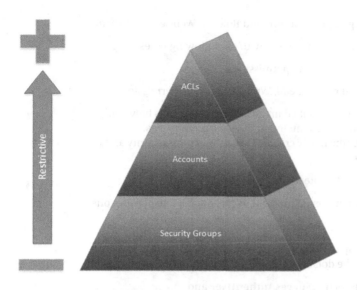

Figure 11-7. *WebCenter Content Security Mechanisms*

- **Role Based - Security Groups**: A folder / content can be assigned with a Security Group. Roles are configured with different permissions over these Security Group.

- **Accounts**: It is used for advanced security models that matches perfectly with hierarchical / departmental-based security models. For example, a user with the Account "Pres" has access to all subaccounts "Pres," "Pres/VP," "Pres/VP/ Dept1,"etc.). Usually this Security Model is implemented manually by Applications connecting to WebCenter Content (such as WebCenter Portal).

- **Access Control Lists (ACLs)**: Used for Content-Level security. The permissions assigned via ACLs overrides any security given by Accounts or Security Groups. The permission can be given to a specific user, group of users, or a specific Role.

■ **Note**   WebCenter Portal already creates the Security Groups and Accounts in WebCenter Content by itself. It is not necessary to create them. However, it is useful to understand the underlying Security Model implemented.

■ **Tip**   For Content-Level security, knowledge of ACLs usage is necessary. Portal Members and Portal Managers need to understand the ACLs model, if enabled.

The above definitions can give you an idea about how Oracle WebCenter Portal implements WebCenter Content Security.

Let's explain how Oracle WebCenter Portal implements the content security model.

WebCenter Portal creates the following Security Groups and Roles in WebCenter Content:

- **PersonalSpaces**: Used only for the Home Portal with the following Roles assigned:
  - **PersonalSpacesRole**: With only Read permissions.
  - **PersonalSpacesAuthenUser**: With Read, Write, and Delete permissions.

- **securityGroupName**: The same as specified in the connection details between WebCenter Portal and WebCenter Content. In our case, we defined it as: WebCenterSpaces. It is used for the newly created Portals as a base security and it has assigned the following roles:
  - **securityGroupNameUser**: With Read permission.
  - **securityGroupNameAuthenUser**: With Read, Write, and Delete permissions.

The Roles defined above are given to the following users:

- **Public** users receive **PersonalSpaceRole** and **securityGroupNameUser** that gives them the capability of reading the documents from the Personal Folders of everyone.

- **Authenticated users** receive **PersonalSpacesAuthenUser** and **securityGroupNameAuthenUser**. It means that they can have full permissions over the content.

As you can see, the base setup with only Security Groups does not fit the security model expected. For that reason, WebCenter Portal implements an Account Security Model on top of it.

Let's try to explain and understand how the Account Model works with WebCenter Portal (Figure 11-8).

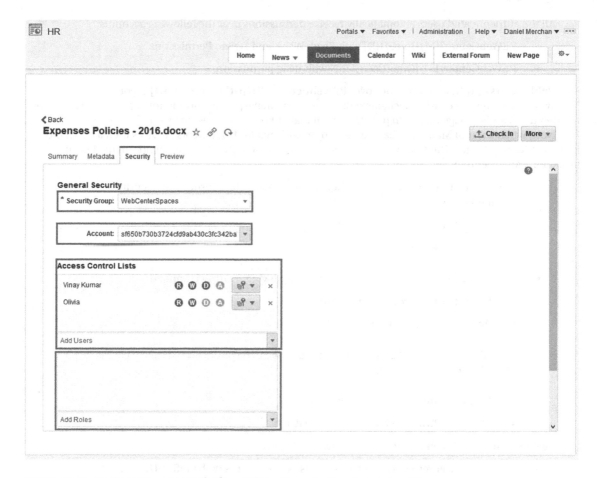

Figure 11-8. *Content Manager Task Flow: Editing Security Permissions to a File*

When a user Logs in in WebCenter Portal for the first time, he has access to the Home Portal (that is like the Personal Portal) and then to the Documents page to access to his own folder for storing and sharing documents.

A folder is created in WebCenter Content with his user name and the following security:

- Security Group: PersonalSpaces.

- Account: PEWebCenter/[UserGUID].

For example: PEWebCenter/5da86807-b93b-40cb-8917-83794802dda2

In addition, another folder is created inside of the user folder – a folder called Public. It has the following security assigned:

- Security Group: PersonalSpaces

- Account: PEWebCenter/PU/[UserGUID].

- For example: PEWebCenter/PU/5da86807-b93b-40cb-8917-83794802dda2

PEWebCenter is the prefix used to indicate that it is a Personal Folder, **PU** is used to indicate that folder / content is Public and the **UserGUID** indicates which the user belongs to.

All the authenticated users automatically receive permissions over the following accounts:

- PEWebCenter/[MyUserGUID] with Read, Write, and Delete Permissions

- PEWebCenter/PU/[OtherUserGUID] with Read permissions

Public users only have permissions over **PEWebCenter/PU/[OtherUserGUID]** account.

With the Accounts security mechanism then a user can make public information from his Public folder to other users and manage their own private content that only can be accessed by him.

Now, when a Portal Manager creates a new Portal and enables Documents Services then a base Folder is created for that Portal. The base Account given to the base Folder / Contents depends on the Portal availability and security:

- If the Portal is marked as private, then it is not accessible by users. The security assigned is:

  - Security Group: *securityGroupName*

  - Account: [Portal GUID]

- If the Portal is online and is *Public*, then the following security is applied:

  - Security Group: *securityGroupName*

  - Account: PUBLIC/[Portal GUID]

- If the Portal is private, but it has documents that can be publicly read then it can have the following account setting:

  - Security Group: *securityGroupName*

  - Account: PUBLIC/AUTHEN/[Portal GUID]

Basically, the permissions to the users are given as following:

- Any Public user receives Read permissions over Accounts with prefix PUBLIC.

- Any Authenticated user receives Read permissions over accounts with AUTHEN prefix.

- Portal Member with Documents rights receives permissions on [Portal GUID] Account for Read, Write, and Delete documents.

In addition, there is another specific **special account prefix called WCILS**. This prefix will be found when a user configures Content-Level security for a Folder / Content using **ACLs**.

Basically any content with ACLs is configured then from *oldaccountvalue* to WCILS/*oldaccountvalue*.

Any authenticated and public user only has Read permissions on WCILS prefix and then only the Users and Roles specified in the User Group List or Roles List will have access to the content.

As a Summary:

- Out-of-the-box WebCenter Portal provides a security model based on Security Groups and Accounts. **There is no need for creating extra security using WebCenter Content UI.**

- If Content-Level security is a requirement, then a WebCenter Content Administrator has to enable ACLs in the system.

■ **Note**   ACLs are not enabled by default.

■ **Caution**   If the number of users is very high, the abuse of allowing all the users to use ACLs can end in an unmaintainable system. Restrict this use.

Working with Content Manager Task Flow

Enable Document Service for a Portal

To make available a Document Services for a Portal, then a Portal Manager needs to make available the Documents Services by enabling it using the Tools and Services option 🔨 when editing a Portal (Figure 11-9).

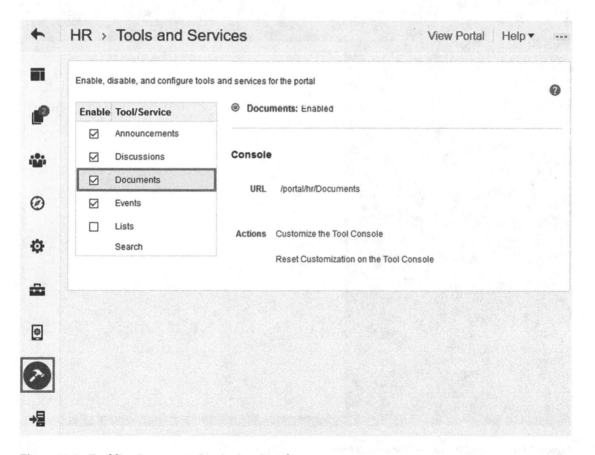

Figure 11-9. *Enabling Documents Service in a Portal*

Add and Configure a Content Manager Task Flow

There are two different ways for adding a Content Manager Task Flow to a Portal:

- By using the Documents System Page that WebCenter Portal provides Out-of-the-box.

- By adding and configuring the Content Manager Task Flow to a custom page.

In case of adding the Out-of-the-box Documents System Page then a Portal Manager should follow the next steps:

- Go to Pages administration ▊▊ (Pages Administration).

- Click ▶ (Page Options) and select **Page Link**. In the Pop-Up, select the Documents page (Figure 11-10).

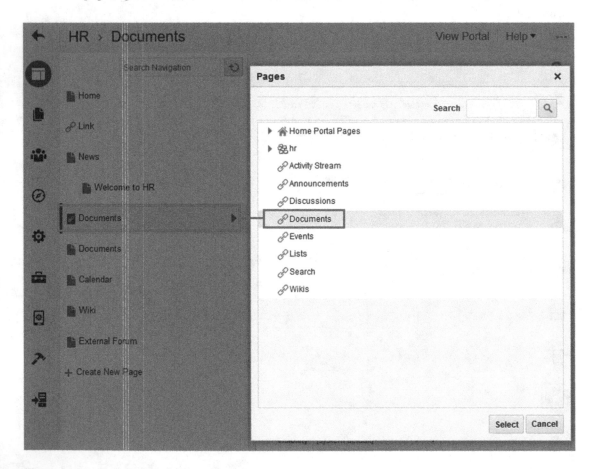

Figure 11-10. *Page Link to the Documents Page*

The other option is to manually add the Content Manager Task Flow to a Page (Figure 11-11).

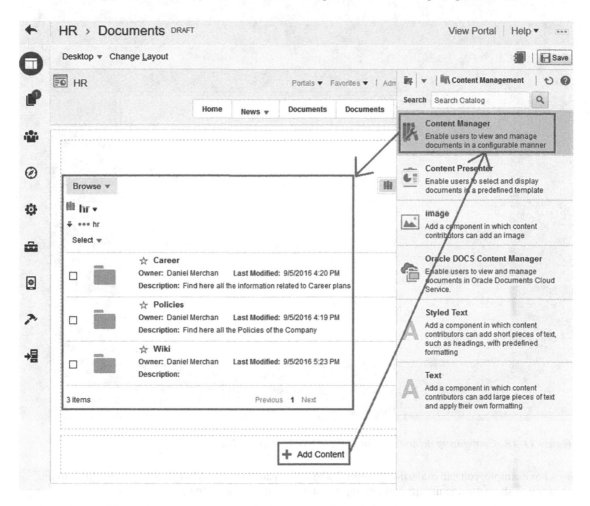

Figure 11-11. *Adding a Content Manager Task Flow to a Custom Page*

Configure Content Manager View

After adding a Content Manager Task Flow to a Page, it can be Configured to its default Look and Feel a little bit.

Click *Configure* to create a Customized View of the Content Manager Task Flow (Figure 11-12)

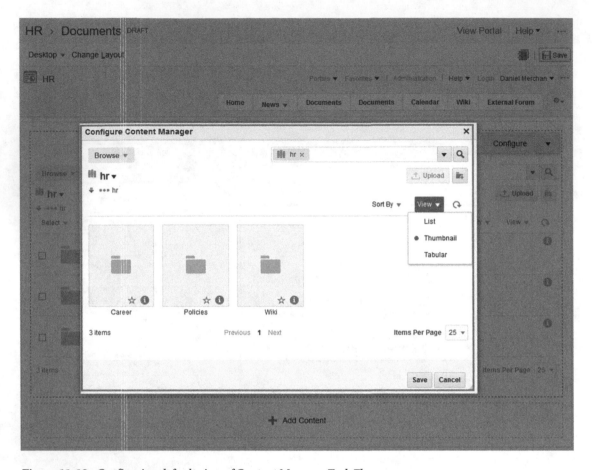

Figure 11-12. *Configuring default view of Content Manager Task Flow*

For example, you can make the Thumbnails View instead of the List View or the Search Filter can be changed to show the documents that Belong to you instead of the root folder.

Content Manager Task Flow Properties

Out-of-the-box, the Content Manager Task Flow is prepared to display the current portal folder. It has the following configurable properties available (Figure 11-13).

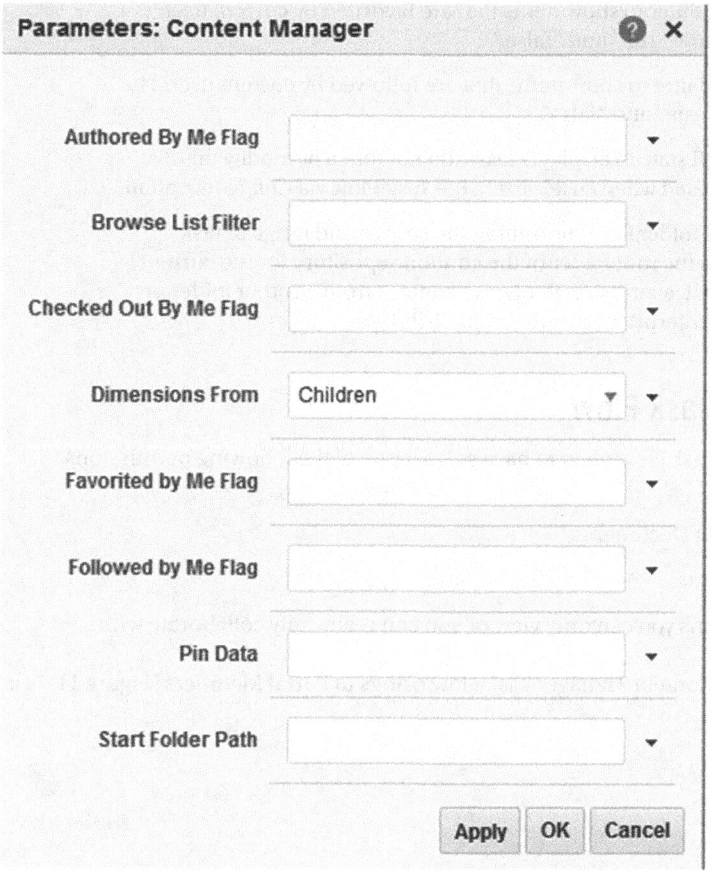

Figure 11-13. *Content Manager Task Flow Properties*

- **Authored By Me Flag**: It can be "true" or "false" and it indicates if the default filter should filter or not by authored content. By default, it is "false."

- **Browse List Filter**: For list folders or only documents. The accepted values are "folders," "documents."

- **Checked-Out By Me Flag**: Filter the content shown by only the Checked Out for the current user. It can be "true" or "false." By default, it is "false."

- **Dimension From**: Specify the geometric dimensions of the Task Flow. You can specify "children" or "parent":

  - If "parent" is selected, then ensure you set up the following Display Options for the Task Flow:

    - **Display Option** - StretchContent property to "true."

    - **Content Style** - Set the height that you want for the Task Flow.

  - If "children" is selected, then let the Display Option and Content Style as default.

- **Favorited By Me Flag**: Filter to show items that are favorited by current user. The supported values are "true" and "false."

- **Followed By Me Flag**: Filter to show items that are followed by current user. The supported values are "true" and "false".

- **Pin Data**: Defines the UI state to display. Please, do not touch or modify this parameter as it is generated when customizing the Task Flow via *Configure* option.

- **Start Folder Path**: The folder for determining the source and range of task flow content. Default is the root folder of the content repository for the current Portal. Enter a path or EL expression to display content from another folder or Portal. For Example: /Enterprise Libraries/daniel/Public

Using the Content Manager Task Flow

Users with access to Content Manager Task Flow need to have at least one of the following permissions assigned:

- Documents: Create and Edit Documents

- Documents: View Documents

Depending on the above permissions you can only view or you can really fully collaborate with documents.

Let's analyze the possibilities that Content Manager Task Flow brings to Portal Members (Figure 11-14):

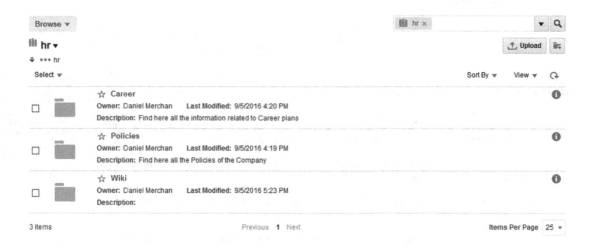

Figure 11-14. *Content Manager Task Flow Default View*

- By clicking Browse ▼ (Browse drop-down) a user can navigate to different functionalities offered:

  - **Search**: Allows the user to enter in an Advanced Search View for searching specific documents within the repository.

  - **Browse**: It goes to a view showing the Root of the repository with useful options for the user such that:

- **Checked-Out Content**: For showing all the content that is checked out for the current user.

- **Content In Workflow**: It displays current user content currently in a Workflow.

- Other Enterprise Libraries has access to (like other Portal documentation, other user documents etc.).

- **Favorites**: List all the Folders and Content that the current user has marked as Favorite.

- **Trash**: This is a new Feature included in 12c version. Deleted content goes to the Trash instead of being deleted forever. It is a great improvement compared to the previous release.

- **Home**: It comes back to the default view for the current Content Manager Task Flow.

- Selecting user by using **Select ▾** or the check boxes enables the following options:

- If a folder is selected:

  - 🔗 (Get Link): To retrieve a link that can be shared with other users to share the selected folder.

  - 🔲 (Move): Allows user to move the selected folder to a different location.

  - 🗐 (Copy): Use it to Copy the current folder with the current content to a different location.

  - 🗑 (Delete): It deletes the current selected folder.

  - ⚙ (Options): The properties section allows user to:

    - Change and show general information.

    - Change the security assigned.

    - Change the metadata.

    - Manage the Shortcuts (only if it has it available).

  - **More ▾** : Advanced options:

    - **Follow**: It marks the folder to be followed and receive notifications when the folder is changed.

    - **Create Shortcut**: Create a Shortcut to the selected folder. It is used by the user to quickly access to specific folders.

    - **Rename**: Rename the current folder.

    - **Propagate**: It is an advanced option used by administrators to propagate metadata and security configurations from the folder to its children.

- If content is selected, the following options are available:

  - ![Upload icon] (Upload): Use it for Check-In a new revision of the selected document.

  - ![Get Link icon] (Get Link): Get a direct link to the content that can be shared with other users.

  - ![Move icon] (Move): Allows user to move the selected content to a different location.

  - ![Copy icon] (Copy): Use it to Copy the current folder with the current content to a different location.

  - ![Delete icon] (Delete): Delete (send to the Trash) the selected content

  - More ▼ : Multiple options such:

    - **Check Out**: Locks the content and other users cannot edit or interact with it.

    - **Check Out and Edit**: Locks the content and opens it for editing.

    - **Download**: Downloads the native version of the document.

    - **View Web Rendition**: Displays the Web Format (transformed by Inbound Refinery) of the selected document. For example, the PDF version of a DOCX.

    - **View Dynamic Conversion**: If Dynamic Converter is enabled in WebCenter Content it displays the HTML rendition / version of the selected content.

    - **Follow**: Follow the selected content to receive notifications when it is modified.

    - **Create Shortcut**: Create a Shortcut to the selected content. It is used by the user to quickly access to specific folders.

    - **Rename**: Rename the selected content.

    - **Unfile Document / File Document**: Used to link/unlink content to its folder / enterprise library. When you unfile a document, you can no longer locate that document by browsing to its parent library or folder.

    - **Upload Similar Document**: Allows user to upload new content that will have the same metadata /security as the selected.

    - **Properties**: Shows the following options:

      - **Summary Tab**: Here you can check the status of the content, download different renditions of it and also add attachments if needed.

      - **Metadata Tab**: Display and Edit the metadata of the current content.

- **Security Tab**: For modifying the current security access.

- **Preview**: It previews the document and allows user to add Annotations if the Imaging capabilities are configured in WebCenter Content.

■ **Note**   If Oracle Document Cloud is configured with WebCenter Content then the Oracle Document Cloud Folders and Content are displayed within Content Manager Task Flow. Check the section of Integration with Oracle Document Cloud for more information.

Working with Content Workflows

By default, Oracle WebCenter Portal configures three simple Workflows in Oracle WebCenter Content:

- **AllUserApprover**: Single-step workflow that requires all the assigned approvers to approve the document to release it from workflow. The approvers cannot edit the file, unless they are the owner.

- **AllUserReviewer**: Single-step workflow that requires all assigned approvers to approve the document to release it from workflow. In this case, the approvers also can modify the content.

- **SingleUserApprover**: Single-step workflow that requires only one assigned approver to approve the document to release it from workflow. The approver cannot edit the content.

A contributor uploading a document using Content Manager Task Flow has to assign manually the Workflow to be assigned to the content / revision and also who are the approvers and reviewers (Figure 11-15).

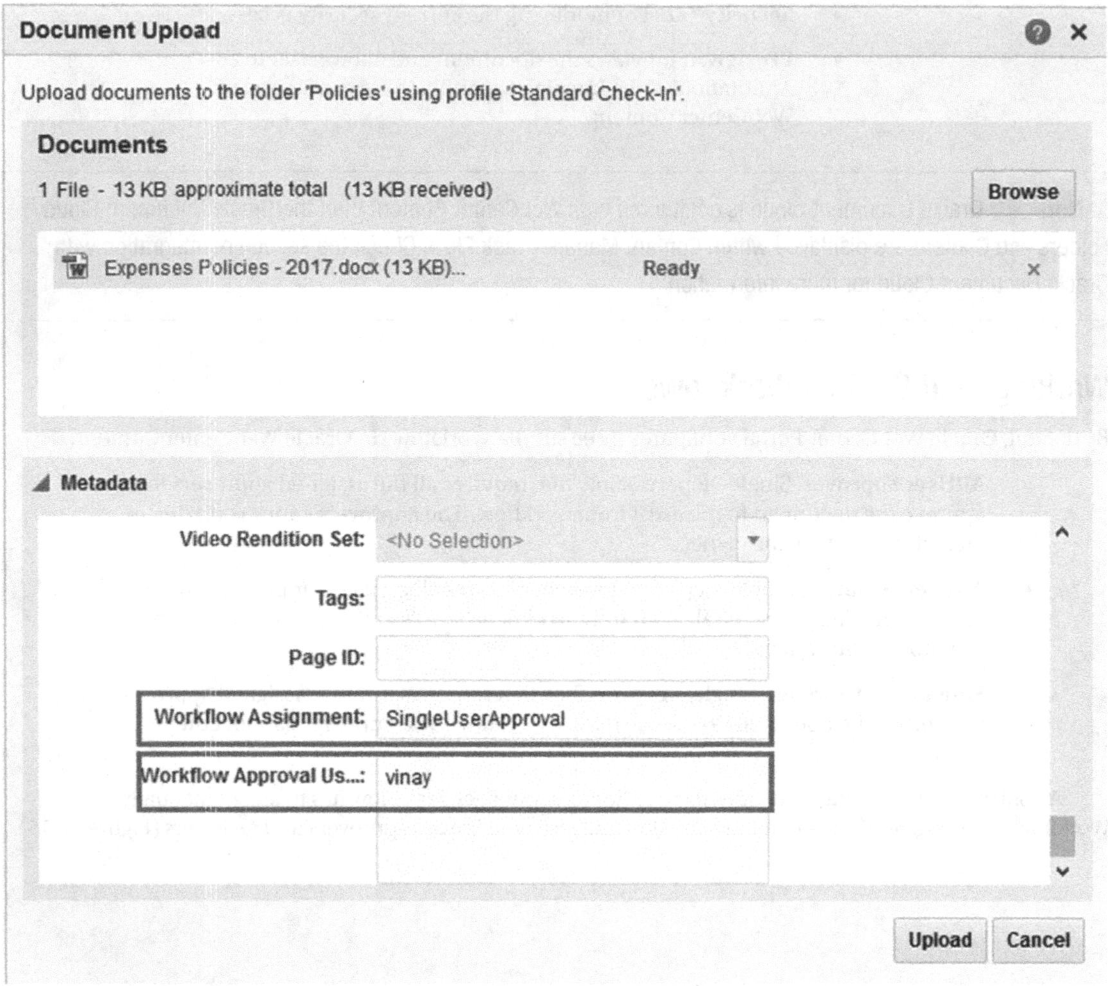

Figure 11-15. Assigning a Workflow and the Approver to a specific document

As you can see the Workflow Assignment and the Approval / Reviewers has to be typed manually, which is really bad.

Once the content is uploaded then an informative message appears that it was assigned to the Workflow as well (Figure 11-16).

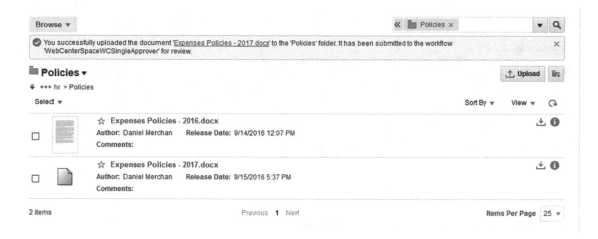

Figure 11-16. *Content Uploaded and Assigned to the Workflow*

Now, the approver has been notified and has to review the content by going to Browse ➤ Content In Workflow (Figure 11-17).

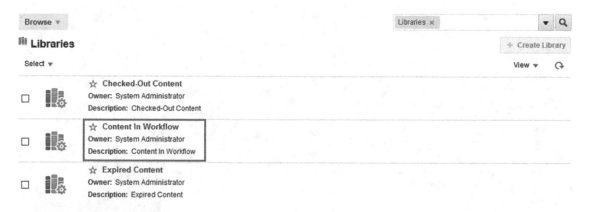

Figure 11-17. *Content In Workflow Option*

Here the approver can review the content he has pending to Review / Approve (Figure 11-18).

Figure 11-18. *All content pending to Approve / Review*

Selecting the check box on the content, new options will be displayed to the approver for Approve (✓) or Reject (⊘).

In addition, he can Approve or Reject by entering the details of the content (Figure 11-19).

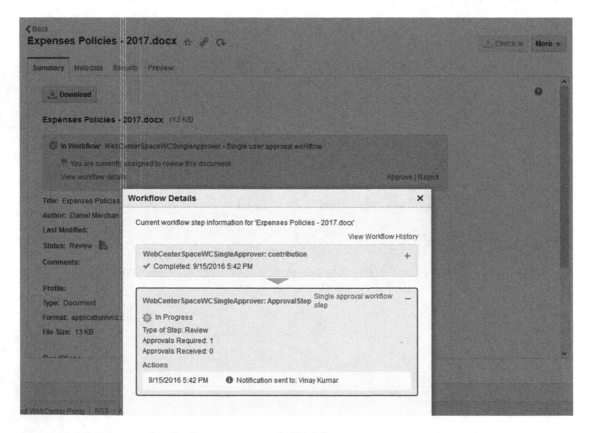

Figure 11-19. *Summary details of a content part of a Workflow*

Working with Web Content: Site Studio

Oracle WebCenter Portal offers WCM (Web Content Management) capabilities by using Site Studio technology.

What Is Site Studio?

Site Studio is an old Oracle WebCenter Component that has been used in the past for building and publishing Web Sites using WebCenter Content (Figure 11-20).

Figure 11-20. *Article Site Studio Data File rendered by Content Presenter*

Since 11g version of WebCenter Portal, the integration with Site Studio has been available by using Content Presenter Task Flow component.

Basically, Content Presenter Task Flow can render Web Content structured data built using on top of the Site Studio Asset Model.

■ **Note** If you are planning for a Web Site focused on content then use WebCenter Sites solution instead of WebCenter Portal.

Oracle is planning to release a Content Presenter Task Flow for consuming WebCenter Sites Assets. However, by now the way for exposing Web Content is by using Site Studio.

Understanding Site Studio Asset Model

The following are the basic Site Studio components that must be used for building Web Content.

- **Element Definition**: The Element Definitions are the smallest pieces of information. They can be reused for defining multiple Region Definitions. The Out-of-the-box Element Definitions are:

  - **Plain Text**: Text editor for providing short texts.

  - **WYSIWYG**: It is a CKEditor for rich content.

  - **Image**: Image selector.

  - **Static List**: Table of elements to be populated manually by the contributor.

  - **Dynamic List**: Auto-populate table based on a Query.

  - **Custom Element**: Based on a Custom Element Form for displaying the Contributor part for this piece of information in a custom way. For example, a check box.

- **Region Definition**: It is the Asset Definition. It uses the Element Definition for defining a structured Asset Type.

- **Data File**: Is the name assigned to an instance of a specific Region Definition.

Maybe the above definitions are confused? Let's try to explain them by using the following example. In this diagram (Figure 11-21), it is shown how to build a "News" asset and have it displayed within WebCenter Portal.

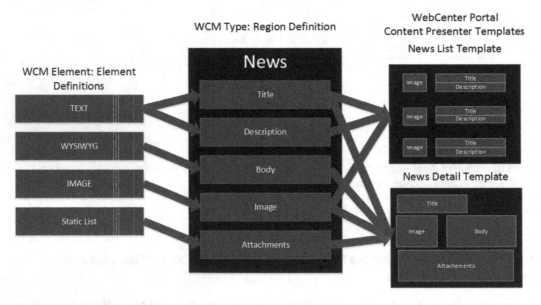

Figure 11-21. *News Asset Definition using Site Studio Asset Model*

As shown in the Figure, we have 4 Element Definitions created and used to build the Region Definition: News:

- The Title and Description are Text Fields.

- The Body is a WYSIWYG component.

- The Image is an Image component.

- Attachments is a Static List to provide links to different documents.

When the Region Definition: News is defined then we can create Data Files that are instances over the News Content Type. A Data File can be, for example, *"The latest CEO update."*

WebCenter Portal by using Content Presenter Task Flow and the following Templates renders the News as the following:

- **News List Template**: It renders a list of News, but not using all the information provided in the Data Files.

- **News Detail Template**: Displays all the information of a specific Data File of type news.

From the above example, you can conclude that you can build your own structured web content by using Site Studio and display it as you want by using Content Presenter Templates.

Creating a Site Studio Asset Type

Developers can model the Site Studio Asset Model by using **Site Studio Designer IDE**.

After enabling Site Studio component, developers can find the Site Studio Designer IDE Installable by accessing to WebCenter Content Console ➤ My Content Server ➤ My Downloads (Figure 11-22).

Figure 11-22. News Asset Definition using Site Studio Asset Model

Using Site Studio Designer, they can easily create Element Definitions and Region Definitions for modeling the Assets (Figure 11-23).

■ **Note**   Site Studio Designer IDE only works in Windows Environments.

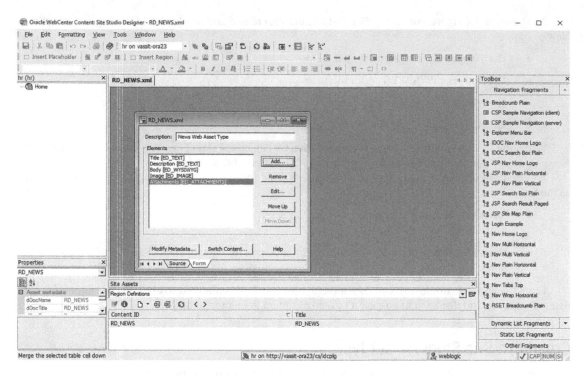

Figure 11-23. Modeling a News Region Definition using Site Studio Designer

---

■ **Note** Element Definitions and Region Definitions are just XML files with specific metadata and content that is filled by Site Studio Designer.

The first time running Site Studio Designer IDE, you need to configure a WebCenter Content connection and create a Web Site for holding the new Web Assets created (Figure 11-24).

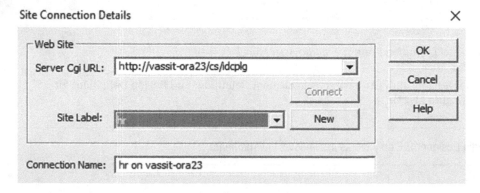

Figure 11-24. Connecting Site Studio Desginer to WebCenter Content for Modeling

After it, in the bottom part there is a Site Assets drop-down that allows you to select which type of Site Studio Asset you want to create (Figure 11-25).

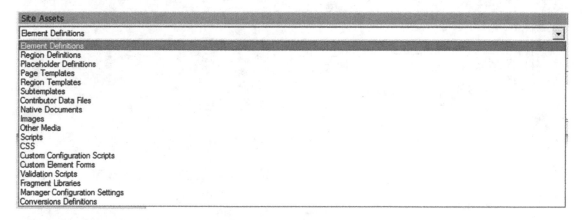

Figure 11-25. *All type of Site Studio Elements. We just need Element Definitions, Region Definitions and maybe Custom Element Forms*

First of all, create all the Element Definitions that you need for creating your Asset Model made by Region Definitions (Figure 11-26).

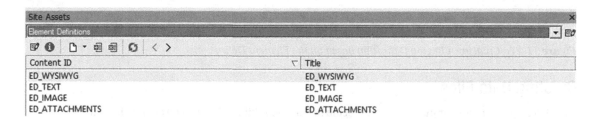

Figure 11-26. *Element Definitions*

Then, model your Asset Type by creating the Region Definition and adding the Element Definition that composes the Region Definition (Figure 11-27).

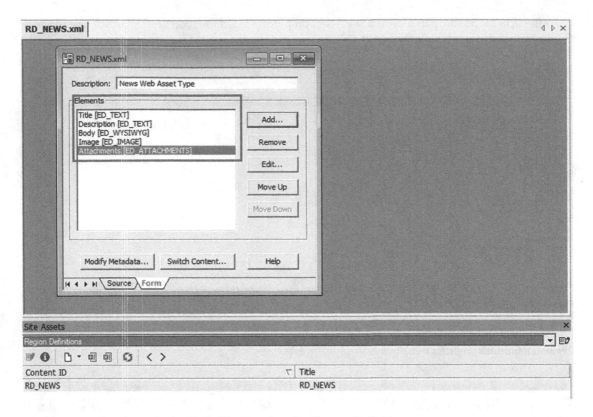

Figure 11-27. *Creating a Region Definition based on the Element Definitions*

Creating Data Files

Data Files are the name for instances of a specific Region Definition. They can be created from three different interfaces:

- **From WebCenter Content old UI**. Not recommended and only should be used by users with administration rights (Figure 11-28).

- **From Content Presenter in Edit Mode**. In Edit Mode a button called Edit Web Content is available if WebCenter Portal and WebCenter Content have been configured for accessing from the same hostname and port (Figure 11-29).

- **From Content Presenter in Contribution Mode**. When a Contributor enters into Contribution Mode and the page contains a Content Presenter then it shows the following options: ✚ (add) and ✎ (edit) that allows users to Create or Edit the current content assigned to the Content Presenter. In case of a Data File it opens Site Studio Contributor (Figure 11-30).

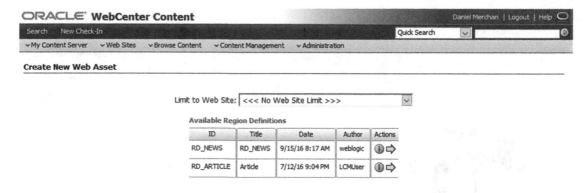

Figure 11-28. *Creating a Data File using WebCenter Content old interface*

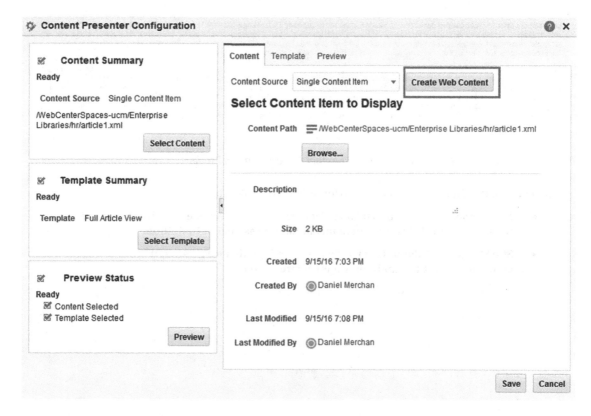

Figure 11-29. *Create a Data File in Content Presenter Edit Mode*

Figure 11-30. *Create a Data File in Content Presenter in Contribution Mode*

Independently of the option selected, two forms have to be filled in:

- **Metadata Form:** Fill important metadata such Title, name of the XML file. **Please, do not touch pre-filled Web Content metadata such as Region Definition.**

- **Site Studio Contributor Form: It displays the form that we generated by configuring the Element Definitions (Figure** 11-31**).**

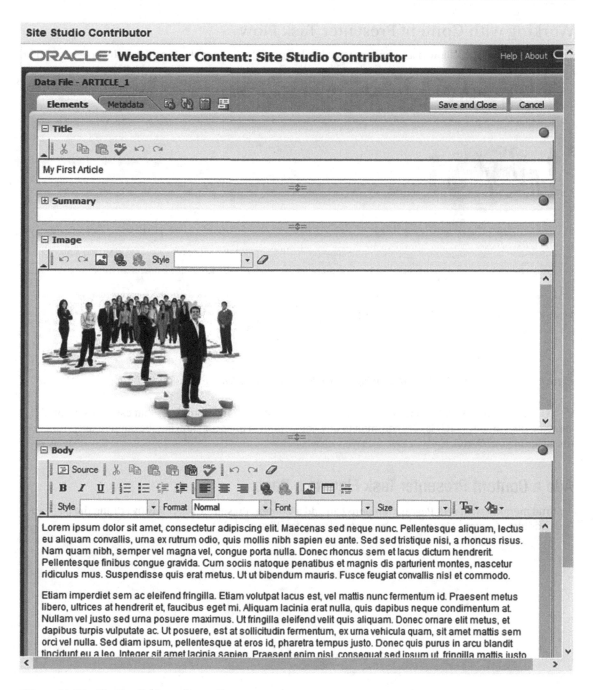

Figure 11-31. *Site Studio Contributor Form*

Working with Content Presenter Task Flow

Content Presenter Task Flow is a component that has been available since the 11g release. It allows user to customize the way that the content is displayed from the Content Repository (Figure 11-32).

Figure 11-32. *Content Presenter displaying an Article using Article Detail View Template*

Out-of-the-box, WebCenter Portal offers a set of Content Presenter Templates that can be used for showing the content, but it is very common to develop your own ones for showing the content accordingly to the styles of your Portal.

Add a Content Presenter Task Flow to a Page

A portal member with *Edit Page* permissions can add a Content Presenter Task Flow by editing the page and then adding a *Content Management* ➤ *Content Presenter* (Figure 11-33).

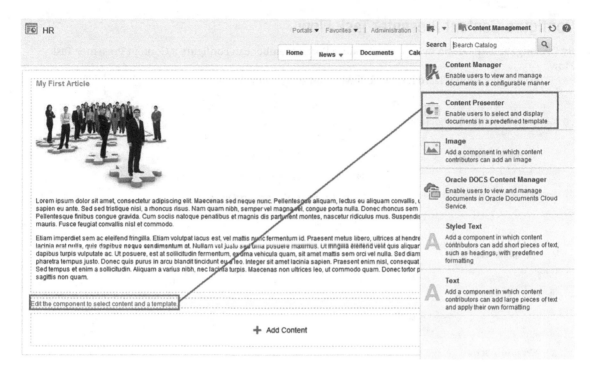

Figure 11-33. Adding a Content Presenter Task Flow

Configure Content Presenter Task Flow

By Clicking the *Edit* button in Page Edit Mode, a Portal Member can configure a Content Presenter Task Flow.

The Configuration Wizard has the following options (Figure 11-34):

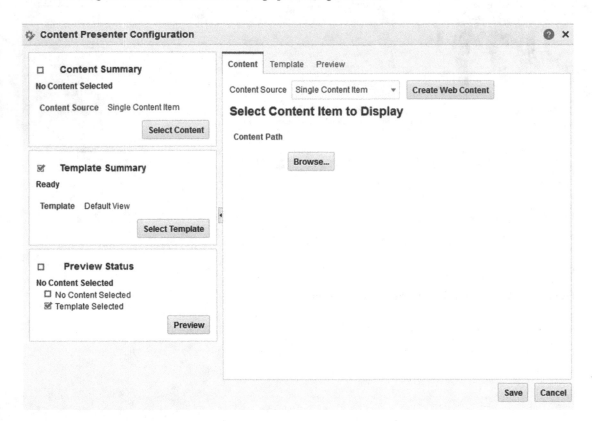

Figure 11-34. *Configuring Content Presenter Task Flow*

- Content Source | Single Content Item ▾ | (Content Source): Allows user to select the type of Content Presenter they are configuring. It can be:

  - **Single Content Item**: Only select one piece of content to be displayed from the Content Repository.

  - **Contents Under a Folder**: It allows user to select a Folder as the root base of the content to be displayed.

  - **Results of a Query**: It retrieves the content from a specific query based on some metadata values.

  - **List of items**: Allows to the contributor to select the specific contents to be displayed.

- **Create Web Content** (Create Web Content): This button is enabled when Site Studio integration is configured. It allows the start of the Site Studio Contributor Wizard for creating new Web Content. It will be automatically assigned to this Content Presenter.

- In the **Template Tab**, it can choose which Content Presenter Template use to display the selected content.

- Finally, the **Preview Tab** allows user to preview the content with the selected content.

In addition, a Content Presenter Task Flow can be configured by editing the **Parameters** option of the Content Presenter Task Flow. The options in Parameters mode are:

- **Data Source**: Selects the content or contents to be displayed. Depending on the **Data Source Type** selected, it is configured in a different way by content:

  - **Single Node**: [connection_name]#dDocName@[content_id]

  - **Folder Contents**: [connection_name]#fFolderGUID:[folder_id]

  - **Query Expression**: To a CMIS Query. For example:

  - select * from cmis:document where cmis:createdBy = 'daniel'

  - **Multi Node**: Specify separated by commas all the content to be displayed following the Single Node mode.

- **Data Source Type**: Specify the type of Content Presenter (Single Node, Folder Contents, Query Expression, Multi Node).

- **Maximum Results**: Used to limit the results when using Query Expression as Data Source Type.

- **Region Template**: Flag to indicate if the Content Presenter Template used is a Site Studio Region Template. This option is used for backward compatibility with Site Studio or when an ADF Content Presenter Template cannot achieve the same results as using a Region Template.

- **Task Flow Instance ID**: Unique identifier for the Task Flow (internal use).

- **Task Flow Category ID**: Used for setting up the category of Content Presenter Template to use.

- **Template View ID**: Here is where the Content Presenter Template is configured. Every Content Presenter Template has a unique ID.

■ **Note** Every configuration made in **Parameters** option overrides any configuration made by the Edit Wizard.

About Content Presenter Templates Development

Content Presenter Templates can be developed by:

- Using JDeveloper for creating ADF Content Presenter Templates.

- Using Site Studio Designer for creating Region Templates.

If possible, always develop your Content Presenter Templates using ADF Content Presenter Templates and JDeveloper.

There are only few things that may make you develop a Region Template, like, for example, to call other WebCenter Content services by using Idoc Script when rendering the template.

Two different types of Content Presenter Templates can be created by using JDeveloper:

- **Content Presenter List Template** for displaying list of items returned by a Query or a Folder.

- **Content Presenter Single Template** for rendering a single content.

Oracle WebCenter Portal offers an API for Content Presenter with multiple EL Expressions that can be used by the developers for accessing all the metadata, rendition, and also to the content of the Web Content.

In order to see what a Content Presenter Template looks like, let's analyze some examples.

The first example is based on a custom News Region Definition and displays the information provided by the Data File.

A sample snippet code of a sample News Detail Content Presenter Template that renders a "News" Data File based on a Region Definition:

```
<dt:contentTemplateDef var="node">
        <div id="newscp">
            <div id="newstitle">
                    <af:outputText value="#{node.propertyMap['NEWS_RD:Title'].value.
                    stringValue}"
                                                  id="outputText1"
                                                  inlineStyle="color:#0E417E;"/>
            </div>
            <div id="body">
                    <div id="image">
                            <!-- Note that using IMAGE Picker stores /cs address, need
                            to remove context access -->
                            <af:image source="/..#{node.propertyMap['NEWS_RD:Image'].
                            value.stringValue}"
                                            shortDesc="#{node.propertyMap['NEWS_
                                            RD:Title'].value.stringValue}"
                                                id="i2" partialTriggers="p1"/>
                    </div>
                    <div id="shortdesc">
                            <af:outputText escape="false"
value="#{node.propertyMap['NEWS_RD:SDesc'].value.stringValue}"                    •
                                                                    id="otSDESC"/>
                    </div>
            </div>
        </div>
  </dt:contentTemplateDef>
```

A sample snippet of code of a List of News calling the above template as nested Content Presenter Template to display each News item:

```
<dt:contentListTemplateDef var="nodes">
        <af:iterator rows="0" var="node" varStatus="iterator" value="#{nodes}"
                     id="i1">
            <dt:contentTemplate node="#{node}" view="daniel.news.detail"
                                nodesHint="#{nodes}" id="ct1"/>
            <af:separator id="s2"
                          rendered="#{iterator.index le iterator.model.rowCount - 2}"/>
        </af:iterator>
</dt:contentListTemplateDef>
```

Now the following example shows how to display a carousel of images by using the ADF Carousel component:

This example is extracted from the Out-of-the-box Carousel Template

```
<jsp:root xmlns:jsp="http://java.sun.com/JSP/Page" version="2.1"
          xmlns:af="http://xmlns.oracle.com/adf/faces/rich"
          xmlns:dt="http://xmlns.oracle.com/webcenter/content/templates"
          xmlns:f="http://java.sun.com/jsf/core">
    <dt:contentListTemplateDef var="nodes">
        <af:carousel id="c1" value="#{nodes}" var="node" emptyText="#{templateBundle.EMPTY_
        NODES}">
            <f:facet name="nodeStamp">
                <af:carouselItem id="ci1"
                                 text="#{node.isFolder ? node.name : (empty node.
                                 propertyMap['dDocTitle'] ? node.name : node.
                                 propertyMap['dDocTitle'].value.stringValue)}"
                                 shortDesc="#{not empty node.propertyMap['xComments'].
                                 value.stringValue ? node.propertyMap['xComments'].value.
                                 stringValue : node.primaryProperty.value.binaryValue.
                                 name}">
                    <af:image id="cimg1"
                              source="#{node.primaryProperty.isImage ? node.primaryProperty.
                              url : node.icon.largeIcon}"
                              shortDesc="#{node.primaryProperty.value.binaryValue.name}"/>
                </af:carouselItem>
            </f:facet>
        </af:carousel>
    </dt:contentListTemplateDef>
</jsp:root>
```

■ **Note**   Sample Content Presenter Templates can be found on a default installation of JDeveloper 12.2.1+ with the WebCenter extension installed on it. Usually, they are located in the folder C:\[ORACLE_HOME_OF_ JDEV]\jdeveloper\webcenter\samples\contentpresenter. They can give you very good tips about how to develop your own Content Presenter Templates.

Desktop Integration Suite

The Desktop Integration Suite also called DIS, is a Client software that can be installed in the Portal Member machine in order to interact with the Content Repository without accessing via WebCenter Portal.

The Desktop Integration Suite requires:

- Enable **DesktopIntegrationSuite** component in WebCenter Content.

- **Install the DIS Client** in your Windows Machine. It can be downloaded from the WebCenter Content old interface ➤ My Content Server ➤ My Downloads. It only will appear if DesktopIntegrationSuite component has been enabled in WebCenter Content.

After installing Desktop Integration Suite, it is required to register the details of WebCenter Content (Figure 11-35).

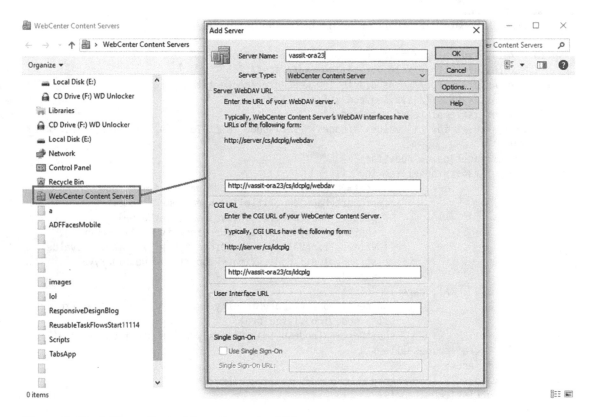

Figure 11-35. *Adding a Content Repository using DIS*

Now, WebCenter Content will be displayed like another drive of your system and you can work with the documents stored on it (Figure 11-36).

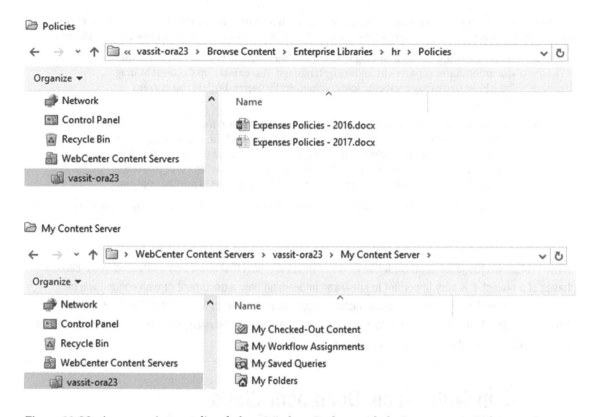

Figure 11-36. *A user can interact directly from Windows Explorer with the Documents in WebCenter Content*

But DIS not only brings the possibility of managing WebCenter Content as another drive In addition, it integrates with the Microsoft Office package allowing the users to upload, download, create, edit documents from WebCenter Content by using their Microsoft Office programs such as Word, Outlook, PowerPoint. (Figure 11-37).

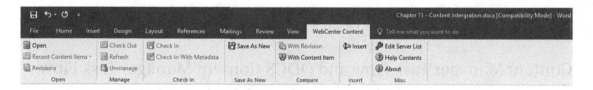

Figure 11-37. *Microsoft Word with WebCenter Content options available*

Multi-Language considerations

It is responsibility of the contributor to upload / create the documents and web content in all the languages required. WebCenter does not translate or create translations for you.

As WebCenter Content does not bring any mechanism for multi-language, then you need to choose a good multi-language strategy. Based on the usage of Content Manager or Content Presenter we suggest:

- If you are using Content Manager Task Flow, for example you can organize the documentation separate in folders by language. You can set up Content Manager Task Flow to display a specific folder dynamically depending on the current language.

- In case of using Content Presenter to display Web Content, for example, it can be created a custom metadata that indicates the language of the content and then configure Content Presenter for querying the content based on the current language. In addition, Content Presenter can be configured for displaying content from a specific folder, separate the web content by language folders is another option.

There are many more possibilities and more complex solutions based on extending or creating custom components.

■ **Tip** Multi-language for documentation or web content is a task that should be addressed in the earliest phases of a project. It is very important to know and understand how a document or web content will be targeted for a specific language. We recommend that you create a Custom Metadata in WebCenter Content to allow contributors to mark the content to a specific language. This can be easily used by Content Presenter for displaying targeted content to the correct audience.

Integration with Oracle Document Cloud

Oracle Document Cloud offers document storage and collaboration capabilities through the Oracle's Cloud. Oracle WebCenter Portal can be integrated with Oracle Document Cloud in two ways:

- **By configuring Oracle Document Cloud with WebCenter Content** it makes the folders and contents of the Oracle Document Cloud available through **Content Manager Task Flow** component.

- Since 12.2.1.1+ (not in 12.2.1), Oracle WebCenter Portal offers the **Oracle Documents Cloud Content Manager Task Flow** that can be added to Pages to embed the Oracle Document Cloud Interface in a WebCenter Portal Page.

Content Manager Task Flow and ODCS Content Manager Task Flow

To enable the Oracle Document Cloud for Content Manager Task Flow then WebCenter Content has to be integrated first with Oracle Document Cloud by following the next steps:

- Enable the **OracleDocumentsFolders** component and restart WebCenter Content Managed Server.

- Configure in WebCenter Content the new Oracle Documents Cloud Settings that can be found on the Administration Menu (Figure 11-38).

- In addition, configure the SSL Settings of the UCM Managed Server for using a Custom Hostname Verifer: weblogic.security.utils.SSWLSWildcardHostnameVerifier

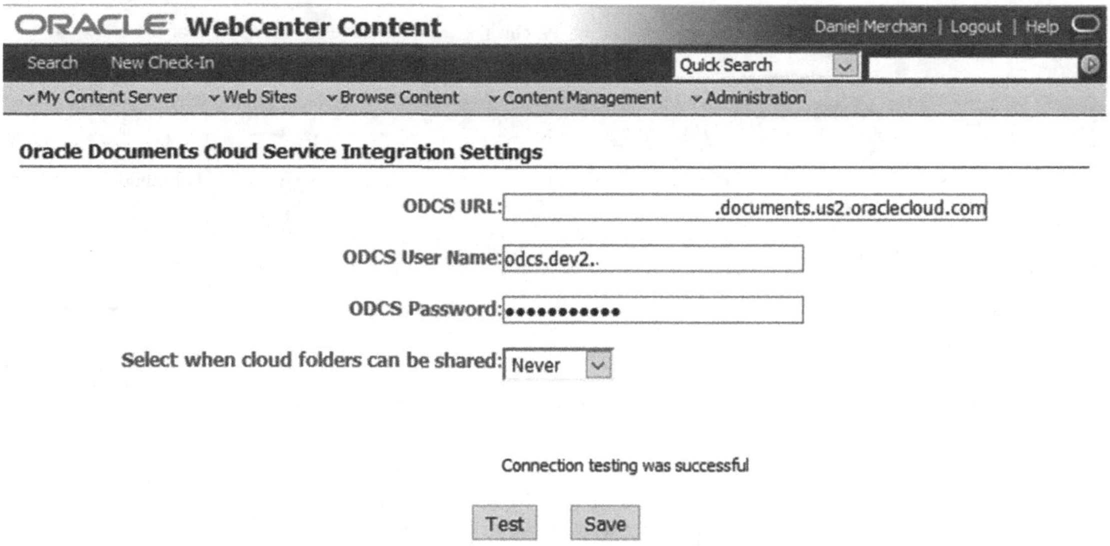

ORACLE® WebCenter Content

Daniel Merchan | Logout | Help ⬭

Search   New Check-In   Quick Search   ⌄

⌄ My Content Server   ⌄ Web Sites   ⌄ Browse Content   ⌄ Content Management   ⌄ Administration

Oracle Documents Cloud Service Integration Settings

ODCS URL: [.documents.us2.oraclecloud.com]

ODCS User Name: [odcs.dev2..   ]

ODCS Password: [•••••••••••   ]

Select when cloud folders can be shared: [Never   ⌄]

Connection testing was successful

[Test]   [Save]

Figure 11-38. Microsoft Word with WebCenter Content options available

We recommend restarting WebCenter Content and WebCenter Portal after this.

Now, the Content Manager Task Flow will allow the users to create and interact with the Document Cloud Folders and Content (Figure 11-39).

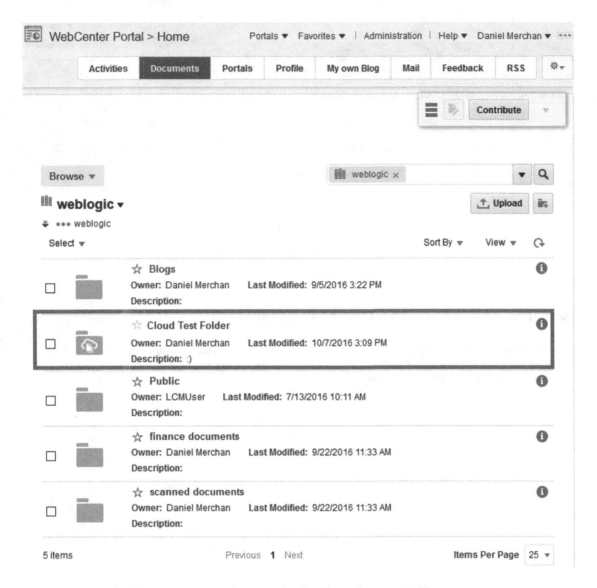

Figure 11-39. *Hybrid Content Manager showing Cloud Folder and Content Folder*

■ **Tip** The same permissions for Documents are applied to the Folders and Content shown from Oracle Document Cloud Service. If you only have permissions for *"View"* then you cannot create or edit documents shown from the Oracle Document Cloud Service.

Document Cloud Content Manager Task Flow

The Document Cloud Content Manager Task Flow is available since the 12.2.1.1+ version of WebCenter Portal.

The integration is simple; it just embeds the "iframe" version of Oracle Document Cloud in WebCenter Portal.

For using Oracle ODCS Content Manager Task Flow is require to configure the following:

- The Administrator of the Document Cloud Account has to enable Embedded Content option and also add the WebCenter Portal domain as a trusted domain.

- A System Administrator of WebCenter Portal has to add the Oracle Document Cloud URL connection by using WLST (by the moment, this connection cannot be done by using the Enterprise Manager Console).

  - Connect via using WLST scripts to WebCenter Portal Domain.

  - Execute the following WLST command by replacing the host and port with your Document Cloud hostname:

```
adf_createHttpURLConnection(appName='webcenter', name='WCP-DCS', url='http://<host>:<port>/Documents')
```

- Add the Oracle ODCS Content Manager Task Flow into a WebCenter Portal Page (Figure 11-40).

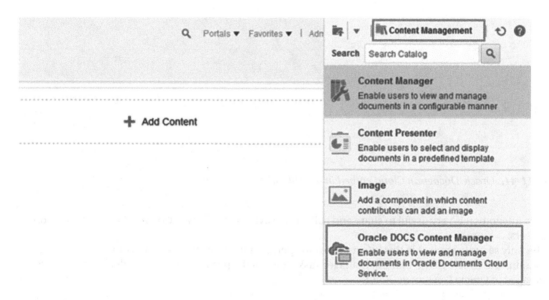

Figure 11-40. *Adding Oracle ODCS Content Manager Task Flow*

- Configure the following parameters of the Task Flow:

  - **DOCS Display Theme**: it is the background and wrapper style used by the Task Flow.

  - **DOCS Folder Path**: Specify a specific folder of DOCS. Remember that the URL must use /documents/embed as part of the URL.

After configuring it, it should display embed the Oracle Document Cloud in the specific folder selected (Figure 11-41):

Figure 11-41. Oracle Docuemtn Cloud embed in a WebCenter Portal Page

This integration is very useful to share and collaborate over documents between Portal users and non-Portal users.

The only security applied in this integration is the permission of the user to access or not to the page that contains the Oracle ODCS Content Manager Task Flow. All the permissions over folders and contents are managed in Oracle Document Cloud.

Publishing Content Using Pages

Oracle WebCenter Portal 12c has introduced a quick way for contributing and publishing pages including simple information such text and images (Figure 11-42).

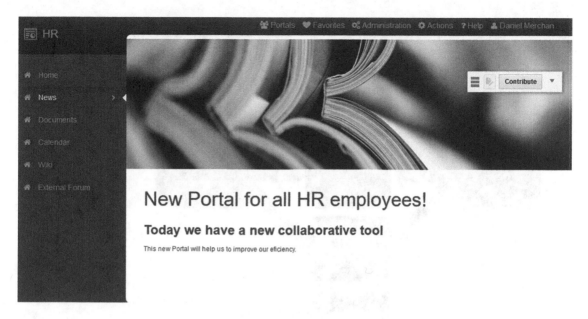

Figure 11-42. Portal Page showing simple information

■ **Note** In previous releases of WebCenter Portal, the *"unique"* way for publishing and contributing web content was using Content Presenter Task Flow and Site Studio for defining structured web content.

In previous releases also exist "text" and "image" components that can be used. However, these components only were available for Administrators in Edit Mode and not for contributors who uses the Contribution Mode. In addition, there were not any mechanisms for Publishing and comparing page versions.

Building Web Content Types Based on Pages Styles

Basically, the key here is to match the concept of Content Type to a Pages Style and then every Page will be an instance of a Content Type / Page Style (Figure 11-43).

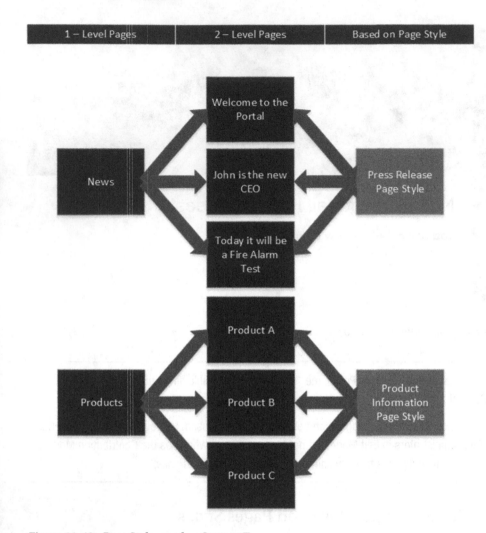

Figure 11-43. *Page Styles used as Content Types*

To make a Page editable in contribution mode then the following editable components should be used when creating the Page Style:

- **Image**: Allows the contributors to use an image from a given URL or from the default content repository.

- **Styled Text**: Use it to allow text section to display a header or short descriptions.

- **Text**: This component allows user to contribute large section of texts providing a powerful WYSIWYG editor (*What you see is what you get*).

The editable components are located in the Content Management Folder of the Default Portal Catalog (Figure 11-44):

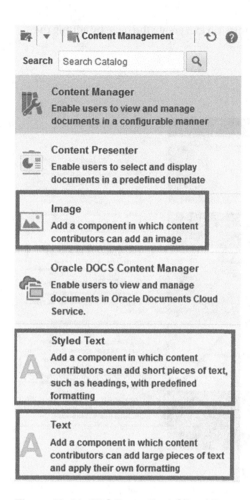

Figure 11-44. *WebCenter Portal Page Content Components*

For example, imagine that we need the following structure for creating content pages, see Figure 11-45 (the same as the Out-of-the-box offered Page Style).

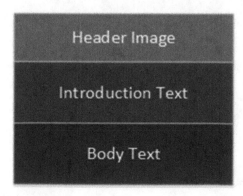

Figure 11-45. *Example of a Page Content that should be replicated multiple times*

Then a Portal Member / Manager with *"Page Creation"* permission can create the page by adding the editable components as shown below in Figure 11-46.

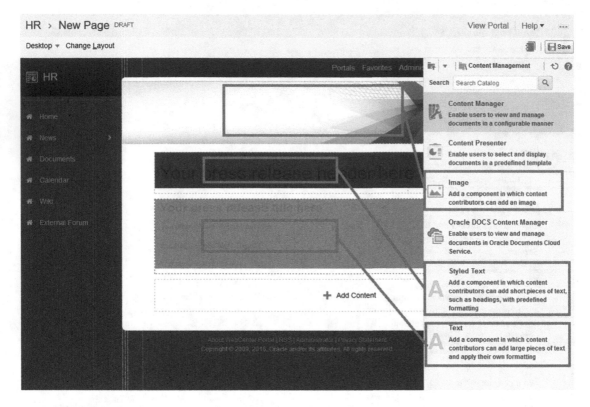

Figure 11-46. *Example of how Press Release Page Style is created*

Now, instead of contributing a real image, real text, or real information, contribute some informational text about what to add in each section to help Contributors add the information (Figure 11-47).

Figure 11-47. *Adding descriptive text for creating a Page Style based on the page*

Once the page is available, remember that the Page can be *"Templated"* by creating a Page Style.

■ **Note**   In Edit Mode. Click ▶ and then *Create Page Style* as it was explained in Chapter 5. After create the Page Style then you may want to Delete the Page used for creating the Page Style.

Now, Contributors with permissions for *"Creating Pages"* and *"Contribute"* can create and contribute content based on the new Page Style (Figure 11-48).

Figure 11-48. *Creating New Content Pages based on the Page Style through Contribution Mode instead of Edit Mode*

Contribution Toolbar and Editable Components

The Contribution Toolbar [≡ ▷ Contribute ▼] has been added in the WebCenter Portal 12c release and it allows the Portal Member with Contributor role for doing the following:

- **Switch between Contribution Mode and View Mode** if they have "Contribution" permissions.

- **Create new Pages** if they have *"Page Creation"* permission.

- **Administrate the Page** if they have *"Edit Page"* permission.

■ **Tip** Contributors can also use the Ctrl + C shortcut (if your WebCenter Portal Administrator did not change the default shortcut) to enter into the contribution mode.

In this mode, the editable components will display the pencil icon ✎ that allows the contributor to modify the editable components shown in the page.

Once the contributor saves the changes made then the Contribution Toolbar will turn to

[≡ ▷ Contribute ▼] that indicates that you are viewing the "draft" mode of the page instead of the published one.

By clicking 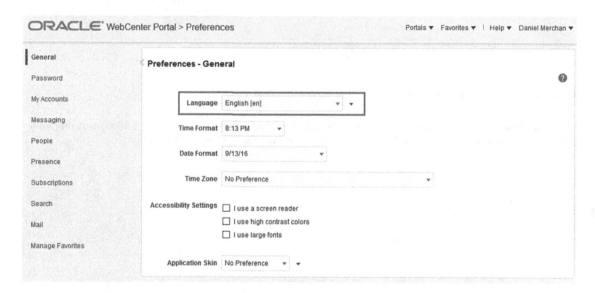(switch between draft / original icon) the page will switch between the *Draft* and the *Published* version of the page.

If the icon appears as *"Disabled"* then it means that there is not a draft version because the page has been published.

By clicking (the arrow icon) a drop-down menu will appear depending on their permissions for **Creating New Pages**, or **Editing the Page** going into the Administration Mode.

■ **Caution**   Remember that if you do not see the Portal Contribution Toolbar it can be because the Page Template does not have the portalToolbar tag included or because you do not have permission to contribute.

Multi-Language Considerations

Here is one of the most confusing parts for WebCenter Portal contributors using Pages for Content Publishing.

Basically, when a contributor contributes a Page it is contributing it for the current Preferred Language of the Contributor (Figure 11-49).

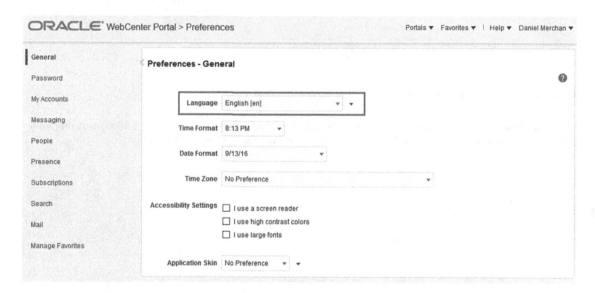

Figure 11-49. *Changing the preferred language*

It means that if a Contributor wants to contribute in a different language then he has to change to:

- Change to the specific language by changing his preferred language.

- Navigate to the Page to be contributed in the new language.

- Enter into the Contribution Mode and override the content. It will store a new version of the content for that specific language.

- Then a Portal Manager with *"Publishing"* permission publishes the Page.

■ **Note** If no localized content was provided for a language, portal members will see the content in the portal's default language.

New localized content is stored in the WebCenter Portal MDS Repository.

Publishing Content Using Data Presenter

Data Presenter is a powerful tool provided by WebCenter Portal 12c for displaying and manipulating data coming from REST and SQL services (Figure 11-50).

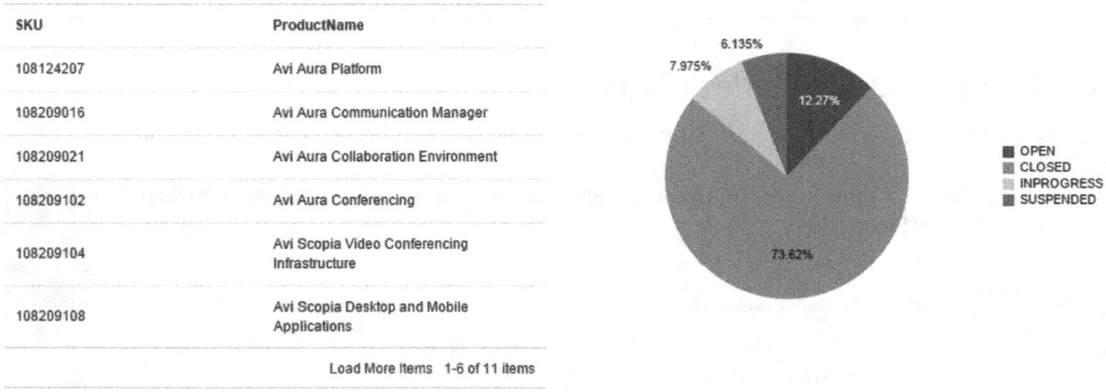
SKU
ProductName
108124207
Avi Aura Platform
108209016
Avi Aura Communication Manager
108209021
Avi Aura Collaboration Environment
108209102
Avi Aura Conferencing
108209104
Avi Scopia Video Conferencing Infrastructure
108209108
Avi Scopia Desktop and Mobile Applications
Load More Items 1-6 of 11 items
6.135%
7.975%
12.27%
73.62%
OPEN
CLOSED
INPROGRESS
SUSPENDED

***Figure 11-50.** Example of Data Presenter retrieving information*

In addition, we cannot forget that there is also another integration via Data Control for consuming Web Services. This one was available in 11g under the name of *"Mashups"* (Figure 11-51).

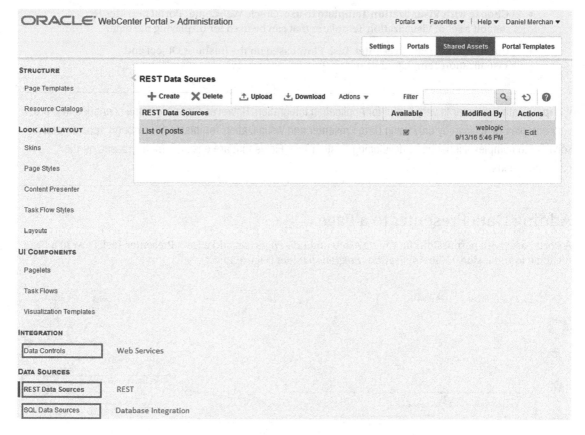

Figure 11-51. *WebCenter Portal Administration for creating Data Sources*

The steps for adding a Data Presenter are the following:

- **Create a Data Source** to retrieve data. You can accomplish this task from:

  - In the WebCenter Portal Administration - Shared Assets.

  - In the specific Portal Administration - Portal Assets.

  - Do it when configuring a Data Presenter Task Flow.

- **Create a Business Object (optional)**. A Business Object makes simple the task for presenting data using visualization templates. A default one is created based on all attributes when creating a Data Source. Business Objects have the following capabilities:

  - Filter the attributes retrieved from the Data Source.

  - Expose operations such, for example, GET, PUT, POST, DELETE for manipulating the data for a REST service.

- **Choose with Visualization Template to use**. Oracle WebCenter Portal provides by default a set of Visualization Templates that can be used for displaying the data.

- **Configure the Data Presenter Task Flow** based on the Business Object and Visualization Template chosen.

■ **Tip** Data Presenter is very useful for Application Integration. However, there are some scenarios that are very complex to achieve by only using Data Presenter and Visualization Templates. We strongly recommend solving the complex scenarios by developing Custom Task Flows that are easier to modify based on the customer needs.

Adding Data Presenter to a Page

A Portal user with permissions for *Create Assets* and *Edit Pages* can add a Data Presenter Task Flow to a Page. It can be found inside of the Application Integration folder (Figure 11-52).

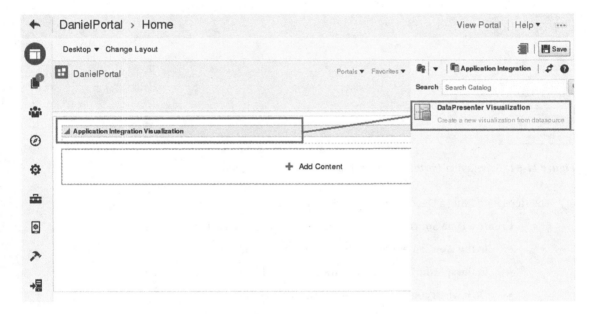

Figure 11-52. *Adding Data Presenter Task Flow*

Configuring Data Presenter Task Flow

To configure the Data Presenter Task Flow, click *Configure* option shown in the component in the Edit Mode of the Page.

The first step is to assign a Data Source. If we do not have the Data Source created yet, then we can create one by clicking **+ Add Data Source**.

When creating a REST Data Source, the following information must be provided (Figure 11-53):

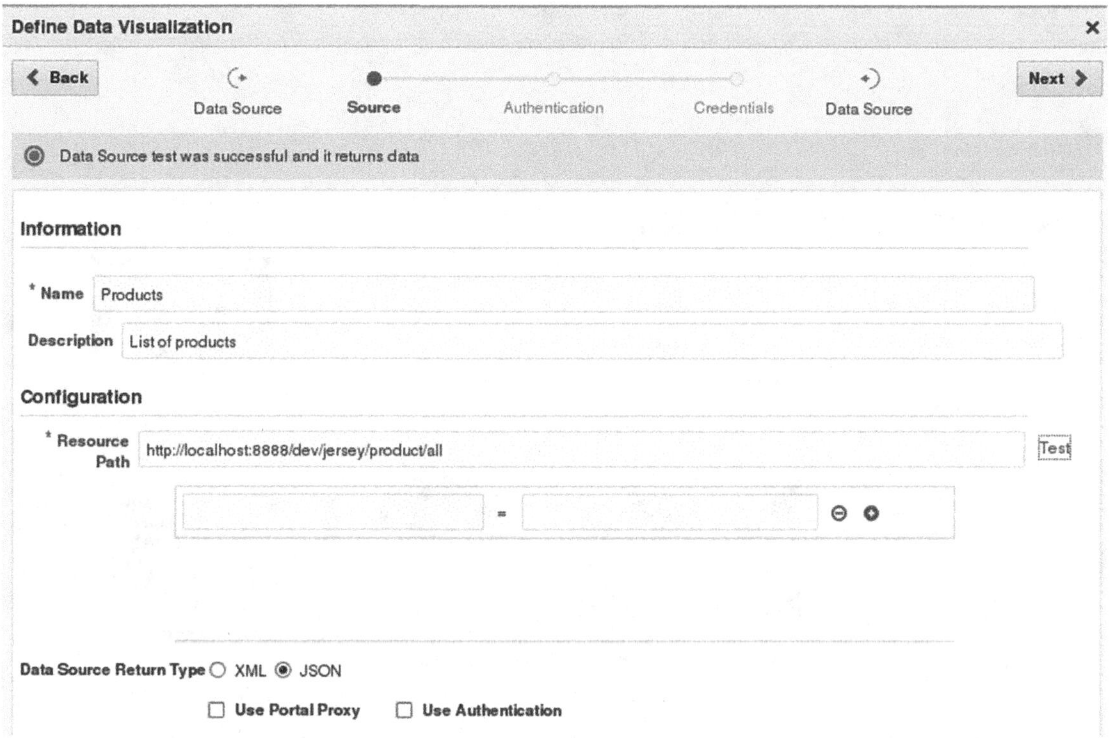

Figure 11-53. *Creating a REST Data Source*

- **Name**: Unique name for recognizing the Data Source
- **Description:** Type here a useful description for other Portal Administrators who are going to use this Data Source
- **Resource Path:** The REST Resource Path (URL).
  - If the REST service accepts parameters, then fill the list below of this option.
- Specify the return format: **XML or JSON**
- Check **Use Portal Proxy** in case of the REST service is external to the Portal network (External Service).
- **Use Authentication**: Check it if the REST service requires authentication. This will enable the Wizard steps for configuring security.

Now select one of the multiple Visualization Templates offered Out-of-the-box by WebCenter Portal or a custom one (Figure 11-54).

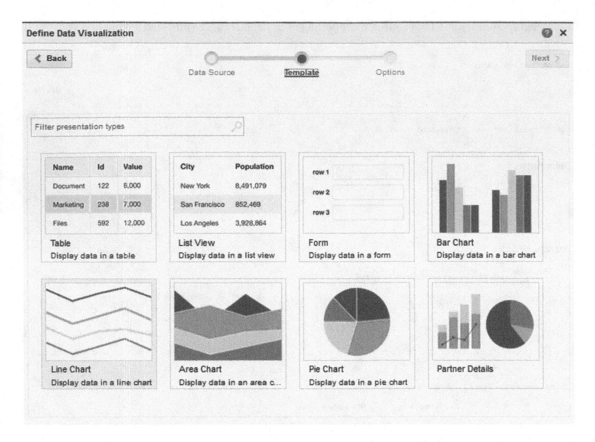

Figure 11-54. Out-of-the-box Visualization Templates + Custom

In the Options Wizard section, there are two important tabs:

- **Settings Tab**: Depending on the Selected Visualization Template, here you can configure which data - attributes must be shown and which ADF components to use for displaying them. For example, for a List View you can configure one of the columns to be a Link to a different WebCenter Portal Page. This is useful if you want to link a List page with the Detail page.

- **Parameters Tab**: Here you find two options:

    - **Visualization Parameters**: Used to get input from other components to the page. Basically, it works like a Task Flow Input Parameter.

    - **Data Source Parameters**: Here you can define Input Components for filling the Input Parameters expected by the Data Source. For example, the REST parameters that the REST Service requires.

After finish the Wizard, you will see your component rendering the data from the external service.

Overview about Custom Visualization Templates

Developing Custom Visualization Templates are very tight to the Business Objects created from the Data Sources.

```
When developing Visualization Templates the clue is to understand the new EL Expression API:
#{owcp.appint}
```

This EL Expression allows the user to map Business Object Attributes and Operations to ADF elements used within our custom visualization template.

For example:

```
<?xml version='1.0' encoding='UTF-8'?>
<jsp:root xmlns:jsp="http://java.sun.com/JSP/Page" version="2.1" xmlns:af="http://xmlns.
oracle.com/adf/faces/rich"

xmlns:f="http://java.sun.com/jsf/core">
    <af:panelGridLayout id="pgl1">
        <af:gridRow id="gr1">
            <af:gridCell halign="stretch" valign="stretch" id="gc3">
                <af:panelHeader text="Update portal details" id="ph3"/>
                <af:panelFormLayout id="pfl4">
                    <af:inputText label="id" editable="always" value="#{owcp.appsint.
                    parameter('id','','','GET.id','')}" id="search1"/>
                    <af:spacer height="20" id="s2"/>
                    <af:button text="Search emp" id="b1" actionListener="#{owcp.appsint.
                    method('Search emp','','None','GET','')}"/>
                    <af:inputText label="name" value="#{owcp.appsint.inoutdata('name','','','GET.
                    employee.name','PUT.employee.name')}"
                                  id="it8" partialTriggers="::b1"/>
                    <af:inputText label="id" value="#{owcp.appsint.inoutdata('id','','','GET.
                    id','PUT.employee.id')}"
                                  id="it10" partialTriggers="::b1"/>
                    <af:spacer height="20" id="s6"/>
                    <af:button text="Update employee" id="b3" actionListener="#{owcp.appsint.
                    method('update employee','','None','PUT','')}"/>
                </af:panelFormLayout>
            </af:gridCell>
        </af:gridRow>
    </af:panelGridLayout>
</jsp:root>
```

As you can see, the new EL Expression has a "complex" format that needs to be understood to use it properly.

If you have experience with Content Presenter Templates for displaying content information from a Content Repository, then you can migrate that concept to Visualization Templates. Here, instead of showing documents with metadata, we are showing data from Data Sources by using Business Objects that are defining the "metadata" of the content (Figure 11-55).

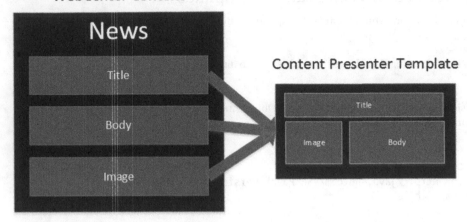

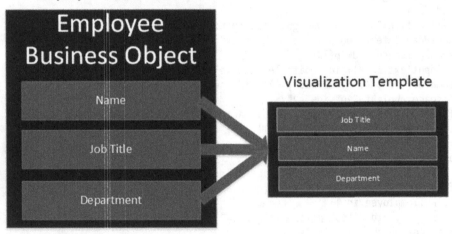

Figure 11-55. Comparison between Content Presenter and Visualization Templates

Multi-Language Considerations

It is responsibility of the back-end systems to provide a mechanism to retrieve the information based on the language send to the service.

For example, a REST service should offer a mechanism for sending via parameter the current language of the Portal.

Publishing Content: Blogs

Another way for publishing content quickly is the use of Blogs.

Blogs are a WebCenter Portal Service that is available when a connection to WebCenter Content is available.

Creating a Blog is just simple as create a Page based on the Page Style: Blog (Figure 11-56).

Figure 11-56. *Creating a Blog Page*

Basically, every port of a specific blog is stored as a HTML file into WebCenter Content. This type of page is very useful for sharing information (Figure 11-57).

Figure 11-57. *Blog Page for publishing quickly Posts*

The blogs can be created in two levels:

- In the Home Portal for publishing a personal Blog.

- In Portal Level for creating Corporative Blogs.

Publishing Content: Wikis

Wikis is another option for publishing content quickly and allowing users to collaborate.

As same as the Blogs, a Wiki is a WebCenter Portal Page created by using the Page Style: Wiki. In addition, it requires that a WebCenter Content connection is available as the Wikis are stored in WebCenter Content as HTML content.

It allows users to edit and collaborate with other users about the content to be displayed in the Wiki page (such as Wikipedia) (Figure 11-58).

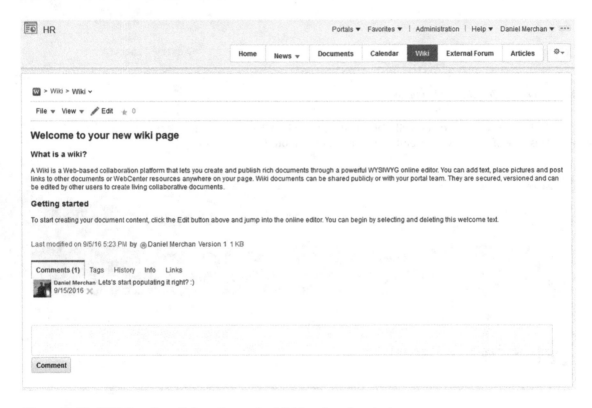

Figure 11-58. Wiki Page for collaborating and publishing shared content

CHAPTER 12

■ ■ ■

Portal Tools and Services

Oracle WebCenter Portal provides multiple components and services for enhancing the collaboration and social networking between users of an organization.

Some of the tools and services are available and works Out-of-the-box. However, there are some services that requires extra back-end repositories to work.

The following table (Table 12-1) contains a summary of the tools and services in WebCenter Portal:

Table 12-1. *Oracle WebCenter Portal Services*

Service	Description	Requires External Repository
Analytics	Gathers and display the most important performance analytics.	Yes
Announcements	Used for posting important announcements for the portal members.	Yes
Discussions	Enable the forums services allowing the users to collaborate by asking / answering questions of other portal members.	Yes
Documents	Provides the content management capabilities for working with documents.	Yes
Events	Calendar service for scheduling and sharing events with other portal members.	Yes* (if enable Personal Events then it requires an Exchange server).
External Applications	Used for allowing the portal members to access external applications that use their own authentication process out of the Single Sign-on of the Portal. For example, access to LinkedIn.	Yes
Instant Messaging and Presence	Allow the users to check the connectivity status (online, busy, away, etc.) and send them instant messages.	Yes
Links	Create relationships between Portal Assets. For example, you can link a document to a discussion thread.	No

(continued)

© Vinay Kumar and Daniel Merchán García 2017
V. Kumar and D. M. García, *Beginning Oracle WebCenter Portal 12c*, DOI 10.1007/978-1-4842-2532-5_12

Table 12-1. (*continued*)

Service	Description	Requires External Repository
Lists	Useful service for creating lists to be shared with other portal members for enhancing the collaboration in some activities. These lists can be created from an Excel Spreadsheet.	No
Mail	For accessing to the email account.	Yes
Messages and Feedback	Provides the capabilities of posting messages (also with attachments) and feedback between portal members or directly to an Activity Stream.	Yes
Notes	Allows the portal members to create their own notes, reminders.	No
Notifications	Subscribe and receive notifications of the portal activities to which you are subscribed.	Yes
People Connections	Social networking capabilities such as profile and connecting with other portal members.	Yes
RSS	Used for displaying feeds via RSS.	No
Search	Enable the search capabilities for searching over the content of the portals.	Yes
Tags	Provides the capabilities for "tagging" / adding keywords to pages.	No

In addition, WebCenter Portal Services can be extended and enhanced by integrating it with other Oracle products.

Table 12-2. *Some of the Oracle WebCenter Portal – Other Oracle Products Integrations*

Oracle Product	WebCenter Portal Integration
Oracle SOA – BPEL	Enable WebCenter Portal Workflows for some basic administration tasks. For example, if Self-Registration is enabled for a Portal then the Portal Manager can review for "Accept" or "Reject" the request.
Oracle BPM	Expose the Task List and business processes of BPM in WebCenter Portal.
Siebel (CRM)	Consume Siebel Web Services by using Data Controls for exposing Siebel information.
E-Business Suite	Expose in WebCenter Portal EBS functionalities via E-Business Suite WSRP Portlets or consume information via Web Services.
PeopleSoft	Integrate PeopleSoft via Web Services or consuming PeopleSoft WSRP Portlets.
Oracle BI (Business Intelligence)	Show the BI Dashboards and graphs by connecting Oracle WebCenter Portal to BI Presentation Services.

As you can see, Oracle WebCenter Portal is highly pluggable with other Oracle products. It is the single secure entry point to all the information and services within an organization (as we mentioned many times in this book).

In this chapter, you will learn and have an overview about the Portal Services shown in the above table (Table 12-1).

■ **Note** The Portal Service: **Polls and Surveys is no longer available in the 12c version**. As an alternative solution maybe you can use Google Forms and expose these forms as an IFrame or Link in WebCenter Portal.

■ **Caution** Documents Service information can be found in Chapter 11 - Content Integration. There is a full chapter for Documents Service as it is one of the most important functionalities in WebCenter.

■ **Note** The Worklist Task Flow has been deprecated in 12c and it has been replaced by BPM Task Flows available via BPM Integration. In this release, the information about Portal - BPM integration is in SOA/BPM official documentation instead of the Oracle WebCenter Portal documentation.

Advanced integrations with BPM, EBS, BI, etc., have not been covered in this book. We strongly recommend the integration with SOA and BPM for enhancing the Portal capabilities.

Analytics

WebCenter Portal Analytics uses Open Usage API for collecting and storing the most important metrics about the usage of WebCenter Portal (Figure 12-1).

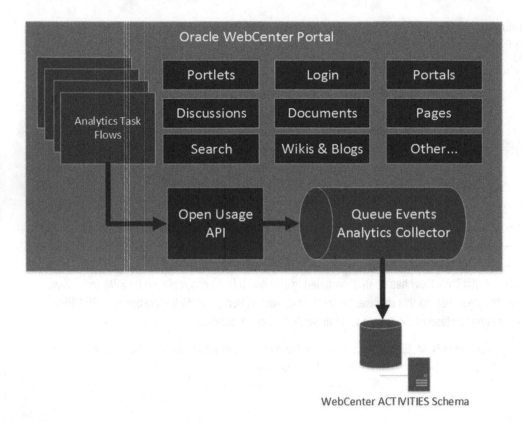

Figure 12-1. *WebCenter Analytics Architecture*

WebCenter Portal Analytics gathers the following performance metrics (Table 12-3).

Table 12-3. *Metrics Gathered by WebCenter Portal*

Metric	Description
WebCenter Portal Traffic	Summary of common events within WebCenter Portal.
Page Traffic	Number of hits and unique hits to Portal Pages.
Login	Login statistics.
Portlet Traffic	Most usage portlets.
Portlet Response Time	Average response time.
Portlet Instance Traffic	Same as Portlet Traffic, but if a Portlet appears in more than one page then each one is considered a different instance of the Portlet.
Search Metrics	Most recent searches and keywords used.
Wiki Metrics	Tracking of the wikis.
Blog Metrics	Tracking of the blogs.
Discussion Metrics	Most popular forums.
Portal Traffic	Tracks the hits by Portal. Which portals are the most used.
Portal Response Time	Average time of the Portals of responding and rendering pages.

Enable WebCenter Analytics

A System Administrator has to configure a connection to WebCenter Analytics by using Enterprise Manager Console or WLST Scripts (Figure 12-2).

The connection requires the following information:

- **Connection Name**: Logical name assigned to the connection. We recommend using the default: WebCenterSpaces-Analytics.

- **Active Connection**: Marks the current connection to be the one used by WebCenter Portal for gathering Analytics.

- **Enable WebCenter Portal Event Collection**: Switch On / Off the analytics gathering.

- **Messaging Mode**: Set as **Unicast** as it is not supported yet by the Multicast mode.

- **Collector Host Name**: IP / Host where WebCenter Analytics is running. The same as the WC_Portal server.

- **Collector Port**: By default, it is 31314.

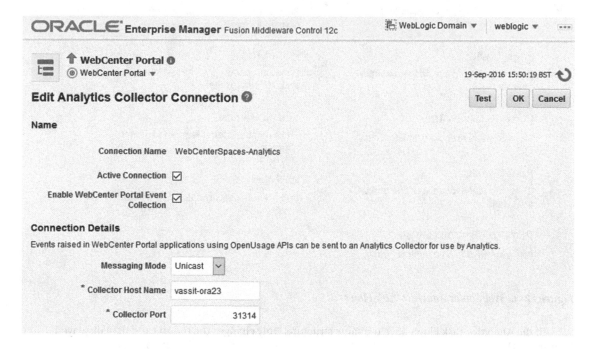

Figure 12-2. *WebCenter Analytics: Connection Details*

■ **Note**   Analytics Collector and WebCenter Portal are both in WC_Portal managed server. WC_Utilities does not exist anymore in 12c version.

In stand-alone installations, WebCenter Portal auto-configures the connection when starting the WC_Portal managed server.

Using Analytics Task Flows

A Portal member with *Edit Page* permissions can add Analytics Task Flows depending on the metrics to be displayed.

In the Resource Catalog in Analytics folder there is one Task Flow per each metric explained before (Figure 12-3).

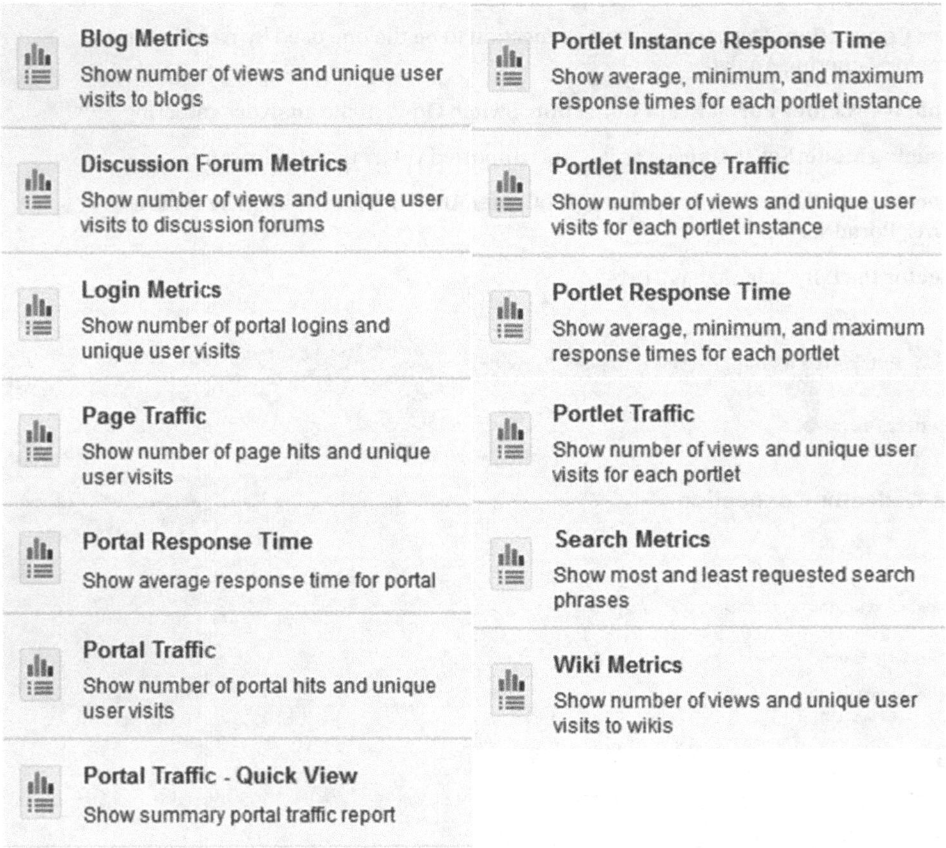

Blog Metrics
Show number of views and unique user visits to blogs

Portlet Instance Response Time
Show average, minimum, and maximum response times for each portlet instance

Discussion Forum Metrics
Show number of views and unique user visits to discussion forums

Portlet Instance Traffic
Show number of views and unique user visits for each portlet instance

Login Metrics
Show number of portal logins and unique user visits

Portlet Response Time
Show average, minimum, and maximum response times for each portlet

Page Traffic
Show number of page hits and unique user visits

Portlet Traffic
Show number of views and unique user visits for each portlet

Portal Response Time
Show average response time for portal

Search Metrics
Show most and least requested search phrases

Portal Traffic
Show number of portal hits and unique user visits

Wiki Metrics
Show number of views and unique user visits to wikis

Portal Traffic - Quick View
Show summary portal traffic report

Figure 12-3. WebCenter Analytics Task Flows

All the Analytics Task Flows have the same structure. Only changes the reports and data displayed (Figure 12-4).

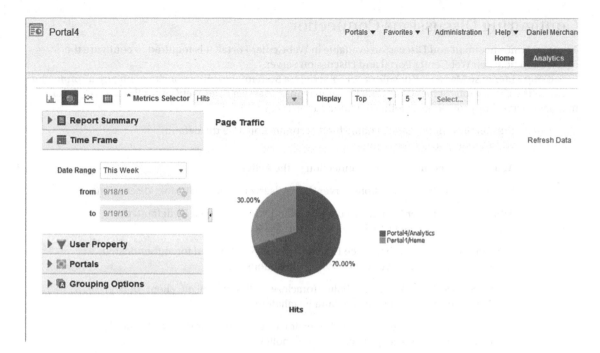

Figure 12-4. *WebCenter Analytics: Page Traffic Task Flow*

The options in the left side and top bar allow the user to filter and display the data.

In addition, the Analytics Task Flow allows the user to export the Analytics data into an Excel Spreadsheet when displaying the Table Mode.

■ **Note** Custom Events can be built over the Out-of-the-box solution provided by Oracle (ACTIVITIES Schema + Open Usage API). However, Oracle discourages that you change / modify the Out-of-the-box ACTIVITIES Schema. If extra analytics are required, then build your own schema and Analytics.

Announcements and Discussions

Discussion Server (WC_Collaboration managed server) enables in WebCenter Portal two important services:

- **Announcements:** This service allow the users to post important activities, events, or information for the Portal members.

- **Discussions:** It enable a Forum Service for WebCenter Portal, which is based on JIVE forums.

285

Configuring Discussions Connection

To make Announcement and Discussion available in WebCenter Portal, it is required to configure the connection between WebCenter Portal and Discussion Server.

Using Enterprise Manager Console or WLST scripts, a System Administrator can configure a connection between the Discussions Server (WC_Collaboration managed server) and WebCenter Portal (WC_Portal managed server) by providing the following information (Figure 12-5):

- **Connection Name**: Logical name for this connection. Use the default: WebCenterSpaces-Discussions.

- **Active Connection**: Mark the connection as the Active.

- **Server URL**: URL to discussions server (http://[servername]:8890/owc_discussions.

- **Administration User Name**: Discussions administration server. By default, the installation creates the LCMUser as administrator.

- **Authenticated User Web Service Policy URI**: Policy to be used for authenticated access to discussions server Web service. The options are:

  - WSS 1.0 SAML Token Client Policy (oracle/wss10_saml_token_client_policy). This is the default value in a default installation.

  - WSS 1.1. SAML Token Message Protection Client Policy (oracle/wss11_saml_token_with_message_protection_client_policy).

  - Global Policy Attachment.

- **Public User Web Service Policy URI**: This client policy connection is used to enforce message security and integrity for public access to the discussions server Web service.

  - None - This is the default value.

  - WSS 1.1 Message Protection Client Policy (oracle/wss11_with_message_protection_client_policy)

  - Global Policy Attachment

- **Recipient Key Alias**: This is the alias to the certificate that contains the public key of the discussions server in the configured key store. It is only available in case of setting a Message Protection Policy.

- **Connection Timeout (seconds)**: It establish the connection timeout when WebCenter Portal consumes Discussions Web Services.

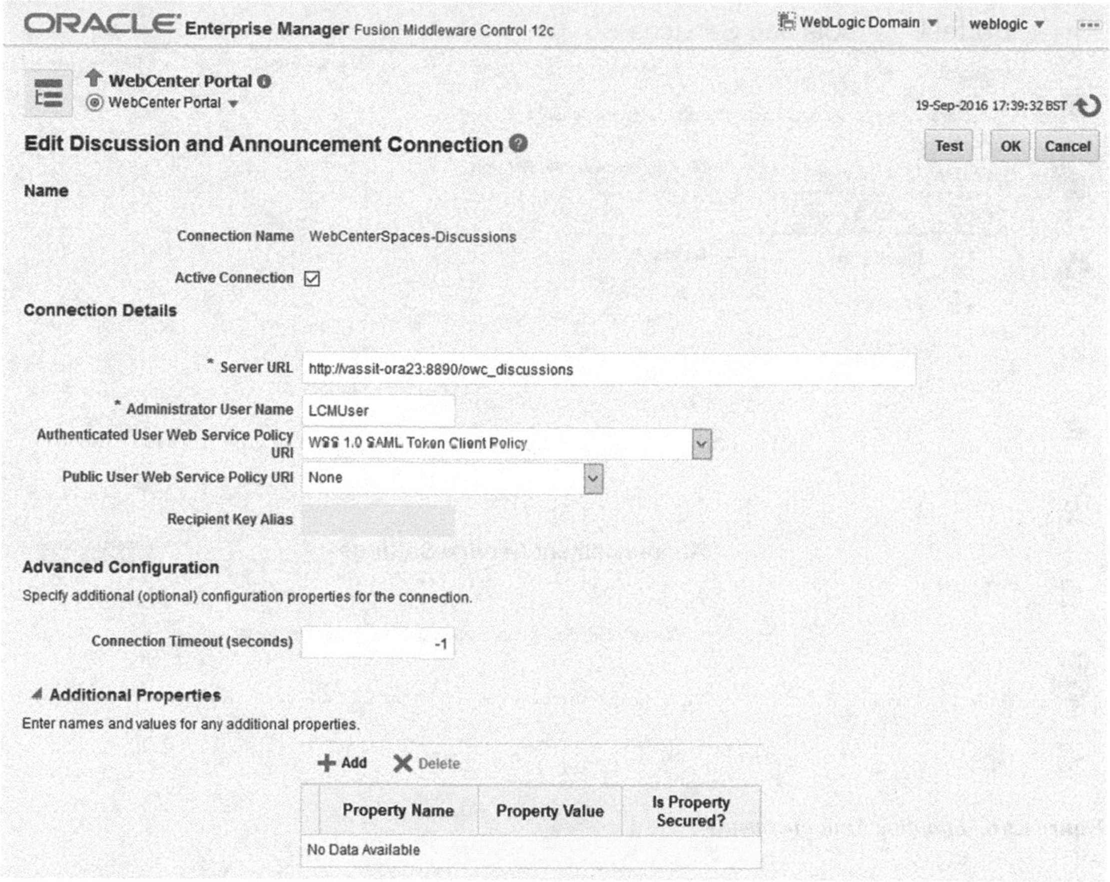

Figure 12-5. *WebCenter Portal - Discussions Connections details*

■ **Caution** For a development environment it is OK if the default configuration is based on WSS 1.0 SAML Token Client Policy. However, for a production environment we recommend you use Message Protected Policy and configure the Java Key Store.

Working with Announcements

Enabling the Announcements in a Portal

A Portal Manager / Administrator has to enable Announcements for the specific Portal by using the Tools and Services administration console ⚒ (Figure 12-6).

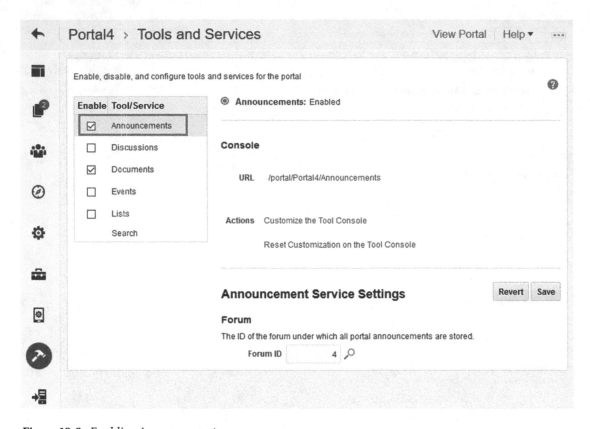

Figure 12-6. Enabling Announcements

About Security

Portal Members that are going to work with Announcements require, at least, the following security permissions:

- *Create, Edit, and Delete Announcements* for Portal Members who are going to Manage the Announcements.

- *View Announcements* for the Portal Members that just can see the Announcements.

Create, Edit, and Delete Announcements

Once a Portal Manager enables the Announcements, there are few ways for accessing to the Announcements Management.

- By accessing to http(s)://[servername]:[port]/webcenter/portal/[PortalName]/ Announcements.

- If the Page Template contains the administration menu included. Click on it and then Manage ➤ Announcements (Figure 12-7).

- Directly from the Announcements Viewer Task Flow by clicking ✏ icon. This icon is only shown if the user has rights for managing Announcements.

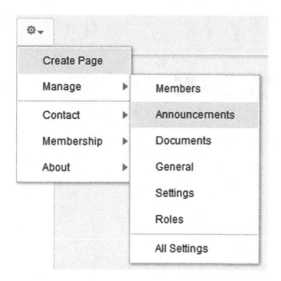

Figure 12-7. *Entering to Administrate Announcements by using the Contextual Menu*

The Announcements administration interface (Figure 12-8) contains the following options:

- **Create** : It allows you to create a new Announcement (Figure 12-9):

  - **Subject**: Title of the announcement.

  - **Body**: It is a rich text editor where the user can add all the information related to the announcement.

  - **Active Date**: Set up when the announcement will be displayed to the portal members.

  - **Announcement Expire Date**: When the announcement is expired and not shown anymore.

- **Show**: It allows to filter the list of announcements depending on:

  - When it was created (Today, Since Yesterday, Last 7 days, Last 30 days).

  - Status of the announcement (Active, Future, Expired).

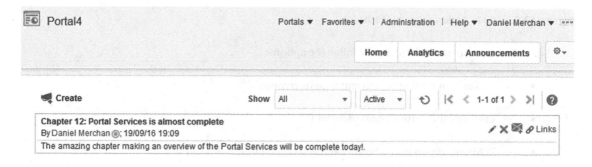

Figure 12-8. *Administration of Announcements*

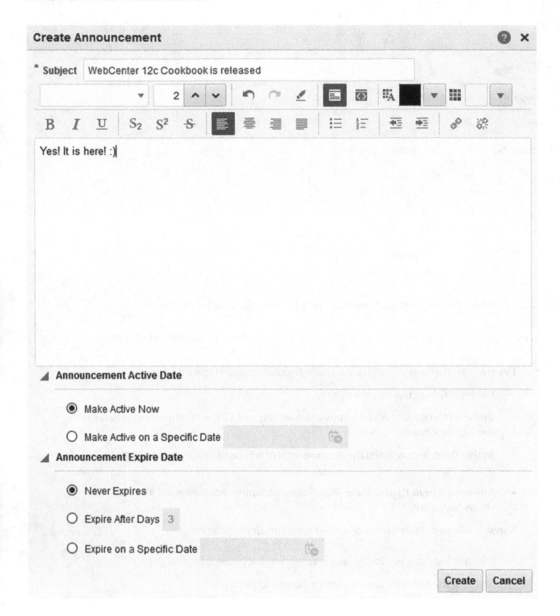

Figure 12-9. *Create Announcement Wizard*

For each announcement there are the following options:

- : Use it for editing the current announcement.

- : Delete the current announcement.

- : Allows you to share the announcement with other users by mail.

- 🔗 : Use the Link Service for linking this announcement to:

  - 📚: Link the announcement to a specific document of the content repository. It is very useful when the announcement is strongly related to some documents.

  - 📄: Link to a new Note. Use it for making a personal reminder.

  - 📤 : Link to an external website.

Adding Announcements Task Flow

Portal Members with Edit Page permissions can add the Announcements Task Flow to Page. It is located under Alerts and Updates of the default Resource Catalog (Figure 12-10).

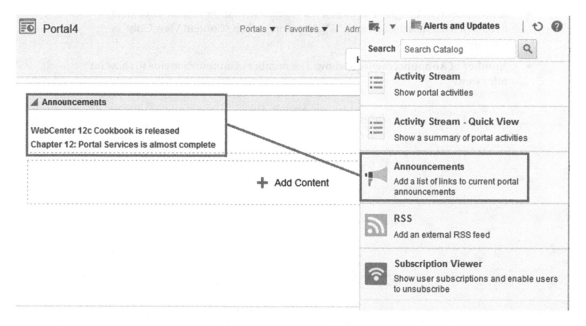

Figure 12-10. *Adding Announcements Task Flow to a WebCenter Portal Page*

The configuration parameters are the following (Figure 12-11):

- **Expand All Announcements in Extended Mini View**: A Boolean value representing whether to display details for all announcements in extended mini view. Default value is false in which case announcements display the announcement title only.

- **Number of Expanded Announcements**: The number of announcements to display announcement details. Announcements exceeding this value display the announcement title only. Use only when "Content View Only" is unchecked.

- **Content View Only**: A Boolean value representing whether to remove the announcement title and display just the announcement content. Check it to remove the title and false to render the title.

- **Hide Toolbar**: Flag for displaying or not the toolbar that has the "Create Announcement" functionality. It can be set up to a Security EL Expression for showing to specific target audience.

- **Navigate to Announcement Viewer**: Controls of display or not the Announcement in a Pop-Up or navigate to the detail page. Check it for navigating to the detail page, uncheck to show the pop-up.

- **Number of Announcements Extended Mini View**: The number of announcements to show in a page on extended mini view.

- **Forum ID**: The Forum ID under which announcements are created in the back-end discussions server. If is not filled then, it automatically takes the configuration for the current portal. Only change it for displaying announcements of others' portals.

- **Announcement Length**: The number of characters to show in announcement details (it truncates the rest with "..."). Use it only when "Content View Only" is checked.

- **Number of Announcements to show**: The number of announcements to show on mini view.

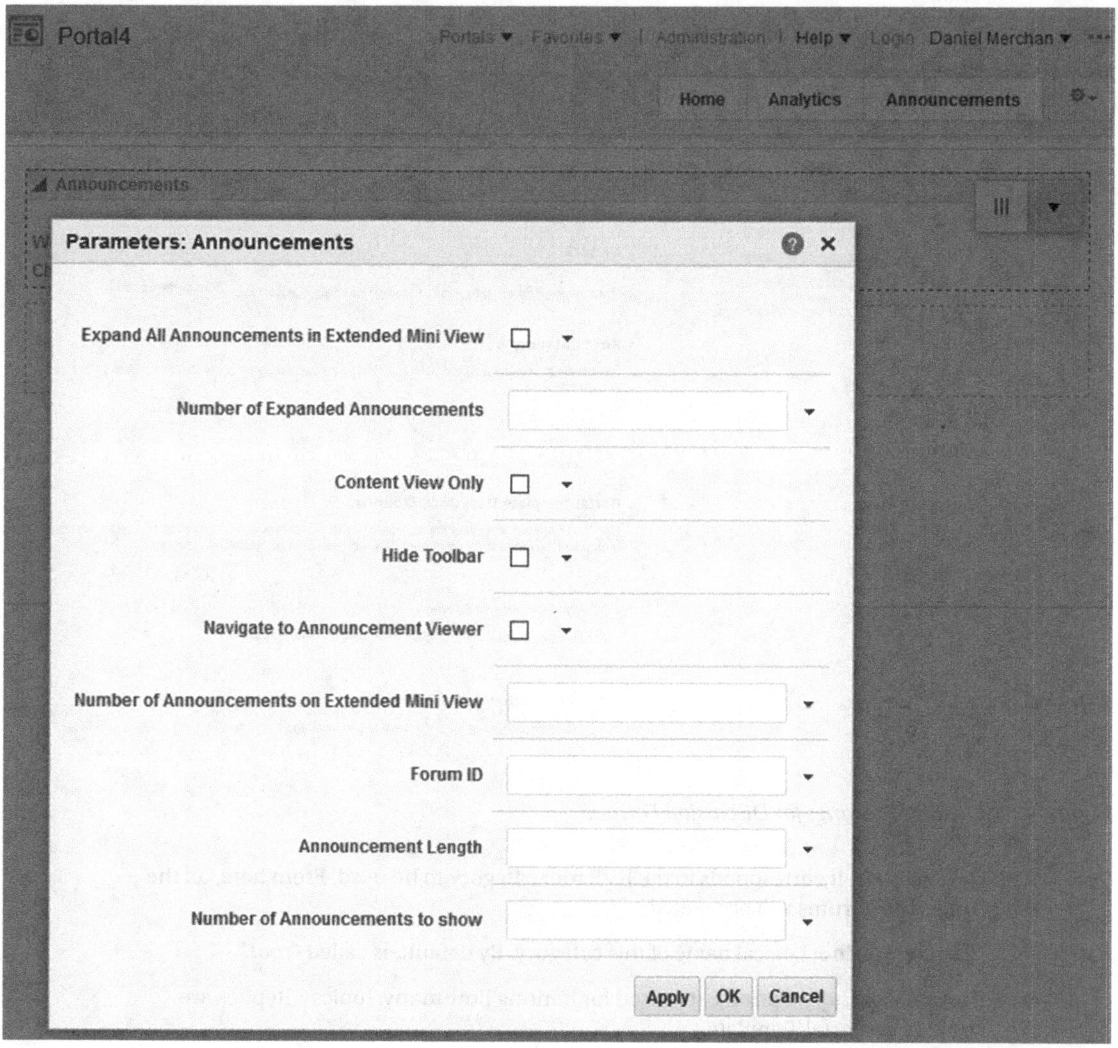

Figure 12-11. *Configuration of Announcements Task Flow*

Working with Discussions

Setup of Global Settings

A Portal Administrator can set up the basic configuration and settings for the discussions forum by accessing to WebCenter Portal Administration Console ➤ Tools and Services ➤ Discussions (Figure 12-12). The global settings are the following:

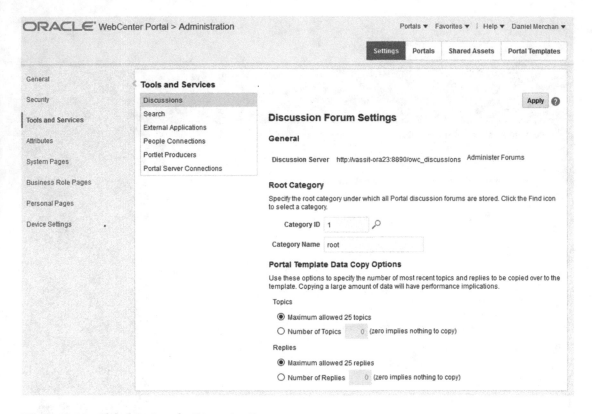

Figure 12-12. *Global Settings for Discussion Forums*

- **Category ID**: It corresponds to the JIVE root category to be used. From here, all the discussion forums will be created.

- **Category Name**: Logical name of this category. By default, is called *"root."*

- **Portal Data Copy Options**: It is used for limiting how many Topics / Replies are copied to a Portal Template.

  - **Topics**: Specify the maximum of topics. If zero, then no data is copied to a Portal Template.

  - **Replies**: Specify the maximum of replies. If zero, then no data is copied to a Portal Template.

■ **Caution**   Do not change the Category ID (root category). In cases of changing it, the forums will continue working, but the links to the discussions or announcements made from other portal services will not work.

Enabling Discussions in a Portal

A Portal Manager / Administrator has to enable Discussions Service for the specific Portal by activating using the Tools and Services administration console ⚒ (Figure 12-13).

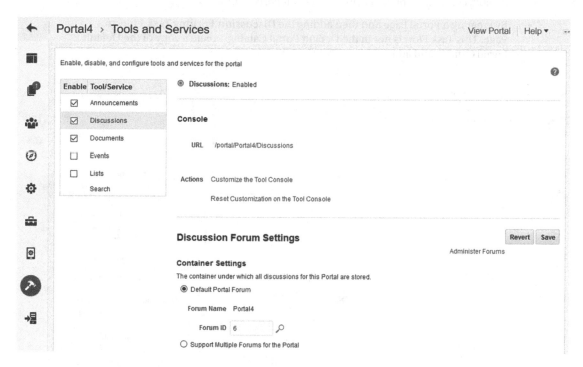

Figure 12-13. *Enable Discussions for a specific Portal*

In the **Container Settings** section, a Portal Manager can enable **Support Multiple Forums** for the Portal option. This option will create a new Category ID for holding all the Forums created in this Portal. **Once enabled, it cannot be reverted to the Default Portal Forum option.**

About Security

The Portal Members who want to work with Discussion Forums require the following permissions:

- *Create, Edit, and Delete / Create, Edit Discussions*: To operate and interact with Discussion Task Flow.

- *Edit Pages*: For adding Discussion Task Flow to a WebCenter Portal Page.

- *Edit Task Flows*: For changing the Discussion Task Flow Parameters, if needed.

Adding Discussions Task Flow

A Portal Manager has many options for adding the Discussions Forums to a Portal:

- By adding a **Page Link** to the **System Page - Discussions**. This system page is, by default, configured for displaying the default Portal Forum.

- By creating a Portal Page and then adding the **Discussion Forums Task Flow** to a Page. This Task Flow is not in the Default Portal Catalog; create a copy of the Default Portal Catalog and add it (Figure 12-14).

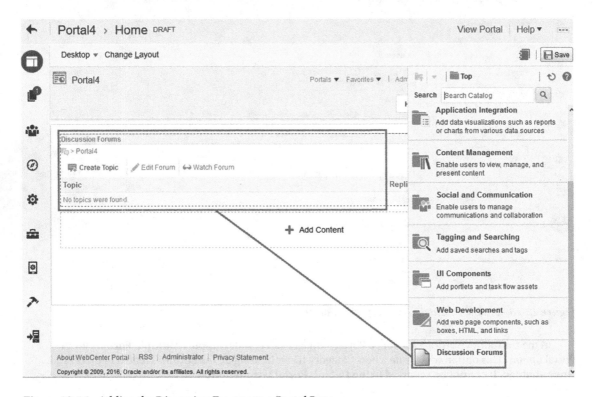

Figure 12-14. *Adding the Discussion Fourms to a Portal Page*

Administrating Discussions Task Flow

Once a Portal Manager enables the Discussion Service, there are few ways for accessing Manage the Forums.

- By accessing to http(s)://[servername]:[port]/webcenter/portal/[PortalName]/ Discussions.

- If the Page Template contains the administration menu included. Click on it and then Manage ➤ Discussions (Figure 12-15).

- By accessing to a Portal Page that contains the Discussion Forums Task Flow (which is not in the Default Portal Catalog).

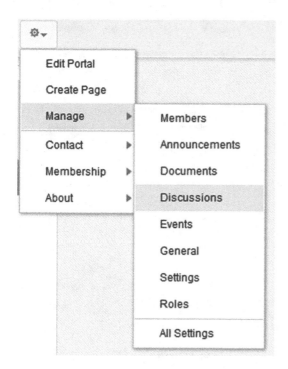

Figure 12-15. *Accessing to the Discussions Management via Portal Options Menu*

In the Discussions Forum Task Flow (Figure 12-16) can be found the following administration options:

- 🖊 Edit Forum **(Only appears if Multiple Forums are allowed for this Portal)**: Allows you to edit the following Forum properties:

  - **Forum Name**: Name of the forum. The default Forum created always uses the same name as the Portal. You can change it to something friendlier.

  - Forum Description: hhh

- ✖ Delete Forum **(Only appears if Multiple Forums are allowed for this Portal)**: Delete the current Forum and all the Topics inside of it.

- 🗃 **(Only appears if Multiple Forums are allowed for this Portal)**: Click this icon to access to the Forums Administration for the current Portal (Figure 12-17):

  - 🗨 Create Forum **(Only appears if Multiple Forums are allowed for this Portal)**: It allows you to create multiple Forums for the current Portal.

Figure 12-16. *Default View of Discussion Forums Task Flow*

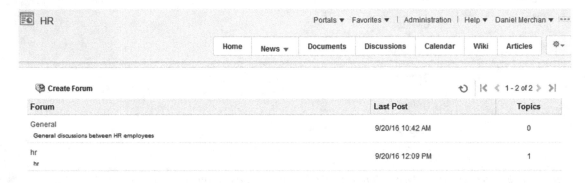

Figure 12-17. *List of Forums for a specific Portal*

Using Discussions Task Flow

The usage of the Forums is very similar to all of the most common Internet Forums.

Let's have a look into the options offered in the Discussion Forum Task Flow for Portal Members (Figure 12-18):

- **Create Topic** : It opens a pop-up for creating a new topic with the following information:

    - **Subject**: Title of the Topic

    - **Body**: Content related to the new Topic.

- Watch Forum / Remove Watch : It allows you to mark a specific Forum as "monitored." *Watched Forums* are displayed in the **Watched Forums Task Flow** for a quick access to the monitored forums.

- Recent Topics 25 : How many topics to be displayed per page.

Figure 12-18. *Discussion Forum Task Flow*

In the **Topic Detail,** a user can collaborate over the original question or replying to the already given replies of other users (Figure 12-19):

- 🖼 **Reply Topic** : Opens a dialog for writing a Reply to the current topic.

- ✏ Edit Topic : Edit the content of the current topic.

- ✖ Delete Topic : Delete the current topic and all the replies.

- 📶 Subscribe / 📶 Unsubscribe : Use it to subscribe to this Topic and receive notifications when someone replies. (It requires you to have Notifications Service enabled in WebCenter Portal.)

- 👓 Watch Topic / 👓 Remove Watch : Marks the current topic as "monitored." Monitored Topics are displayed in the **Watched Topics Task Flow.**

- 🔗 : Opens the Links Service for linking the current thread, topic, reply to another thread, document, event, etc.

- ✉ : Share the current thread via Email.

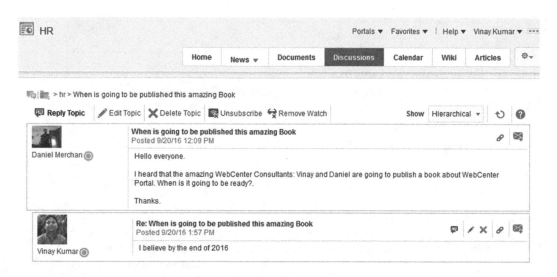

Figure 12-19. *Discussion Forums: Topic Detail Page*

299

Other Discussions Task Flows

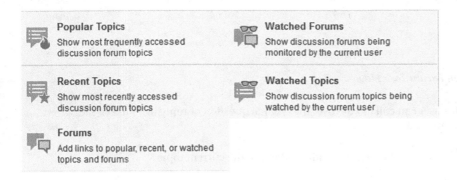

Figure 12-20. *Other Discussions Task Flows of the Resource Catalog*

As mentioned before, Forums and Topics can be marked as "Watched." There are two Task Flows that show direct links to the monitored Forums and Topics by the current user called: **Watched Forums Task Flow** and **Watched Topics Task Flow**. In addition, there are another two Task Flows for displaying the most recent and the most popular topics: **Recent Topics Task Flow** and **Popular Topics Task Flow**.

Another option is the **Forums Task Flow** that merges the above concepts into a single Task Flow. The user can select what to see using the drop-down (Watched Topics, Watched Forums, Popular Topics, Recent Topics).

◢ **Watched Forums**

ↄ

hr

◢ **Watched Topics**

ↄ

When is going to be published this amazing Book

◢ **Recent Topics**

ↄ

When is going to be published this amazing Book

◢ **Popular Topics**

ↄ

When is going to be published this amazing Book

◢ **Forums**

Watched Topics ▾ ✎ ↄ

When is going to be published this amazing Book

Figure 12-21. *Other Discussion Task Flows added to a WebCenter Portal Page*

External Applications

External Applications are any application that implements its own authentication process and does not take part of the Single Sign-On of your WebCenter Portal.

Users accessing External Applications via WebCenter Portal only have to Log in once. WebCenter Portal stores securely the credentials of the user for that specific External Application in the **Credential Store** (Figure 12-22).

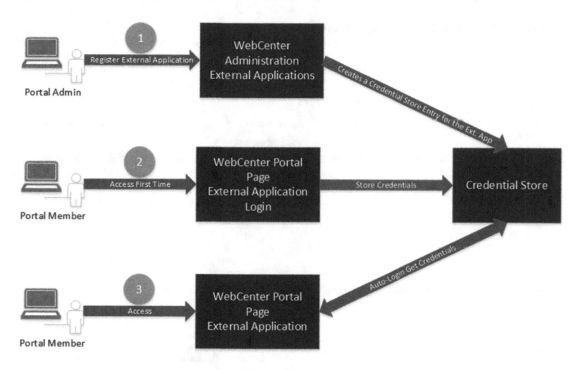

Figure 12-22. *How External Applications Works*

Registering External Applications

There are two different places where External Applications can be registered:

- By using the Connections Management via Enterprise Manager Console (Figure 12-23).
- Directly in WebCenter Portal Administration Console (Figure 12-24).

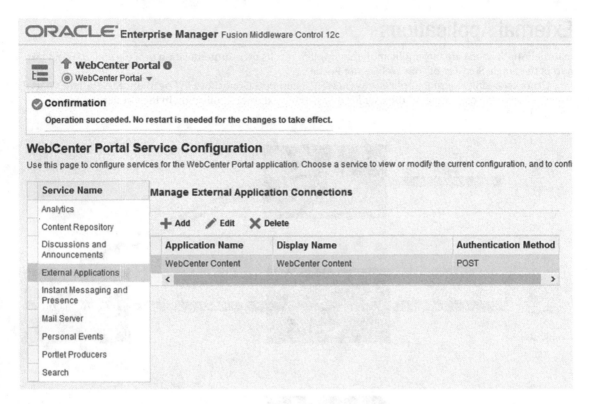

Figure 12-23. Registering External Applications via Enteprise Manager Console

Figure 12-24. Administering External Application through WebCenter Administration Console

In both cases, the information to be provided when creating an External Application is the following:
Name

- **Application Name**: The unique name that will identify the External Application.

- **Display Name**: The logical name used to be displayed in a friendly way to the users.

Login Details:

- **Enable Automatic Login**: It enables the Single Sign-on once the user Logs in the first time. It means the credentials are securely stored in the Credential Store and used for the following times that the user accesses this External Application.

- **Login URL**: Enters the URL that exposes the Login of the Application.

- **HTML User ID Field Name**: Exploring the HTML, fill it by using the name attribute of the input field that holds the User Name / User ID of the Login form.

- **HTML User Password Field Name**: Exploring the HTML, fill it by using the name or the input field that holds the Password of the Login form.

Authentication Details:

- **Authentication Method**: Use it for configuring a POST, GET, or BASIC authentication against the External Application.

Additional Login Fields:

- In case of there is any other field to be submitted in the Login process, then there is a table where the user can populate extra information that will be submitted during the authentication process.

Shared Credentials: Activate if a shared user's credentials are going to be use for authenticating against the External Application.

- **Enable Shared Credentials**: Check it for enabling shared credentials.

- **User Name**: User to be used for the authentication process.

- **Password**: Password used for the authentication process.

Public Credentials: If the External Application is enabled for Public access, then it will be use the following credentials for non-authenticated people:

- **Enable Public Credentials**: Check it for enabling Public Users to use the following credentials when accessing a WebCenter Public Portal Page containing the External Application.

- **User Name**: User to be used for the authentication process.

- **Password**: Password used for the authentication process.

Adding an External Application to a Portal

An External Application can be added to the Portal Navigation by creating a Link to it (Figure 12-25).

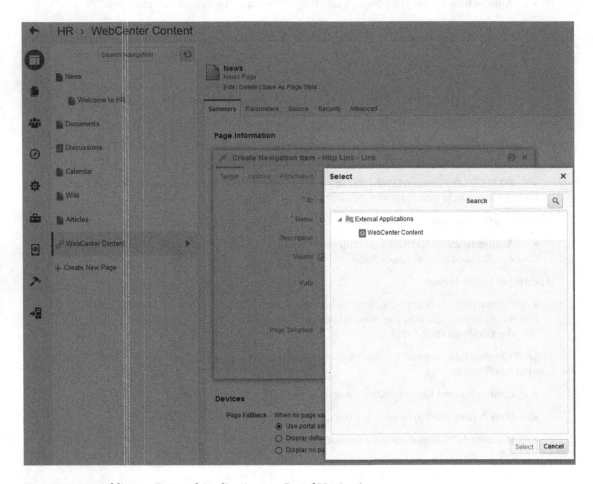

Figure 12-25. *Adding an External Application to a Portal Navigation*

The first time that a user will access this page, he will find the following Login form (Figure 12-26). After Login, subsequent access will retrieve the credentials from the Credential Store.

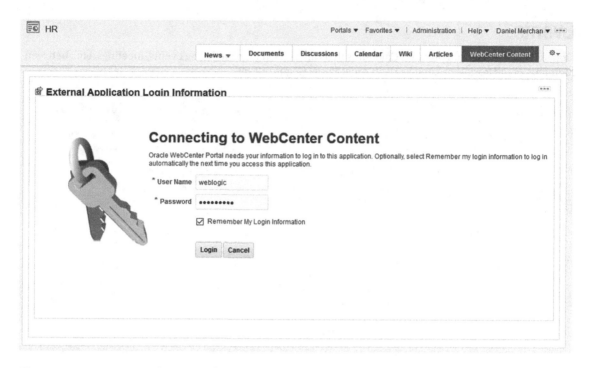

Figure 12-26. *Login Form for External Application*

Manage External Applications Credentials

Portal Members can manage their stored credentials by accessing their User Preferences ➤ My Accounts (Figure 12-27)

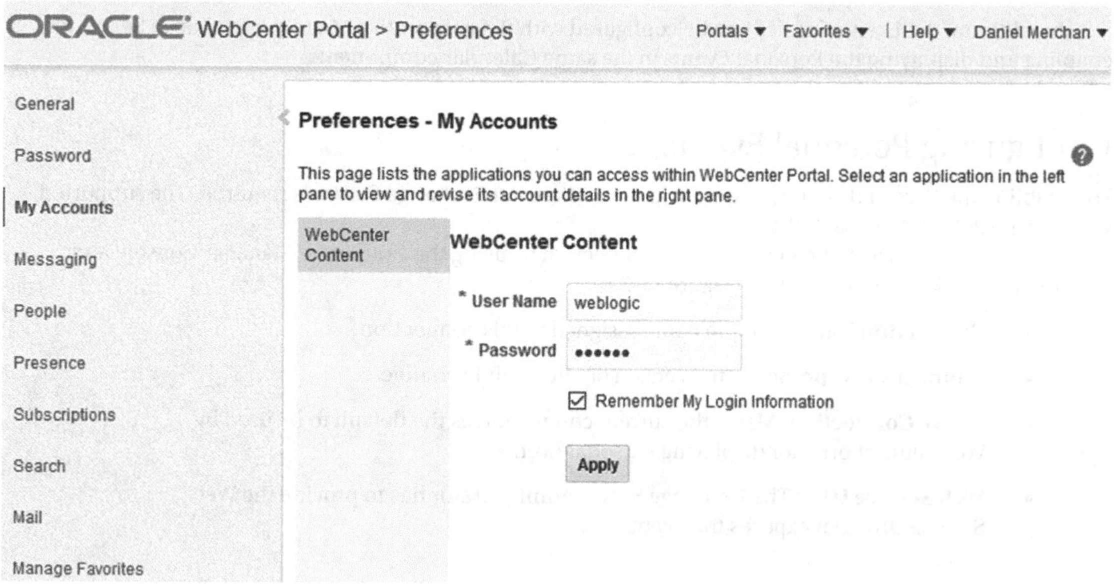

Figure 12-27. *User Preferences for managing Accounts on External Applications*

Events

Oracle WebCenter Portal provides Calendars that can be used for scheduling events, meetings, etc., between Members of the Portals created by WebCenter Portal (Figure 12-28).

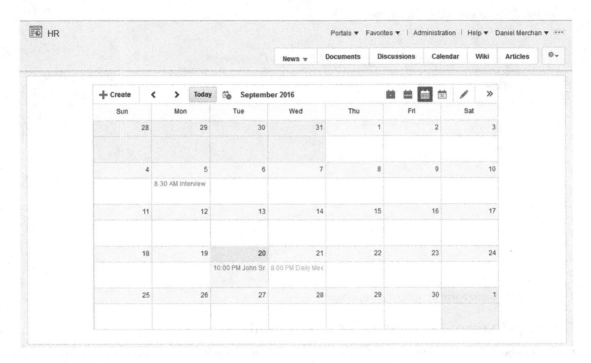

Figure 12-28. *Events Task Flow in a Portal Page*

In addition, the Events Service can be configured with the corporative Microsoft Exchange Server for enabling and displaying the Personal Events in the same Calendar components.

Configuring Personal Events

For enabling the Personal Events, a connection to a Microsoft Exchange Server is required. The supported versions are 2007, 2010, and 2013.

A System Administrator can configure a connection by using the Enterprise Manager Console and providing the following information (Figure 12-29).

- **Connection Name**: Unique name assigned to this connection.

- **Connection Type**: Select the version of Microsoft Exchange.

- **Active Connection**: Marks the current connection as the default to be used by WebCenter Portal for displaying Personal Events.

- **Web Service URL**: The Exchange Server Administrator has to provide the Web Service URL that exposes the Events.

- For example: `http://myexchange.com:80/EWS/Services.wsdl`

- **Associated External Application**: Create an External Application for being used to authenticate against the Exchange Web Service.

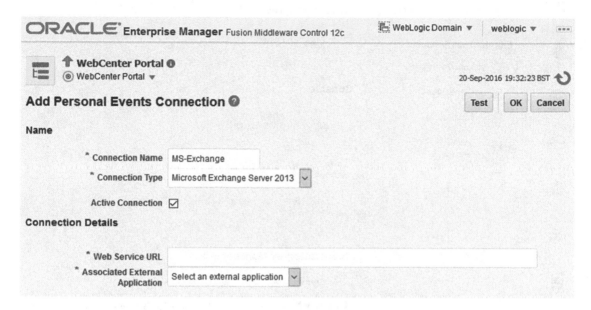

Figure 12-29. *Configuring a Personal Events Connection to a MS Exchange Server*

■ **Note** The required configuration in the Exchange Server can be found in the official Oracle Documentation.

About Security

Portal Members that are going to work with Events require some of the following permissions to be assigned:

- *Create, Edit, Delete Events*: Full permissions over the Events.
- *Create Events.*
- *Edit Events.*
- *Delete Events.*
- *View Events.*

Enabling Events for a Portal

To enable the Events Service in a specific Portal, a Portal Manager has to enable it by accessing to the Tools and Services interface 🔧 and enabling the Events (Figure 12-30).

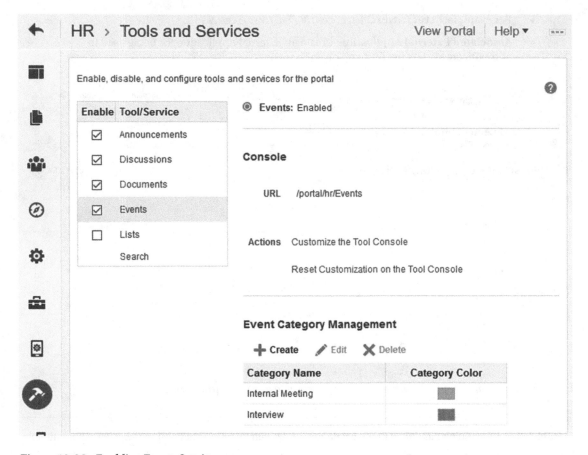

Figure 12-30. *Enabling Events Service*

In addition, in this Administration Interface, a Portal Manager can create the **Event Categories** for the Events of this specific Portal.

By creating categories, the Portal Members can create events based on one of these categories. The events mapped to a category are also mapped to a specific color for recognizing them easily inside of the calendar.

Adding Events Task Flow

There are multiple ways for adding the Events Task Flow:

- When enabling the Events Service, the **Events System Page** is available via / webcenter/portal/[PortalName]/Events. It can be directly exposed in the Portal Navigation by using a **Page Link**.

- Portal Managers can access to Events by using the Portal Menu (⚙▼) by accessing to Manage ➤ Events

- Adding the Events Task Flow to a WebCenter Portal Page (Figure 12-31)

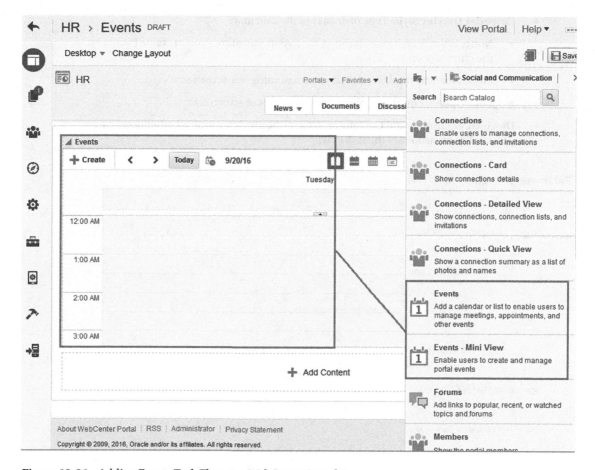

Figure 12-31. *Adding Events Task Flow to a WebCenter Portal Page*

The Events Task Flow can be configured by changing the following parameters (Figure 12-32):

- **Calendar Style Class**: Use it for assigning a custom-style class to the ADF Calendar component used by this Task Flow.

- **Default Current Date**: By default, it is today. But it can be used to establish the current date to a different one.

- **Customization ID**: Internal ID used by WebCenter for customizing this instance of the Events Task Flow. Leave it as default or change it to reset the customizations.

- **Group Space**: By default, it is configured to display the current portal events. Use the helper tool ( ) to search for another Portal.

- **Maximum Enabled Calendars**: The maximum number of calendars that can be shown in this Task Flow.

- **Maximum Calendars**: The maximum number of calendars to allow. The default is 20.

- **Calendar Overlay Style**: Type of display of the calendar:

  - **None**: Is the default view. It shows the Events and allows you to create Events for the current portal.

  - **Mini**: Calendar overlay enabled, but consuming less screen size.

  - **Full**: Calendar overlay enabled, consuming lot of screen size.

- **Disable Personalize and Customize**: A check box to determine whether users can personalize or customize the task flow.

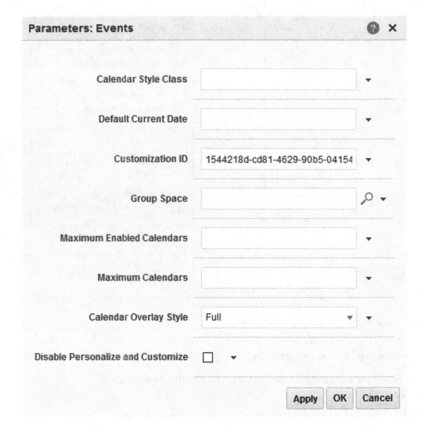

Figure 12-32. *Configuring Events Task Flow*

■ **Tip**   Use the Events Task Flow in the Home Portal for displaying Personal Events and relevant Portals Events.

Use the Events Task Flow in a specific Portal to display only the Events relevant to the Portal.

Working with Events Task Flow

The following options are available in the Events Task Flow (Figure 12-33)

- Right-Click in a specific interval of hours or ╋ **Create** : Shows a Pop-Up for creating a new event:

  - **Title**: Subject of the Event.

  - **Location**: Where the event will be.

  - **Start Time - End Time - All day event**: How long the event will be.

  - **Priority**: Assign a priority to the event.

  - **Category**: Assign to a custom-created category. It will display the event with the category color in the calendar.

  - **Details**: Further information.

- ╋ **Add Calendar** : A user can add other calendars for displaying the events of other Portals.

- ▣ ▦ ▦ ▤ : Switch between the different modes to display the calendar.

- View |All ▼| : Filter the events by categories.

- ✎ : Edit custom preferences for displaying the events in the calendar.

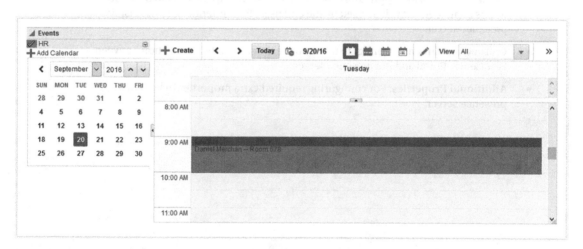

Figure 12-33. *Full Overlay version of Events Task Flow*

Instant Messaging and Presence

WebCenter Portal can be configured with a Presence server. Oracle WebCenter Portal is certified with Microsoft Communications Server for enabling Instant Message and Presence capabilities to the users.

Configuring Presence Server

WebCenter Portal requires you to configure a connection to a Presence Server by using Enterprise Manager Console or WLST scripts (Figure 12-34). For registering a Presence Server, the following information is needed:

- **Connection Name**: Unique name for this connection.

- **Connection Type**: The only available option is Microsoft Office Communications Server.

- **Active Connection**: Mark for selecting this connection as the default to be used by WebCenter Portal for presence capabilities.

- **Server URL**: URL of the server hosting instant messaging and presence services. Use the format <protocol>://<host>:<port>

- **User Domain**: Enter the user domain associated with this connection. The domain specified is the Active Directory domain on the OCS server.

- **Pool Name**: Enter the name of the Microsoft Live Communication Server pool used for this connection.

- **Associated External Application**: Register an External Application to be associated to this connection. It will be used by the end users for authentication against the presence server.

- **Connection Timeout**: Configure to set up the timeout of the connection between WebCenter Portal and the presence server.

- **Additional Properties**: For configuring required extra properties to be sent to the presence server.

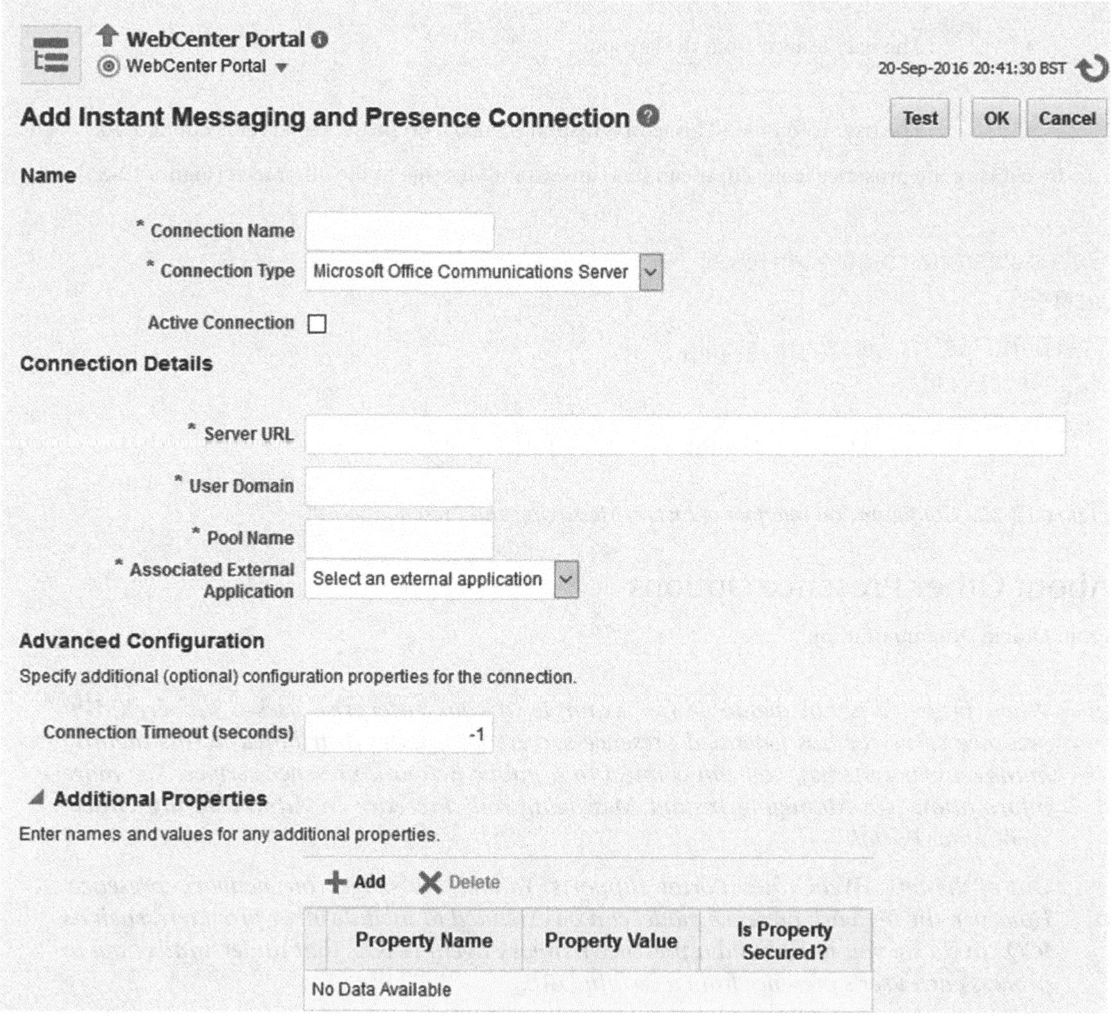

↑ **WebCenter Portal** ❶
◉ WebCenter Portal ▼

20-Sep-2016 20:41:30 BST ↻

Add Instant Messaging and Presence Connection ❔

Test | OK | Cancel

Name

* Connection Name [   ]

* Connection Type [Microsoft Office Communications Server ▾]

Active Connection ☐

Connection Details

* Server URL [   ]

* User Domain [   ]

* Pool Name [   ]

* Associated External [Select an external application ▾]
  Application

Advanced Configuration

Specify additional (optional) configuration properties for the connection.

Connection Timeout (seconds) [-1]

◢ **Additional Properties**

Enter names and values for any additional properties.

➕ Add   ✖ Delete

Property Name	Property Value	Is Property Secured?
No Data Available		

Figure 12-34. *Configuration Interface of Instant Messaging and Presence Server*

■ **Note**   The required configuration in Microsoft Communications / Lync can be found in the official Oracle Documentation.

Using Presence and Instant Messaging

Once Instant Messaging and Presence connection is configured, then users can see the other user profiles with the following presence status:

- 🔵 : The user is currently "online."

- ➖ : The user is busy.

- ⏰ : The user is away from the keyboard.

- ◎ : The user is "offline." This icon is displayed also if no presence server is configured.

By clicking the presence icon, a user can send an Instant Message to the other user (Figure 12-35):

Figure 12-35. *Configuration Interface of Instant Messaging and Presence Server*

About Other Presence Options

From Oracle Documentation:

> *When presence is not available (for example, if your enterprise uses a Jabber/XMPP presence server or has federated presence servers with users distributed across identity management systems), you can connect to a public network presence service. For more information, see Managing Instant Messaging and Presence in Administering Oracle WebCenter Portal.*
>
> *Out-of-the-box, WebCenter Portal supports Yahoo! Messenger on network presence. However, the network presence model can be extended to include other providers, such as ICQ. To do so, you must build a presence network agent (PNA) that understands how to process each user's presence from a certain URL.*

Basically, WebCenter Portal can make use of other presence providers, such as Yahoo!. If you need to connect to different ones, then you need to develop your own **Presence Network Agents (PNA)** by using Java.

There is an option called "Presence" in the User Preferences options of WebCenter Portal (Figure 12-36). The users can here set up their Presence users it they are not using the default IMP configured. The information to be provided is:

- **IM Address**: It is very important as it will be processed by the Out-of-the-box and the Custom Presence Network Agents for handling the presence status. For example, Yahoo! is implemented Out-of-the-box. It means that xxx@yahoo.com will be processed if the Yahoo! PNA.

- **Display Name**: Which display name to use when rendering the Presence Status icon.

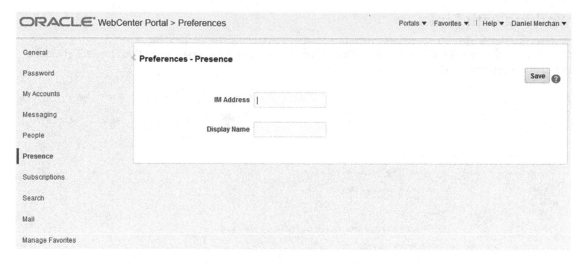

Figure 12-36. *Configuration Interface of Instant Messaging and Presence Server*

Maybe the information above is confusing, let's try to clarify:

- If a Microsoft Presence server is configured, then it will be used for Presence and Instant Messaging.

- If there is no Presence server configured, then a user can configure an IM Address in their preferences for enabling presence. Out-of-the-box, for example, Yahoo! is available as possible Presence Network Agent. If you use a different one, then your developers have to develop a new one.

Links

The Links Service allows the portal members to create relationships between Portal Assets and then maintain the information linked and easy accessed.

Configuring Links

The Links Service is provided Out-of-the-box by WebCenter Portal.

About Security

The Portal Members that are going to work with Links requires them to have some of the following security permissions:

- *Create* and *Delete Links*: Full management over create and delete the links.

- *Create Links*: Only can create links.

- *Delete Links*: Only can delete links.

Working with Links

Links Service 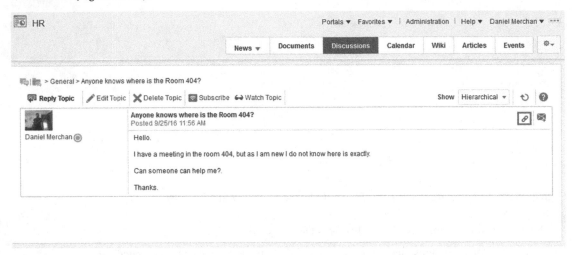 is offered in most of the Out-of-the-box components (Task Flows) that Oracle WebCenter Portal offers (Figure 12-37).

Figure 12-37. Example of Link Service in a Discussion Topic

The options offered by the Links Service are the following (Figure 12-38):

- **Link to New**: This option allows to link the current asset to a new asset:

  - **Discussion**: It opens or creates a pop-up for creating a topic linked to the current asset.

  - **Document**: Allows you to upload a new document linked to the current asset.

  - **Event**: For creating and event linked to the current asset.

  - **Note**: Allows you to create a Note linked to the current asset.

  - **URL**: Links the current asset to an external site.

- **Link to Existing**: Use it for search and link the current asset to an existing one:

  - **Announcements**: Link the current asset to an announcement.

  - **Discussions**: Link the current asset to a topic / discussion thread.

- ![] **Document**: Link the current asset to an existing document in the content repository.

- ![] **Event**: Link the current asset to an existing Event.

- ![] **Delete**: Use this option for deleting a link.

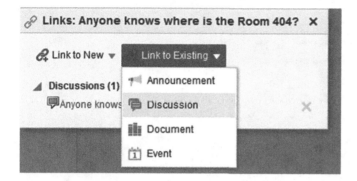

Figure 12-38. *Link Service options*

■ **Note** The available assets to the link depend on what portal services are enabled and the current permissions of the user. For example, if you cannot create Topics in the Discussion Service then the option of Link to New Discussion will not be available.

Lists

The Lists Service provides to the portal members the capabilities for creating lists and shares them with other portal members for collaborating in tasks and activities.

For example, imagine that you and a colleague are writing an amazing WebCenter Portal book. You can create a list for creating the milestones based on the chapters of the book.

Configuring Lists Service

Lists Service is provided Out-of-the-box with WebCenter Portal. It does not require any external integration.

Enabling Lists Service

To enable the Lists Service in a specific Portal, a Portal Manager has to enable it by accessing to the Tools and Services interface ![] and enable the Events (Figure 12-39).

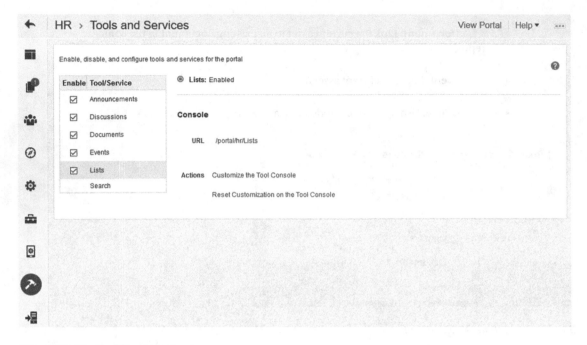

Figure 12-39. *Enabling Lists Service*

About Security

The portal members require you to have some of the following permissions for creating and interacting with Lists Service:

- *Create, Edit* and *Delete Lists*: Full permissions for creating, editing and deleting lists.

- *Create Lists*: Allow you to create lists.

- *Edit Lists*: Allow you to edit existing lists.

- *Delete Lists*: Allow you to delete any list.

- *Edit List Data*: Allows you to edit the data inside of the lists.

- *View Lists*: Allow you to see the lists.

Working with Lists Administration Task Flow

There are multiple ways for accessing to the Lists Administration Task Flow (Figure 12-40):

- When enabling the Lists Service, the **Lists Management System Page** is available via /webcenter/portal/[PortalName]/Lists. It can be directly exposed in the Portal Navigation by using a **Page Link**.

- Lists administrators can access to Lists by using the Portal Menu (⚙ ▾) by accessing to Manage ➤ Lists.

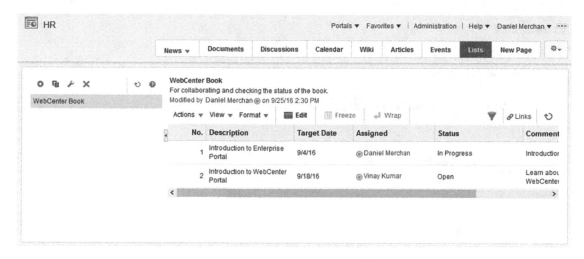

Figure 12-40. *Lists Administration Task Flow*

The options available are:

- 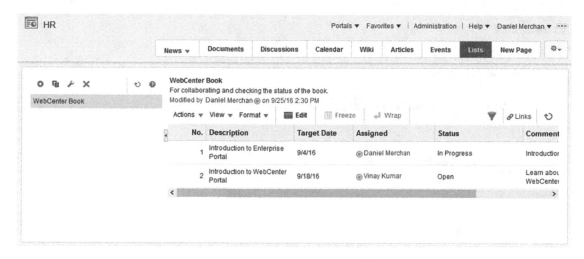 **Create List**: It allows you to start the dialog for creating a new list.

- **Copy List**: Copy the selected list into a new one.

- **Edit List**: Use it for edit the selected list.

- **Delete List**: Delete the selected list.

Create a List

The lists can be created manually (editing the columns one by one) or from an Excel Spreadsheet. After click in Create List, the following dialog is displayed (Figure 12-41):

- **Name**: The logical name of the list.

- **Description**: Descriptive text about the list.

- **Create from**: Here you can select the pre-built and custom List templates available or create a list from an Excel Spreadsheet.

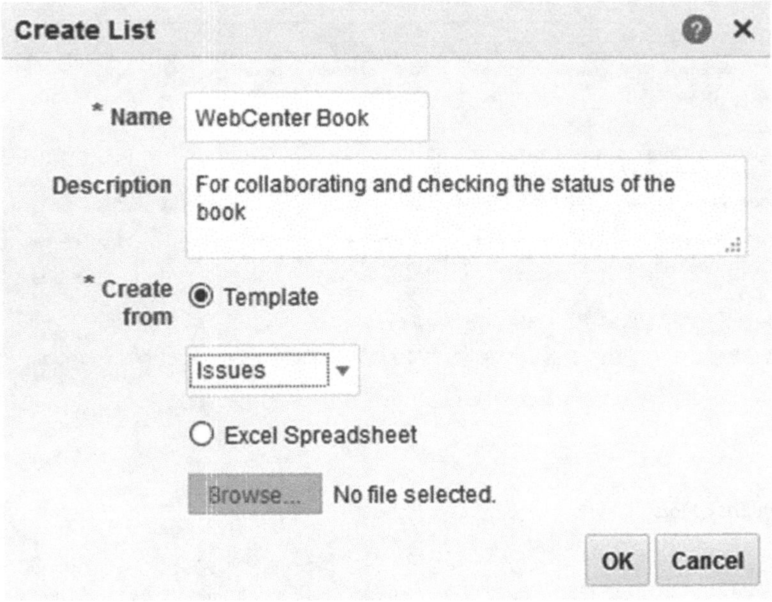

Figure 12-41. *List creation Dialog*

The available pre-built templates are:

- **Custom List**: Allows you to create a list without a specific template (from zero).

- **Issues**: Create a list based on project issues including the following columns: Number of Issue, Description, Target Date, Assigned, Status and Comments.

- **Milestones**: Create a list based on project milestones including the following columns: Date, Description and Status.

- **Objectives**: Create a list based on project objectives including the following columns: Title and Description.

In case of loading a Spreadsheet, take into consideration the following format:

- The first row of the spreadsheet will be use as column headers.

- The columns will be created as Plain Text. Using the Lists Service tools, you can modify if the columns is another type such Date etc...

When a list is created, an administrator can create, edit or modify columns by using the edit list option ✏ (Figure 12-42):

- ➕ **Create**: Use it for adding a new column into the list. The following information has to be provided when creating a column:

  - **Name**: Name of the column

  - Data Type: The type of data used for the column. The allowed types are:

    - **Plain Text**: Text column that also provides options for creating a link on it.

- **Rich Text**: Rich text editor for formatted text.

- **Number**: For only allowing numerical values.

- **Date Time**: Date and Time displayed in the format configured in the WebCenter Portal Preferences.

- **Boolean**: To display a checkbox.

- **Picture**: For providing a URL to display an image inside of the column.

- **Person**: This column will display a helper for assigning a Portal User. It will display a link to the Profile of the Portal User.

- **Edit**: Use it for changing the configuration of the column.

- **Delete**: Delete the current column.

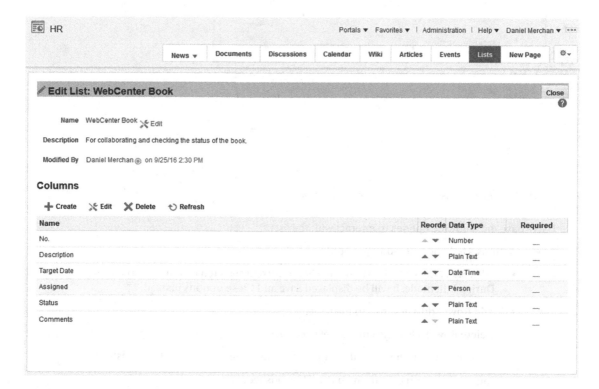

Figure 12-42. *Editing a List*

■ **Tip** Edit the columns when no data has been imported yet. Changing the Data Type or other properties can be dangerous when a List is in use.

Working with Lists

Lists can be added to WebCenter Portal Pages by editing the page and adding the List from the Resource Catalog. The Lists are in Social and Communications ➤ Lists ➤ [Name of the List] (Figure 12-43).

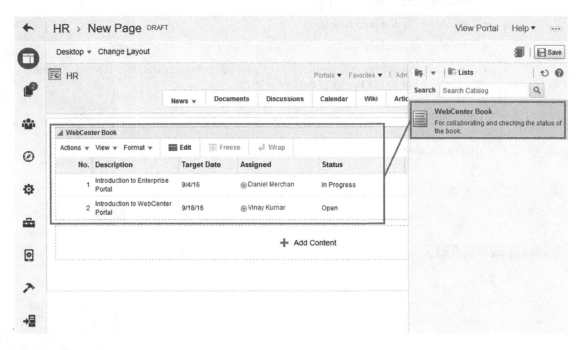

Figure 12-43. *Adding a List to a WebCenter Portal Page*

Users have the following options to interact with the list:

- **Actions**: Here there are multiple options:
  - **Edit, Save, Close**: It allows you to edit the current selected row in the table. During Edit mode, it will be displayed Save and Close options instead.
  - **Add Row**: Add a new row to the table.
  - **Delete Row**: Delete the current selected row.
  - **Export...**: Export the current data shown in the table into an Excel Spreadsheet.
  - **Import...**: Import data from an Excel Spreadsheet.
  - **Filter Rows:** Enable the filtering. Shows an input text for searching specific text over the data shown in the table.
  - **Links...**: Opens the Links Service for linking the List to a Portal Asset.
  - **Send Mail:** Share the List via email.
  - **Refresh List**: Refresh the data in case of it has been edited by another user.

- **View**: Options to personalize how the table is displayed:
    - **Columns**: Select which columns to be displayed.
    - **Sort**: Sort the list by specific columns.
    - **Reorder Columns**: To reorder the columns in the table. This can be also made by Drag & Drop columns.
- **Format**: Use it for resizing the columns if needed.
- ▦ **Edit**: Enters into Edit Mode to manage the data displayed in the table. The options after enabling editing mode are:
    - 💾 **Save**: It saves the edited data.
    - ✖ **Close**: Switch from Edit Mode to View Mode.
    - ➕ **Add**: Add a new row to the table.
    - ✖ **Delete**: Delete the current row.
- ▥ **Freeze**: If the table is too big and you can scroll left to right, then you can freeze a column to mark it as displayed even if scrolling.
- ↵ **Wrap**: Control whether to allow column data to wrap in a selected list column. Data that wraps breaks onto additional lines if it would otherwise exceed the column width.
- ▼ **Filter**: Opens the filter section to filter the data based on the text provided in the filter.
- 🔗 **Links**: To use the Links Service for linking the current list to a specific portal asset.

■ **Note**   Each row can be also linked to a portal asset by click in the Link column that is always displayed by default.

Mail

By enabling the Mail Service, users of WebCenter Portal can:

- Do **basic operations** such view, compose, reply emails within WebCenter Portal (Figure 12-44).
- Enable to create **distribution lists**. This option only works with Active Directory Exchange Server users.
- **Share and Send** portal assets by email. Great number of the Portal Components has the ✉ **Send Mail** feature (like Links).

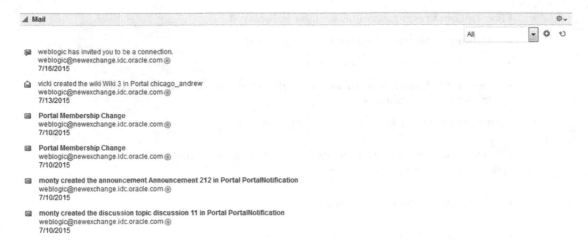

Figure 12-44. *Mail Access through Mail Task Flow*

WebCenter Portal supports Exchange Server or any mail server which supports IMAP4 or SMTP protocols.

Configuring Mail Service

By default, Oracle WebCenter Portal is configured to allow the users for sending the emails by the option **Send Mail**. It uses, by default, their local mail clients such Outlook (Figure 12-45).

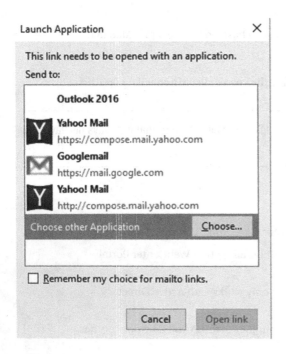

Figure 12-45. *Launch of local Mail clients for sharing portal assets*

Using Enterprise Manager Console or WLST scripts, a System Administrator can configure Mail Server Connections for WebCenter Portal. When a Mail Server connection is configured, then portal members can Send Email and share portal assets in the same context of the Portal instead of the local clients. Connections are configured by providing the following information (Figure 12-46):

Name:

- **Connection Name**: Unique name assigned to this connection. Use a representative name as users can use it by changing their Mail Preferences.

- **Active Connection**: Mark this connection as the default one used when WebCenter Portal is configured to use a Mail Server.

Mail Server Connection Details: Fill IMAP or SMTP depending on the mail server support.

- **IMAP Host**: Host / IP where IMAP server is running

- **IMAP Port**: Port used by IMAP

- **IMAP Secured**: Mark for using SSL over the connection

- **SMTP Host**: Host / IP of the SMTP server

- **SMTP Port**: Port of the SMTP server

- **SMTP Secured**: Mark for using SSL over the connection

- **Associated External Application**: Create and associate an External Application to this connection. It will be used to store securely the credentials of the users when accessing to their email accounts by using this connection.

LDAP Directory Server Configuration: Configure for enabling distribution list. WebCenter Portal supports Microsoft Exchange where distribution lists are managed on an Active Directory server.

- **LDAP Host**: Host / IP of the LDAP.

- **LDAP Port**: Port used to connect to the LDAP.

- **LDAP Base DN**: Base Distinguished Name of the LDAP schema.

- **LDAP Domain**: Domain + distribution list names. For example, imagine @pigeon. co.uk as the domain, for a portal named HR then the distribution list of email will send the emails to HR@pigeon.co.uk. **It is very important to know this for configuring the distribution lists properly.**

- **LDAP Administrator User Name**: Enter a user with privileges for create entries in the LDAP Schema.

- **LDAP Administrator Password**: Enter the password of the above user.

- **LDAP Default User**: Comma-delimited users that will become members of every portal distribution list that is created.

- **LDAP Secured**: Indicate if the LDAP connection is secured over SSL.

Advanced Configuration

- **Connection Timeout**: Setup a timeout in seconds for a connection to the mail server.

Additional Properties: Use it for adding extra Java Mail Properties required for making the IMAP or SMTP connection.

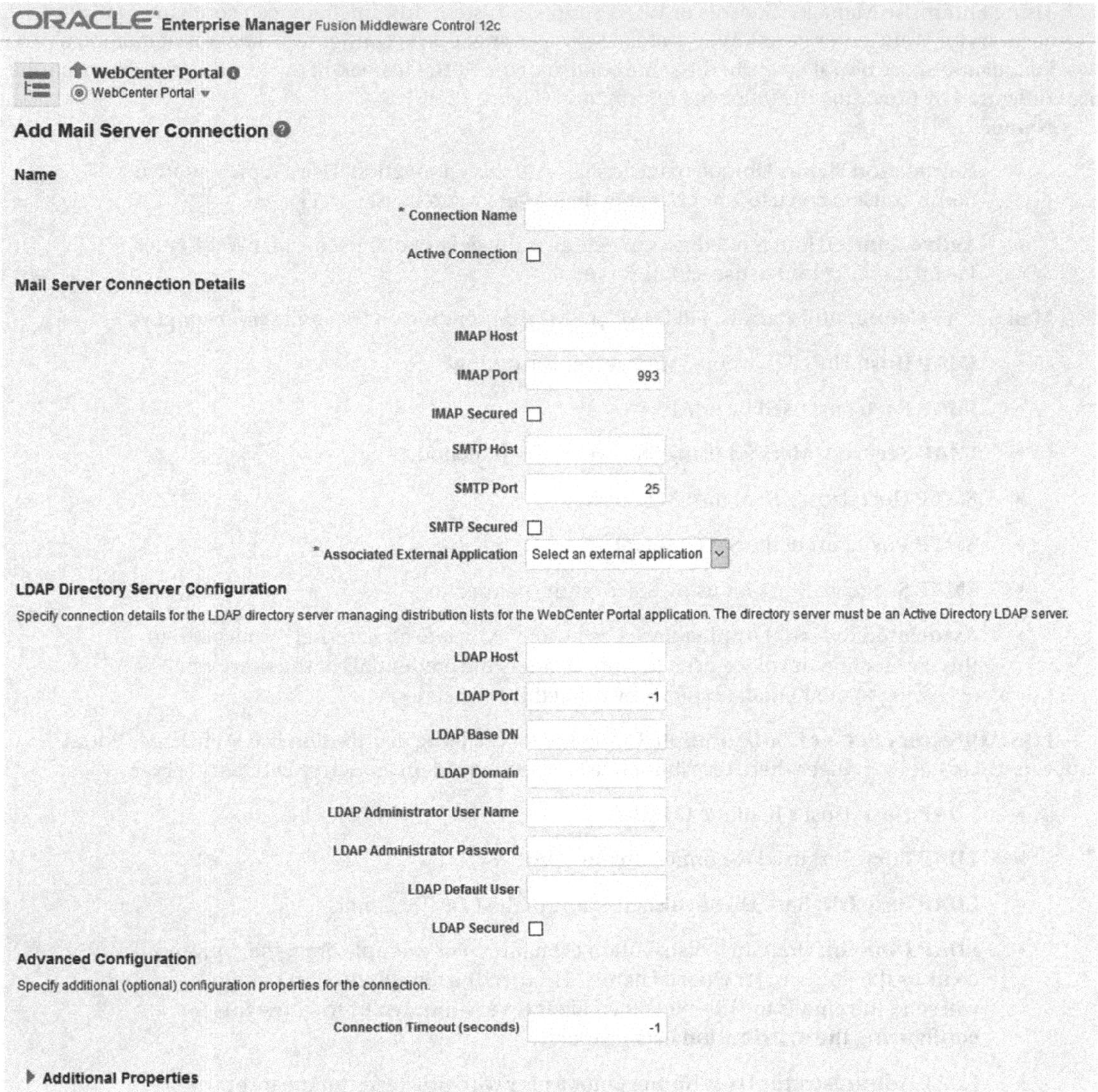

Figure 12-46. *Mail Server configuration via Enterprise Manager*

■ **Note** Multiple Mail Servers can be configured in WebCenter Portal, but only one can be marked as active.

Users can change to a non-default Mail Server by changing it in their user preferences (if they have permissions to do it).

Global Settings

Once, at least an active mail connection is available, then a Portal Administrator can set up the global settings for Mail Services by accessing to WebCenter Portal Administration ➤ Tool and Services ➤ Mail (Figure 12-47). The following options are available:

Default Mail Client for Send Mail ( ):

- **Local Mail Client**: It will display the dialog for selecting a local mail client for sending the email (GMAIL, Yahoo!, Outlook...)

- **WebCenter Portal's Mail Service**: In this case, it will use WebCenter Portal Mail Component for sending the email.

Override:

- **Allow Users to Override the Default Mail Client Setting**: Mark it if you want to allow the users the capabilities for changing their Mail settings via User Preferences.

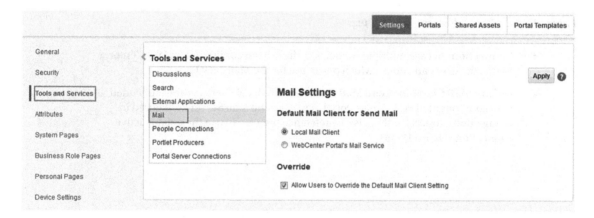

Figure 12-47. *WebCenter Portal Mail Global Administration*

Personal Settings

In case of the Global Settings are set up to *Allow Users to Override the Default Mail Client* Setting, then a portal member can change by himself the Mail Service preferences for using the Send Email action. By navigating to the User Preferences ➤ Mail. (Figure 12-48).

Figure 12-48. *User Preferences, Mail Settings*

- **Connection**: In case multiple connections have been configured for WebCenter Portal, the user can choose which one to use for the Mail Task Flow.

- **Default Mail Client for Send Mail**: Choose to use local clients or the embedded mail component of WebCenter Portal. It will use the Mail Server configured in Connection property, if there is no preference then it will use the default active connection (Figure 12-49).

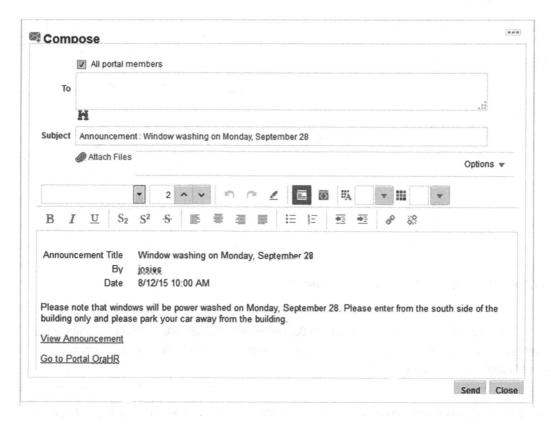

Figure 12-49. *Send Email using the embed WebCenter Mail Service*

About Mail Task Flow

Not only can portal assets be shared by using the Send Mail option (with the embed component or using the local client). In addition, WebCenter Portal brings the Mail Task Flow, which allows the users to manage their emails account directly inside WebCenter Portal.

This component can be added to a Portal Page by adding the Mail Task Flow (Figure 12-50).

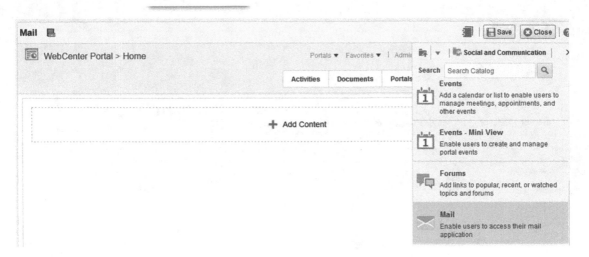

Figure 12-50. *Mail Task Flow in the Resource Catalog*

___

■ **Note**   By default, this Task Flow is included in the Default Home Portal Catalog. If you need to add the Mail Task Flow to a specific portal (different to the Home Portal), then you have to add the Mail Task Flow to the configured Resource Catalog in use.

___

This Task Flow provides the typical capabilities for working with emails such as **Send**, **Reply**, **Reply All,** Add attachments, etc.

However, this Task Flow has limitations compared to desktop clients such Outlook. For example, it does not render embedded images. They always appear as attachments.

The first time a user accesses the Mail Task Flow, a link called "*Login to Mail*" will appear. The user has to enter his email address and credentials (Figure 12-51). The credentials will be stored securely in the credential store and used for auto-log in the user the next time.

Figure 12-51. *Email Task Flow ask for credentials the first time*

■ **Tip**   Allow the users to decide their preferred Mail Settings and how the Send Email feature will work. Not all the users are happy or comfortable with WebCenter Portal Mail Service and they still prefer using client tools such as Outlook.

People Connections

People Connections enables social networking capabilities to WebCenter Portal through the following components:

- **Activity Stream**: For tracking any activity that happens to the user connections, portals etc.

- **Connections**: Enable the user to link with other users.

- **Profile**: To view and edit personal information or view and interact with other connections or users.

- **Message Board**: The message board is something similar to Facebook wall; here users can post and view messages from other connections or portal members.

- **Feedback**: Provides a means of viewing, posting, and managing feedback remarks.

Enabling People Connections

People Connections is enabled Out-of-the-box when installing WebCenter Portal. For production environments, the Identity Store (repository of users) must be configured to use an External LDAP such Oracle Internet Directory or Active Directory.

People Connections Settings

A WebCenter Portal Administrator can configure the default People Connection settings by accessing to WebCenter Portal Administration ➤ Tools and Services ➤ People Connections (Figure 12-52).

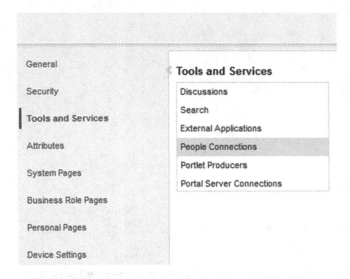

Figure 12-52. *Accesing to People Connections Global Settings*

The settings configured here will be the base for all People Connection components.

Portal members can override some of these settings via their Preferences ➤ People interface (Figure 12-53).

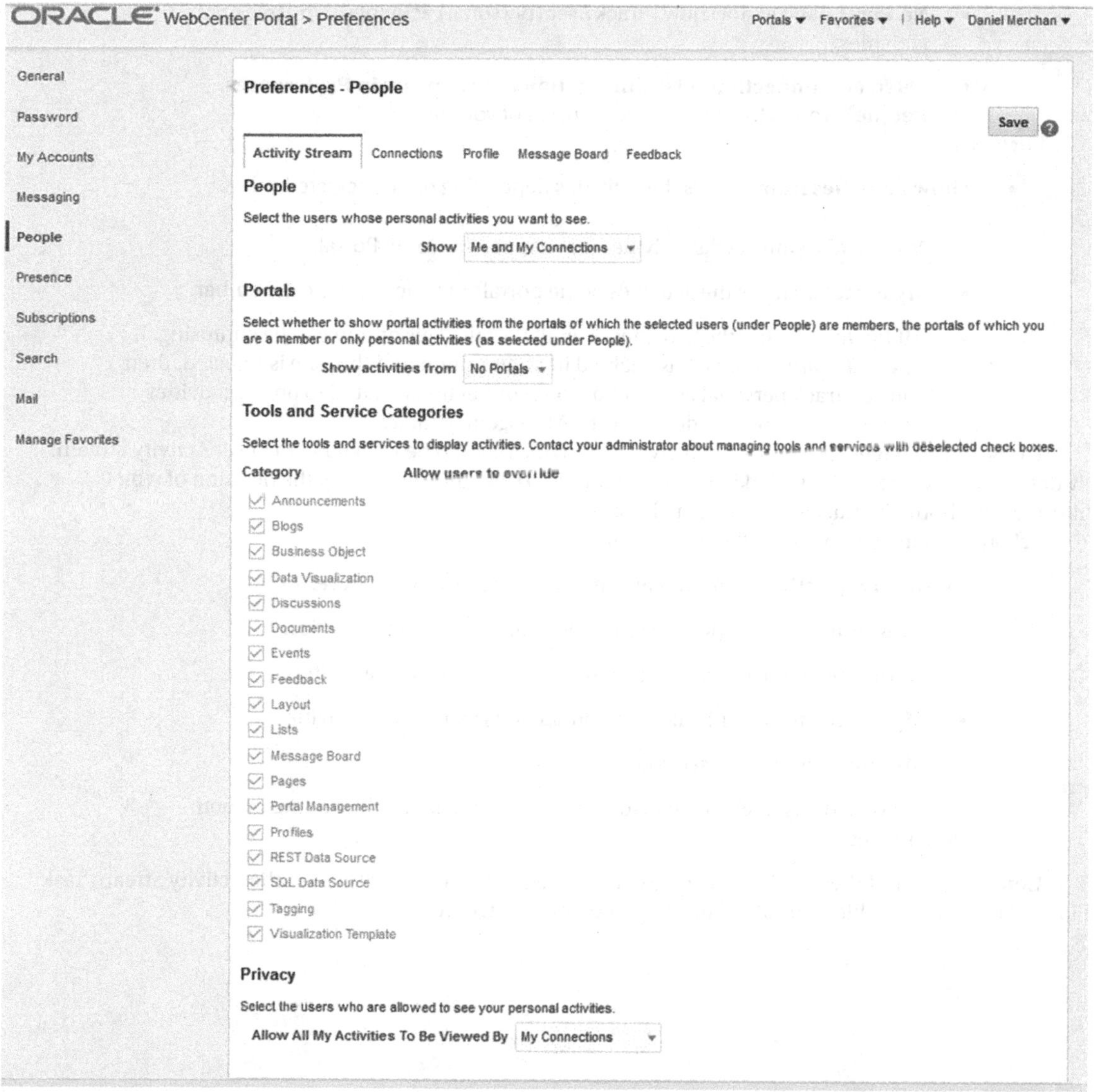

ORACLE WebCenter Portal > Preferences

Portals ▼ Favorites ▼ | Help ▼ Daniel Merchan ▼

General

Password

My Accounts

Messaging

| People

Presence

Subscriptions

Search

Mail

Manage Favorites

Preferences - People

Save ❓

Activity Stream   Connections   Profile   Message Board   Feedback

People

Select the users whose personal activities you want to see.

Show   [Me and My Connections   ▼]

Portals

Select whether to show portal activities from the portals of which the selected users (under People) are members, the portals of which you are a member or only personal activities (as selected under People).

Show activities from   [No Portals ▼]

Tools and Service Categories

Select the tools and services to display activities. Contact your administrator about managing tools and services with deselected check boxes.

Category   Allow users to override

☑ Announcements

☑ Blogs

☑ Business Object

☑ Data Visualization

☑ Discussions

☑ Documents

☑ Events

☑ Feedback

☑ Layout

☑ Lists

☑ Message Board

☑ Pages

☑ Portal Management

☑ Profiles

☑ REST Data Source

☑ SQL Data Source

☑ Tagging

☑ Visualization Template

Privacy

Select the users who are allowed to see your personal activities.

Allow All My Activities To Be Viewed By   [My Connections   ▼]

Figure 12-53. *People Connections user Preferences*

Activity Stream Settings

The following settings can be configured for the Activity Stream components (Figure 12-53):

People

- **Show:** Select from who do you want to see updates in the Activity Stream:

  - **Me and My Connections:** Is the default value. Track your own activities and your connection activities.

  - **Only me:** Only my activities will be tracked in the activity stream.

- **No Personal**: Do not show / track user (personal) activities, only track portal activities.

- **Selected Connections Lists (this option only appears in Preferences - People):** To track only the selected users of your lists.

Portals

- **Show activities from**: Filters the activities depending on the selected value:

  - **No Portals**: Only tracks activities that happen in Home Portal.

  - **My Portals**: Tracks the activities of the portals of which you are a member.

  - **All Portals**: Tracks the activities over all Portals. This option can be confusing. If *Selected Connection Lists* is enabled in *Show* option and this one is selected, then you can track personal activities of your connections related to portal activities (for example, when he does a Portal Management activity).

Tools and Services Categories: Mark which Activities should be tracked in the user Activity Stream. By default, all are enabled. By marking *"Allow user to override"* then we can let the decision of which information should be tracked in their activity stream.

Privacy: Secure settings over the user activities.

- **Allow All My Activities To Be Viewed By**: The possible values are:

  - **Everyone**: All users (logged or public) can see the user activities:

  - **Authenticated Users**: All logged users can see the user activities.

  - **My Connections**: Only the user connections can see his activities.

  - **Myself**: Only you can see your activities.

- **Allow override by users**: Enable to allow the users change this setting in their Preferences.

Comments and Likes: Activities can be commented and marked as "like" in the Activity Stream Task Flow. They can be enabled / disabled in this part of the configuration.

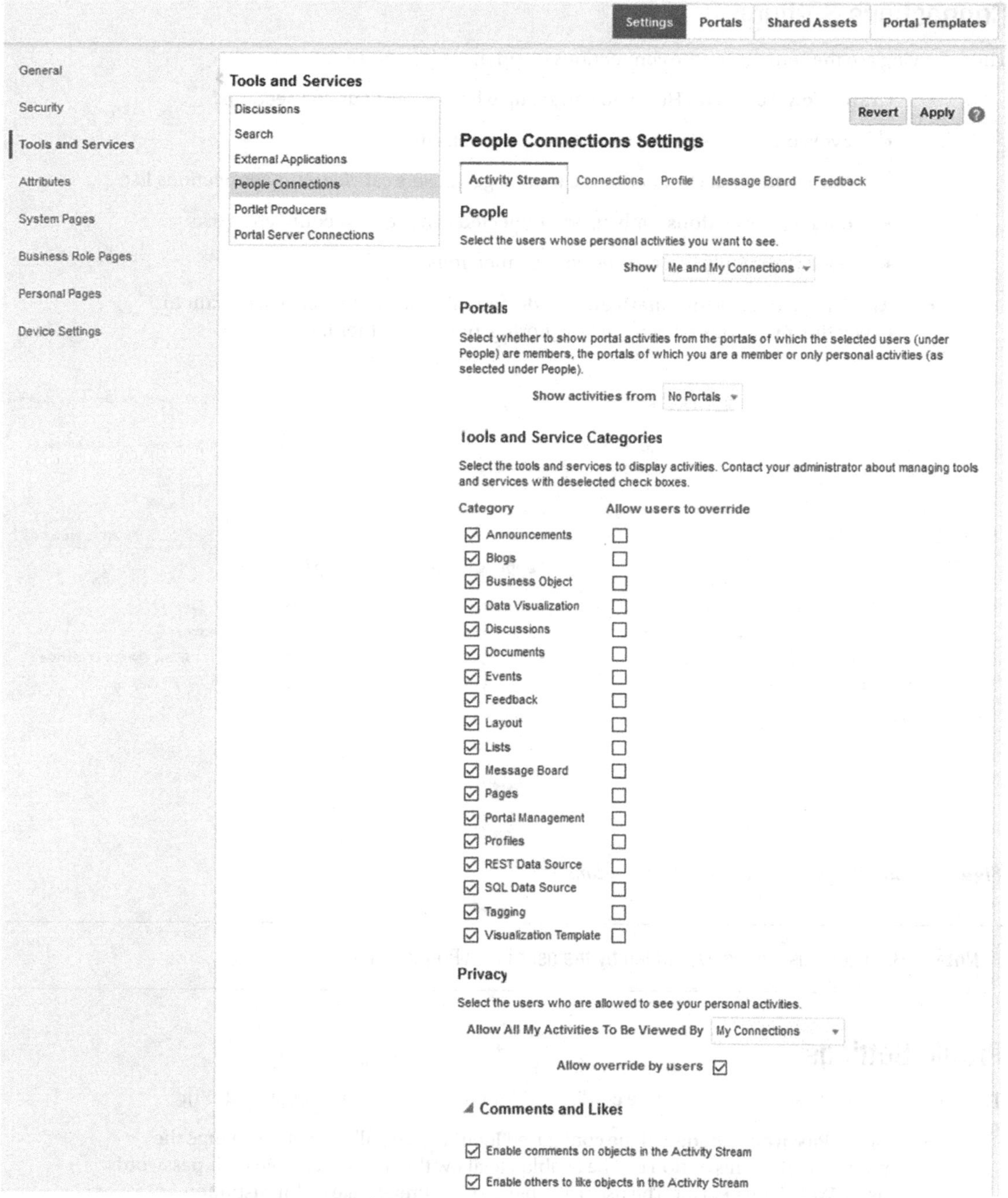

| Settings | Portals | Shared Assets | Portal Templates |

General

Security

Tools and Services

Attributes

System Pages

Business Role Pages

Personal Pages

Device Settings

Tools and Services

Discussions

Search

External Applications

People Connections

Portlet Producers

Portal Server Connections

Revert   Apply   ❓

People Connections Settings

Activity Stream   Connections   Profile   Message Board   Feedback

People

Select the users whose personal activities you want to see.

Show   Me and My Connections ▾

Portals

Select whether to show portal activities from the portals of which the selected users (under People) are members, the portals of which you are a member or only personal activities (as selected under People).

Show activities from   No Portals ▾

Tools and Service Categories

Select the tools and services to display activities. Contact your administrator about managing tools and services with deselected check boxes.

Category	Allow users to override
☑ Announcements	☐
☑ Blogs	☐
☑ Business Object	☐
☑ Data Visualization	☐
☑ Discussions	☐
☑ Documents	☐
☑ Events	☐
☑ Feedback	☐
☑ Layout	☐
☑ Lists	☐
☑ Message Board	☐
☑ Pages	☐
☑ Portal Management	☐
☑ Profiles	☐
☑ REST Data Source	☐
☑ SQL Data Source	☐
☑ Tagging	☐
☑ Visualization Template	☐

Privacy

Select the users who are allowed to see your personal activities.

Allow All My Activities To Be Viewed By   My Connections ▾

Allow override by users ☑

◢ **Comments and Likes**

☑ Enable comments on objects in the Activity Stream

☑ Enable others to like objects in the Activity Stream

Figure 12-54. People Connections: Activity Stream Settings

Connections Settings

The following are the settings for the connections component (Figure 12-55):

- **Grant View Access to**: Here you can set up who can see your connections:

  - **Everyone**: All users can see your connections list.

  - **Authenticated**: Only authenticated / logged users can see your connections list.

  - **User's Connections**: Only users connected can see your connection lists.

  - **User Only**: Only you can see your connections list.

- **Accept Invitations Automatically**: By default, disabled as usually users want to check the invitations for accepting, ignoring, or refusing them.

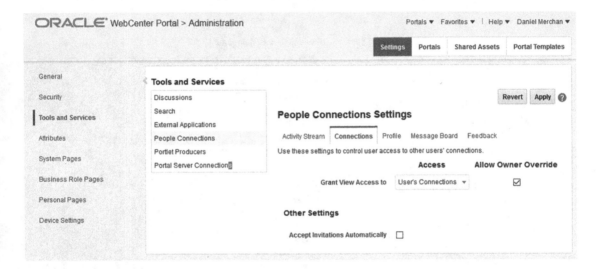

Figure 12-55. *People Connections: Connections Settings*

■ **Note**   Both settings can be overridden by the user in his Preferences.

Profile Settings

The following are the settings that can be configured for the Profile feature (Figure 12-56):

- **Allow Password Change**: If the configured Identity Store allows you to change the password, then this option can be enabled to allow the users to change their passwords using WebCenter Portal. The user can change it via Preferences administration.

- **Profile Access**: Security settings for specific Profile sections. The following sections can be secured:

- **Summary**: General information of the user like the Name, Email, Department, etc.

- **Employee:** Information about the employee such as Employee Number, Organization, Expertise, etc.

- **Business Contact:** Information to contact the user within the company. It is the job mobile number, city, fax, etc.

- **Personal Information:** Information of the user like the Home Address, Date of Birth, etc.

- **Profile Section:** Here can be configured which attributes can be edited by a user in his Profile.

- **Profile Synchronization Settings**: Set up some of the Profile - LDAP synchronization settings:

  - **LDAP read batch size for profile synchronization**: By default, 1000.

  - **Synchronize user profile photos with LDAP when the cache expires**: Turn on /off the synchronization of the profile photo with the Identity Store (LDAP) data when the cache of the Profile expires.

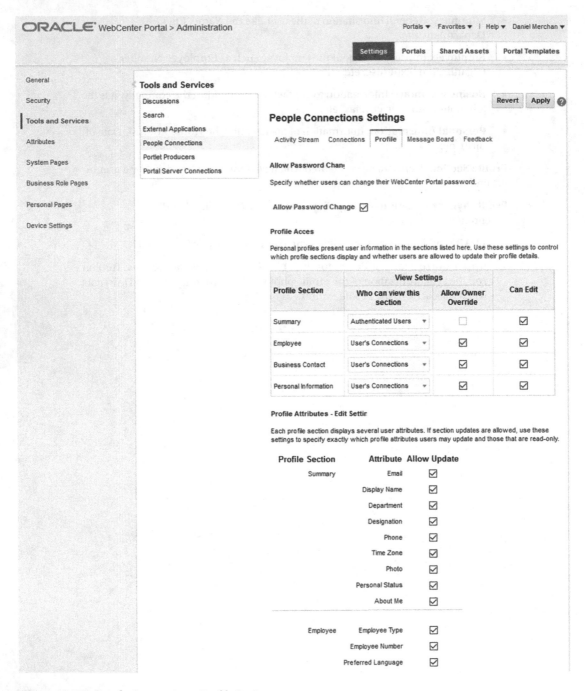

Figure 12-56. *People Connections: Profile Settings*

■ **Note**   Only Profile Access: Employee, Business Contact, and Personal Information options can be overridden via User Preferences.

■ **Tip**   By using WLST Scripts, the System Administrators can change the Profile Cache Size and how many times a day the Profile information is synchronized). It is important to change these properties if the profile information will be changed very frequently.

Message Board Settings

The following are the settings for the Message Board (Figure 12-57):

- **Grant View Access to**: Set who can view your Message Board:
  - **Everyone**: All can see the posts.
  - **Authenticated** Users: Only logged in users.
  - **User's Connections**: Only the user connections.
  - **User Only**: Only the user.
- **Grant Post Access to**: Set who can post in your Message Board:

  - **Everyone**: All can see the posts.
  - **Authenticated** Users: Only logged in users.
  - **User's Connections**: Only the user connections.
  - **User Only**: Only the user.

  Additional Access Settings:
  - **Permissions of users who post in other Message Boards:Edit Messages**: Allow the users to edit their messages.
  - **Delete Messages**: Allow the users to delete their messages.
- **Permissions of users over the messages received from other users**:
  - **Delete Messages received from others**: Allow the user for deleting the messages received.
  - **Change the visibility of the messages**: Allow the user for hiding / showing messages from specific users.

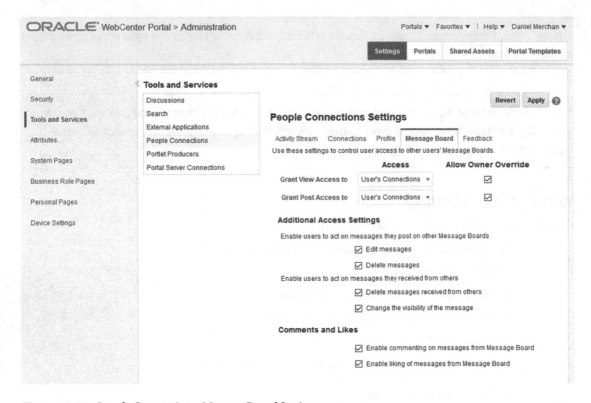

Figure 12-57. People Connections: Message Board Settings

Comments and Likes: Messages can be commented and marked as "like" in the Message Board Task Flow. They can be enabled / disabled in this part of the configuration.

■ **Note**   Only the Grant options can be configured for being overridden by users in their Preferences.

Feedback Settings

The following are the settings that can be configured for the Feedback functionality (Figure 12-58):

- **Grant View Access to**: Set who can view the feedback you have given.

  - **Everyone**: All can see the posts.

  - **Authenticated** Users: Only logged in users.

  - **User's Connections**: Only the user connections.

  - **User Only**: Only the user.

- **Grant Post Access to**: Set who can post a Feedback to you.

  - **Everyone**: All can see the posts.

  - **Authenticated** Users: Only logged in users.

- **User's Connections**: Only the user connections.

- **User Only**: Only the user.

- **Grant View Feedback Given Access to**: Set who can view the Feedback that you have received.

  - **Everyone**: All can see the posts.

  - **Authenticated** Users: Only logged in users.

  - **User's Connections**: Only the user connections.

  - **User Only**: Only the user.

Additional Access Settings

- Permissions over the Feedback given:

  - **Delete Feedback**: If checked, it allows the user that has given feedback to delete it.

- Permissions over the Feedback received:

  - **Change the visibility of the feedback**: Enable to hide / show a feedback.

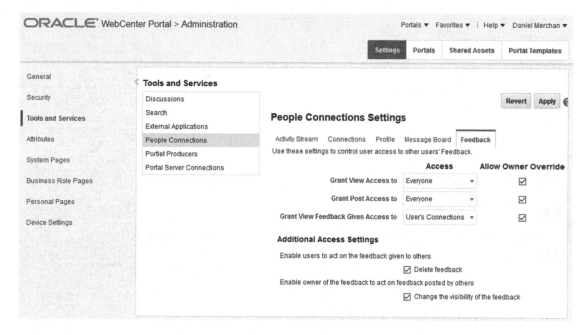

Figure 12-58. *People Connections: Feedback Settings*

■ **Note**   Only the Grant options can be configured for being overridden by users in their Preferences.

Working with Connections

Connections enable the portal users for building their own social networks by connecting with other portal users.

By connecting with other users then you are allowing them to access to some of your personal information such as Message Board, Connections Lists, Feedbacks, etc/., as we talked before on People Connection: Settings.

Out-of-the-box, Oracle WebCenter Portal offers the following Connections Task Flows (Figure 12-59):

- **Connections**: This component allows you to manage your connections lists, pending invitations, sent invitations.

- **Connections - Card**: Displays the contacts as cards by offering small details and options.

- **Connections - Detailed View**: Component that allows you to manage your connections with a different look and feel compared to Connections component.

- **Connections - Quick View**: Only displays the user picture and a link to their profile.

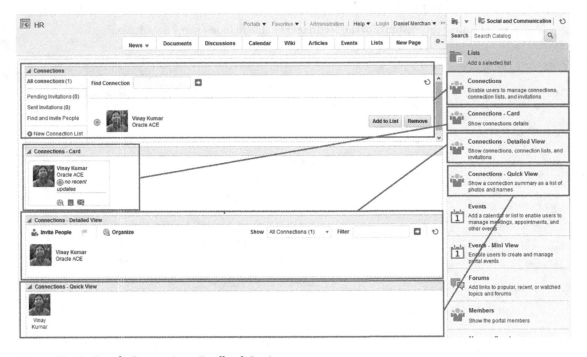

***Figure 12-59.** People Connections: Feedback Settings*

Connections Task Flow

The Connections Task Flow brings the following functionalities (Figure 12-60):

- **All Connections**: Display all the connections you have made.

- **Pending Invitations**: Display the users that have sent you an invitation.

- **Find and Invite People**: Allow for searching and inviting a portal member to your connections.

-  **New Connection List**: Create connections lists for organizing your contacts. The connection lists are displayed on between *Pending Invitations* and *All Connections* option.

Figure 12-60. *Connections Task Flow*

The configurable parameters for this Task Flow are (Figure 12-61):

- **Current View**: What is the default view to show when Connections Task Flow is displayed:

  - Connections

  - Received Invitations

  - Pending Invitations

  - People

- **Number of Rows (list layout)**: How many rows to show non-paginated in the list of users.

- **User Name**: By default, it is configured to the current logged user. Leave it as it is.

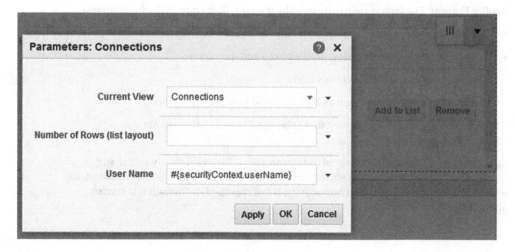

Figure 12-61. *Connections Task Flow Parameters*

Connections – Card Task Flow

The Connections – Card Task Flow offers the following options (Figure 12-62):

- **Connections**: Access directly to the connections page of the selected user. (Only if you have permissions to see the connections of your connection.)

- **Lists**: This functionality permits the user to add the selected user to a specific connection list.

- **Send Email**: Send an email to the selected user.

Figure 12-62. *Connections – Card Task Flow*

The configuration parameters for the Connections – Card Task Flow are (Figure 12-63):

- **Connections List Name**: For opening only the connections of a specific connection list for the current user.

- **Number of connections per page**: How many connections will be displayed at once in a page.

- **Number of Columns**: How many columns display the grid.

- **Number of Rows**: How many rows display the grid.

- **Profile Format**: The layout style to be used by the grid. Enter one of the following:

    - **Virtual Business Card**: Display the connection in a virtual business card.

    - **Iconic**: Display the connection profile photo and user name.

    - **List**: Display a list with the connections.

    - **Tiled**: Display the connection as tiles arranged in a flowing layout.

- **Allow Remove**: Check it if you want to display the *Remove* option within the connection layout.

- **Sort Criteria**: To change the order of the connections. For example, by specifying 'LAST_ACTIVITY_TIME' then it sorts the connections in descending order of date at which they were last involved in any activity. If not specified, by default it is sorting alphabetically by name.

- **Filter Pattern**: It allows you to filter the content. For example, if you specify "Managers" then it will show connections from connection lists containing that word.

- **Hide Footer**: Whether the display of the footer should be turned off. Specifying #{true} will prevent a link to launch the Connections Main View from showing at the bottom of this screen if the Maximum Connections parameter has been specified and there are more connections available than that number.

- **Hide Name**: Whether the display of the name should be turned off for iconic view. Specifying #{true} will prevent a name link from appearing in the connections iconic view and the image will turn to a link.

- **Launch Style**: The way it works when a user clicks in the user name:

  - **Snapshot**: Opens a dialog with user details and some options such Go to Profile or Send a Message.

  - **Profile**: Opens the user profile in the current page.

- **Profile Launched on Selection**: Whether to launch or not profile pop-up upon selection. Specifying #{false} will not launch the profile pop-up upon selection.

- **Show "See all your connections" in footer always**: If turned off, it will not be paginated and only will show the most relevant users.

- **User Name**: By default, it is configured to display the current logged user connections. Do not touch this parameter.

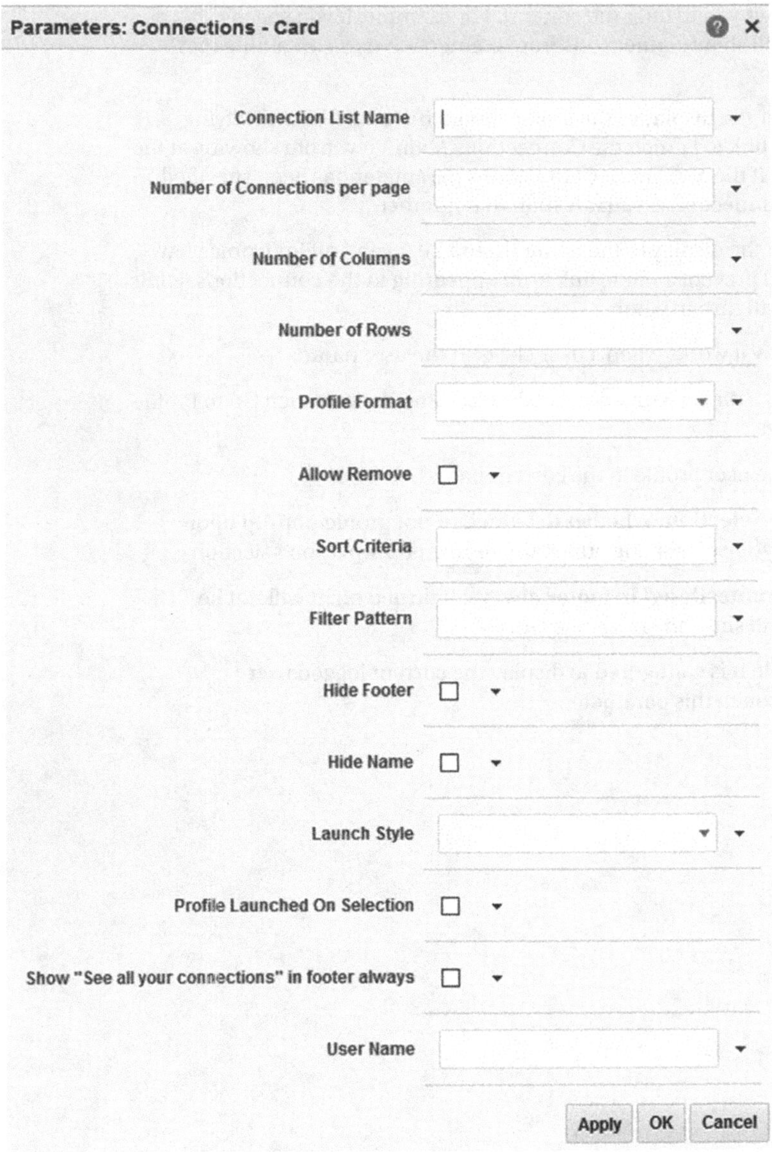

Parameters: Connections - Card

Connection List Name

Number of Connections per page

Number of Columns

Number of Rows

Profile Format

Allow Remove

Sort Criteria

Filter Pattern

Hide Footer

Hide Name

Launch Style

Profile Launched On Selection

Show "See all your connections" in footer always

User Name

Apply   OK   Cancel

Figure 12-63. *Connections Card Task Flow Parameters*

Connections – Detailed View

This is the default Task Flow shown in the Connections Tab of the Profile page in the Home Portal.
It offers all the functionalities for connecting and managing your social network (Figure 12-64).

- **Invite People**: Opens a dialog very similar to *Connections Task Flow* for searching and inviting people.

- **Pending Invitations**: Displays if there is any pending invitation.

- **Organize**: Opens a dialog very similar to *Connections Task Flow* for managing the connection lists.

- **Show**: Allow the user to filter the connections by the connection lists, pending invitations, or users to who you have sent an invitation.

- **Filter**: Introduce text for filtering and searching in the current user list.

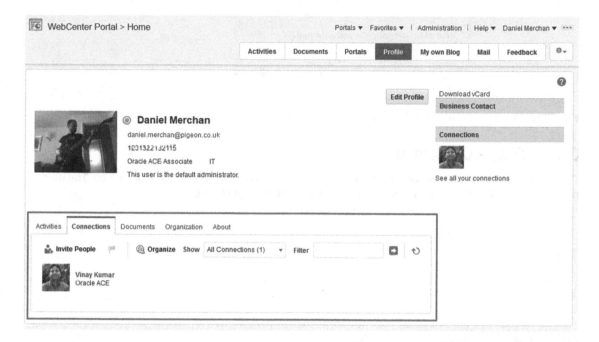

Figure 12-64. *Connections – Detailed Task Flow*

The Connections – Detailed Task Flow has the following configurable parameters (Figure 12-65):

- **Number of Connections per Page**: How many connections to display in the list before it shows the pagination.

- **Sort Criteria**: To change the order of the connections. For example, by specifying 'LAST_ACTIVITY_TIME' then it sorts the connections in descending order of date at which they were last involved in any activity. If not specified, by default it is sorting alphabetically by name.

- **User Name**: By default, the current logged user. Do not change it.

Figure 12-65. *Connections Detailed Task Flow Parameters*

Connections – Quick View

This is the smallest connections component and it only displays the users you are connected on. The user name is just a link to their profiles like in the other components (Figure 12-66).

Figure 12-66. *Connections – Quick View Task Flow*

The configuration parameters for Connections Quick View Task Flow are (Figure 12-67) are:

- **Number of Connections per Page**: How many connections will be shown in a single page.

- **Number of Columns**: To set the number of columns to be displayed in the grid.

- **Number of Rows**: To set the number of rows to be displayed in the grid.

- **Hide Footer and Hide Header**: Whether the display of the footer should be turned off. Specifying #{true} will prevent a link to launch the Connections Main View from showing at the bottom of this screen if the Maximum Connections parameter has been specified and there are more connections available than that number.

- **User Id**: The user whose connections are shown. By default, it takes the current logged user.

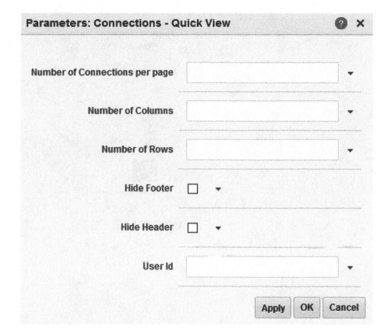

Figure 12-67. *Connections Quick View Task Flow Parameters*

Working with Profile

The Profile is your personal area within WebCenter Portal. We need to differentiate two types of profiles:

- **Your Profile**: Which means your information, documents, messages, connections, etc.

- **Other User Profile**: You can see and interact with other user profiles depending on the security and permissions they have set for their Profiles.

About Your Profile

Your Profile can be accessed by:

- Accessing to the Home Portal ➤ Profile page (Figure 12-68).

- Via user menu options ➤ User Profile.

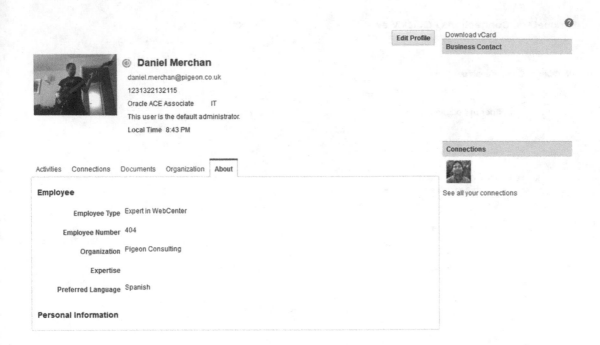

Figure 12-68. *Connections Quick View Task Flow Parameters*

Here a user has the following options:

- **Edit his profile information**. Only if he has permission to do it. Remember that we were talking before about Profile Settings where a Portal Administrator can set up which attributes can be overridden by the user.

- **Download a Business Card in vCard format**.

- **Quick view over his connections**: A Connections Quick View is configured for showing the current connections.

- **Activities Tab**: Displays a personal Activity Stream Task Flow to track connections and personal activities.

- **Connections Tab**: For managing the connections list and social network.

- **Documents Tab**: To access and manage personal documents.

- **Organization**: It displays a Hierarchical View of you within the company. It displays who is your manager and who are you managing (Figure 12-69).

- **About**: Employee and Personal Information is displayed here.

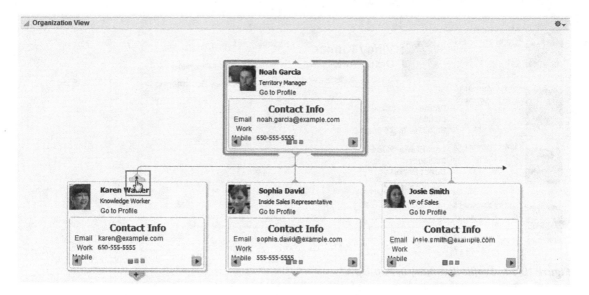

Figure 12-69. *Organization View*

■ **Note**   The information displayed in the Profile comes from the Identity Store (LDAP).

The Organization View requires the "manager" attribute set up in the LDAP.

About Other Profiles

Users can enter into the other user profiles by clicking in their user names.

When clicking in a user name two things can happen:

- **Open the Profile Summary in a Pop-Up**. Here there is a summary of the User Profile. Other options appear such *Go To Profile, Add Message*, etc. (Figure 12-70).

- **Open the Profile page of the selected user**. Depending on the permissions preferences of the user. You can check the information, post a message, etc. (Figure 12-71).

Figure 12-70. *Profile Summary in Pop-Up*

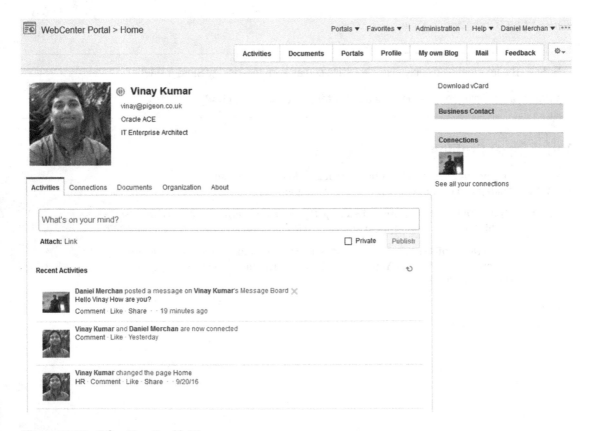

Figure 12-71. *Other User Profile View*

About Profile Task Flows

Oracle WebCenter Portal provides some Profile Task Flows that can be added to the Portal Pages (Figure 12-72):

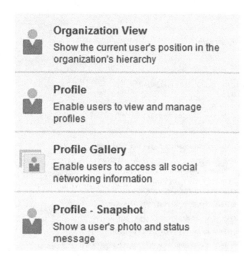

Organization View
Show the current user's position in the organization's hierarchy

Profile
Enable users to view and manage profiles

Profile Gallery
Enable users to access all social networking information

Profile - Snapshot
Show a user's photo and status message

Figure 12-72. *Resource Catalog – Profile Task Flows*

- **Organization View**: For showing your position within the Organization by using a Hierarchy Viewer. It is the same as displayed in the Home Portal -> Profile -> Organization Tab.

- **Profile**: This component displays all the user information and the *Publisher Task Flow* for posting and sharing an activity via Activity Stream.

- **Profile Gallery**: This component offers a complete functionality as it mixes multiple Portal Services into a single one (Figure 12-73):

  - **Profile – Snapshot**: It displays basic information. In addition, it allows you to publish messages in the message board by the embedded *Publisher Task Flow*.

  - **Profile**: Displays a summary of personal information (Email, Phone, Time Zone).

  - **Connections**: It is a changed version of the Connections – Card Task Flow where the user can manage his social network.

  - **Feedback**: It displays the Received / Given feedback.

  - **Activity Stream**: Mini View version of the Activity Stream for tracking the activities of you and your contacts.

  - **Message Board**: Displays the latest messages posted.

- **Profile – Snapshot**: It displays basic information. In addition, it allows you to publish activities in the Activity Stream by the embedded *Publisher Task Flow*.

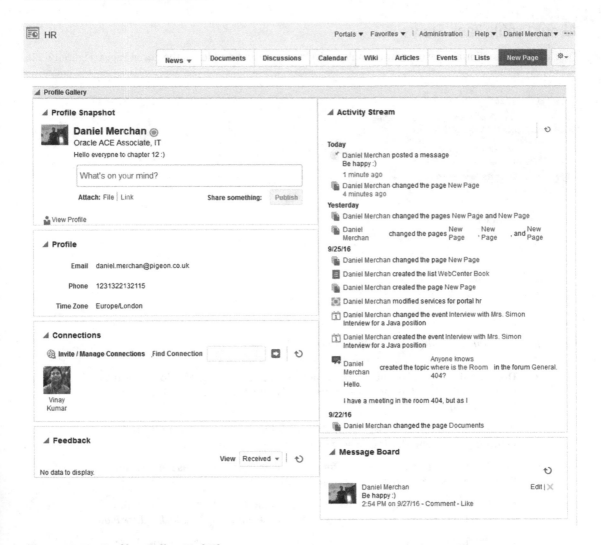

Figure 12-73. *Profile – Gallery Task Flow*

Working with Message Board

The Message Board enables the users to post, view, and send messages between them (Figure 12-75).
These messages / posts are "scoped" to the Portal that it belongs to.
What does it mean "scoped" to the Portal belongs to?

- The Message Board in the **Home Portal** is something similar to your Facebook wall of your profile. Only your messages and the messages sent to you are displayed here. Remember two things:

  - You need to add the Message Board Task Flow to a Personal Page as it is not added Out-of-the-box.

  - Permissions and privacy settings can be set in your User Preferences.

- If the Message Board is added to a **specific Portal** (not the Home Portal) it acts like the wall where all the portal members can post message and interact between them.

■ **Caution**   Activity Stream and Message Board may be confused by their concepts. The Message Board posts can be streamed to the Activity Stream as another portal activity depending on the permission settings.

If the messages are being streamed to the Activity Stream, be aware that even those messages you *mark private* will still show up in the Activity Streams of your connections and the poster's connections.

Message Board Task Flow

As commented before, the Message Board Task Flow can be added to a Personal Page in the Home Portal or to a Portal Page (Figure 12-74).

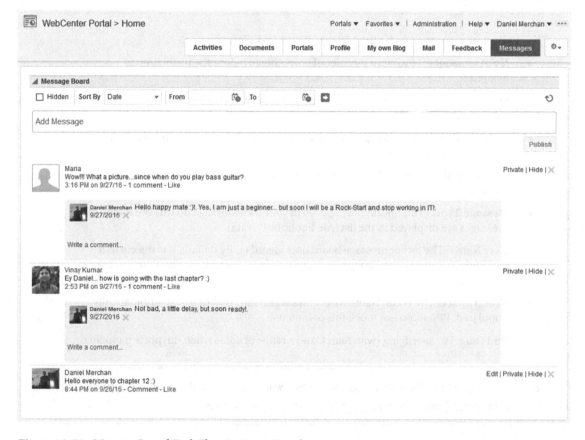

Figure 12-74. *Message Board Task Flow in Home Portal*

The options displayed in this component are:

- **Hidden**: Check it to display all the messages independently if they were marked as *Hide*.

- **Sort By**: Sort the list by Date or by a specific user.

The options displayed in the posts:

- **Edit**: Edit your comment. Only if you have permissions.

- **Private / Share**: To mark the message as private or allow it to be shown to the others.

- **Hide**: Mark the post as hidden.

- ✖ **Delete**: Delete the post. Only if you have permission.

■ **Note** Likes and Comments are only shown if they are enabled by a Portal Administrator.

The configuration parameters for the Message Board Task Flow are:

- **No of messages**: Maximum number of posts shown before the pagination is displayed.

- **Start Date**: For specifying (with End Date) a range of dates when the posts happened.

- **Hide Header**: Show / Hide the header of the component that includes the Hidden check box and the Filters.

- **Hide Publisher**: Hide the publisher making impossible to post new messages in this component.

- **Message Type**: (This option only applies in your own Message Board) What type of messages are displayed in the list (All, Public or Private).

- **User Name**: The owner message board user identifier. By default, it is the current authenticated user. If the Group Space parameter is contributed, then this parameter is ignored.

- **Group Space**: The Portal Name where Message Board is added. It is automatically populated. Please, do not touch this parameter.

- **End Date**: For specifying (with Start Date) a range of dates when the posts happened.

■ **Note** Do not touch User Name and Group Space as it will be automatically populated depending on where you added the Message Board Task Flow (Home Portal or a Custom Portal).

Message Board – Quick View Task Flow

The Message Board - Quick View Task Flow is a component very similar to the Message Board Task Flow (it does not include the filtering) (Figure 12-75).

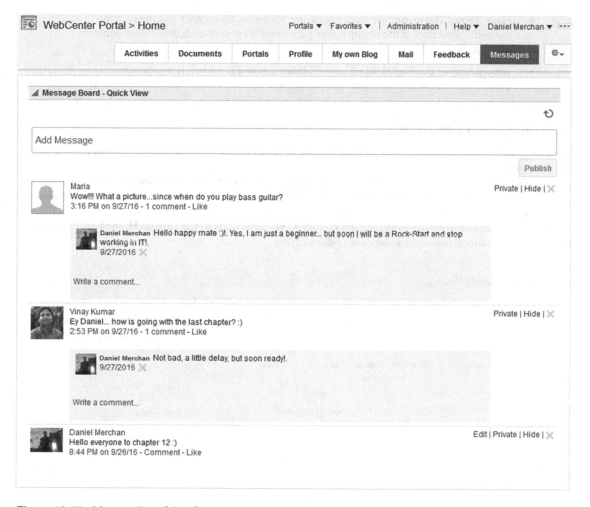

Figure 12-75. *Message Board Quick View Task Flow in Home Portal*

The configuration parameters for this Task Flow are:

- **No of messages**: Maximum number of posts shown before the pagination is displayed.

- **Hide Actions**: Hide the post options toolbar (Edit | Private | Hide).

- **Hide Footer**: It does not make any difference.

- **Hide Header**: Hides the refresh button shown in the header.

- **Hide Publisher**: Hides the publisher making it impossible to post new messages in this component.

- **Message Type**: (This option only applies in your own Message Board) What type of messages are displayed in the list (All, Public or Private).

- **User Name:** The owner message board user identifier. By default, it is the current authenticated user. If the Group Space parameter is contributed, then this parameter is ignored.

- **Group Space:** The Portal Name where Message Board is added. It is automatically populated. Please, do not touch this parameter.

Working with Feedback

The Feedback component enable the portal members to post feedback to other users. It is very similar to the Message Board.

For example, if you created a workshop for your colleagues then maybe you need to receive feedback about how it was. As a Portal Member, then you can create a Personal Page with the Feedback component and share it with your connections or portal users for posting Feedback about how it was.

Feedback Task Flow components are not included Out-of-the-box in the Default Home Portal Catalog. They must be included manually to be used (Figure 12-76).

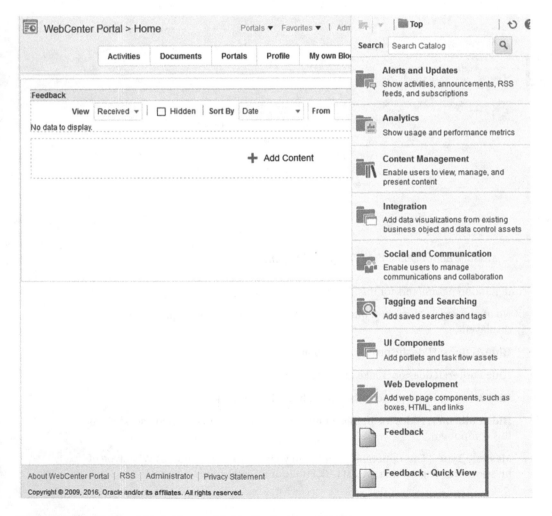

Figure 12-76. *Feedback Task Flows added to the Resource Catalog*

■ **Caution** If the feedback posts are being streamed to the Activity Stream, be aware that even those messages you *mark private* will still show up in the Activity Streams of your connections and the poster's connections.

When a Personal Page is created with the Feedback component then it can be shared by using the Send Mail feature in your Personal Page. Remember to give first permissions to the users for accessing and post in your personal page (Figure 12-77). The URL for access to your Feedback page will be:

```
http://host/webcenter/portal/profile/[username]/page/[PersonalPageName]
```

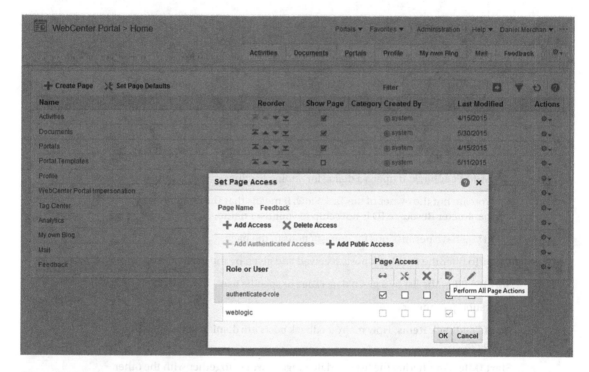

Figure 12-77. Security Settings for the Feedback Personal Page

■ **Caution** If the permission *Perform All Page Actions* is disabled, then the user will never see the Add Feedback button of the component.

Feedback Task Flow

The Feedback Task Flow allows you to show and filter the Feedback that we have given or received (Figure 12-78).

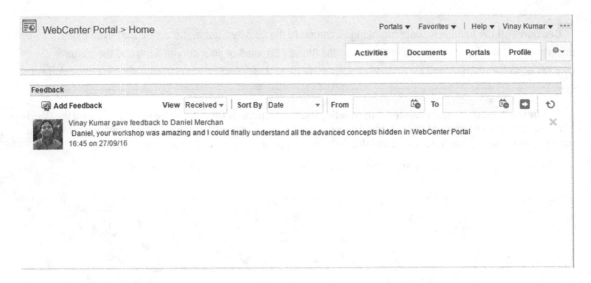

Figure 12-78. *Feedback Task Flow accessed by non-owner user*

The following options are displayed:

- **Add Feedback**: It opens a dialog for adding Feedback. This is only shown if:

    - You are not the owner of the Task Flow. It means that the configuration parameter Resource ID is not setup to your user name.

    - If you have permissions for doing actions in the page.

- **View**: To filter the Feedback posts received and given by the user.

- **Sort By**: Filter the list by a given date range or specific user.

The configuration parameters are:

- **No of Feedback Items**: How many feedback posts are displayed before being paginated.

- **Start Date**: For filtering the list in a date range. It works together with the other parameter *End Date*.

- **Hide Given**: To not allow display of given feedback.

- **Hide Header**: Hides the top toolbar.

- **Resource Id**: It must be set up to your user name. For example: #{securityContext. userName}

- **End Date**: For filtering the list in a date range. It works together with the other parameter *Start Date*.

Feedback Quick View Task Flow

This is a small version of the Feedback component removing filtering and more customizable for smaller window size (Figure 12-79).

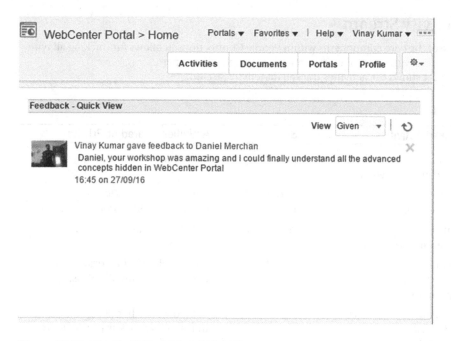

Figure 12-79. *Feedback Task Flow Quick View*

The configuration parameters are the following:

- **No of Feedback Items**: How many feedback posts are displayed before being paginated.

- **Display Message Size**: A number representing the size of the message to be displayed. A More link appears at the bottom of the message and when clicked can view the full message.

- **Start Date**: For filtering the list in a date range. It works together with the other parameter *End Date*.

- **Hide Actions**: Hide the Private | Hide options of the post.

- **Hide Footer**: To hide the footer of the Task Flow.

- **Hide Given**: Hides the option of displaying the given feedback.

- **Hide Header**: Hides the header (Filter and Refresh options).

- **End Date**: For filtering the list in a date range. It works together with the other parameter *Start Date*.

- **User Id**: The user id the Feedback component belongs to.

Working with Activity Stream

The Activity Stream is one of the core components within People Connections. It allows for tracking all type of activities that are happening with your contacts or portals of which you are part.

The following Table 12-4 shows the activities tracked in Activity Stream:

Table 12-4. Activities Tracked

Tool / Service	Tracked Activities	Scope	Activities Shared or Private
Announcement	New created announcements. Edited announcements.	Portal	Shared with the portal members.
Blogs	Create blog. Update blog.	Portal Home Portal	The activities in a Portal will be shared with other Portal Members.
Connections	Invitations. Invitations accepted.	Home Portal	It is shared with the inviter and the invitee's connections.
Discussions	Create a Forum. Create new topic. Reply to topic.	Portal	Shared with all the Portal Members where the Forum / Topic is.
Documents	When uploading a document via *Publisher Task Flow*. (Not Content Manager.)	Portal Home Portal	Shared with other Portal Members. In Home Portal, it is private to the user and his connections.
Feedback	Give feedback. Receive feedback.	Home Portal	Shared with the users that can access and view your activities.
Lists	Create a List.	Portal	Shared with portal members where the List is created.
Message Board	Post message. Receive message.	Home Portal	Shared with the users that can see your messages.
Pages	Create Page. Edit Page. Add Tag. Remove Tag.	Portal Home Portal	Activities happened within a Portal are shared to the Portal Members Activities in Home Portal are private to the user.
Profiles	Update photo. Update profile. Update personal status.	Home Portal	Shared with other users that have access to personal activities.
Portal Events	Create a new Event. Edit an Event.	Portal	Shared with other Portal Members.
Portals Management	Portal Activities like Create, Change membership role, join, update portal configuration etc, etc. In addition, any post comment and like to a portal asset.	Portal	Shared with other Portal Members.
Tagging	Add a Tag Remove a Tag	Portal Home Portal	In a portal, the activities are shared with Portal Members. In your Personal Home Portal only the users with permissions to see it.

As you can conclude from the above table, we need to differentiate between accessing to the Activity Stream via:

- **Home Portal or Profile Page (Activities Tab)**: Here will be displayed all the personal activities and activities of our connections or users with permissions.

- **Custom Portal**: Here the Activity Stream component is used for tracking all the activities within the scope of the portal. Something similar to a community of people or Facebook fan page.

■ **Tip**   Use Activity Stream for tracking activities and sharing documents and links with your contacts or other portal members. If you just need to post a message, consider using Message Board instead.

Activity Stream Task Flow

Let's have an overview over what options offer the Activity Stream Task Flow (Figure 12-80):

- **Publisher**: The *Publisher Task Flow* in the top allows you to share a message with a File or Link attached.

- **Recent Activities Posts**: For each post there are the following options:

  - **Comment**: Comment on the current activity.

  - **Like**: Like the current activity.

  - **Share**: Share the activity (like retweet in Twitter) or send it via email.

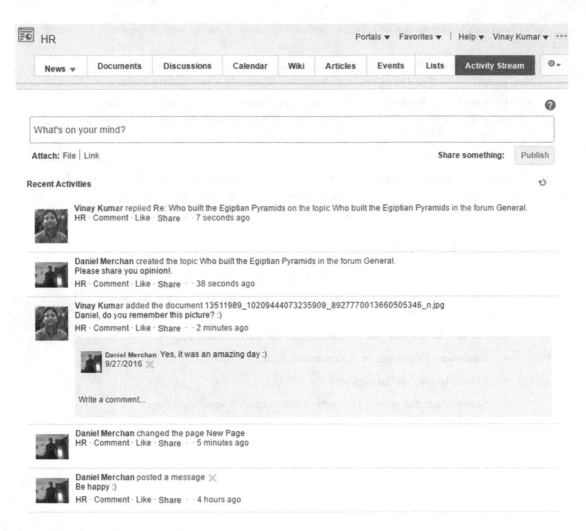

Figure 12-80. *Activity Stream Task Flow*

Depending of the configuration parameters, it can be also the following options:

- **Date Range**: For filtering the list of activities.

- **Options**: For personalizing the activities displayed. Remember that it depends on the global configuration of Activity Stream as we mentioned in the settings section.

Configuration parameters for the Activity Stream Task Flow:

- **Advanced Query**: Allow to set up a complex query for displaying exact type of portal activities. This is a complex task that may require the help of a developer. For example, OD.OBJECT_TYPE = \'wiki\' AND AD.ACTOR_NAME = \'#{securityContext. userName}\' will display only the wikis of the current logged user.

- **Enable Context Info**: To enable / disable see the activities in a context info pop-up when clicking them.

- **Hide Comments**: To hide the comments section of the posts.

- **Hide Configuration Button**: Hide the options button. Users cannot override the activities displayed in this component.

- **Hide Inline Preview**: To hide preview of streamed files.

- **Hide Like**: Hide the like functionality.

- **Hide Share**: Hide the share option for sharing the portal activity.

- **Hide Portals Options**: The Portals option allow users to switch to see the activities from all portals, current portal or just personal.

- **No of activities to display per page**: Number of activities displayed in the list before the pagination is displayed.

- **Pagination**: Enable / Disable pagination.

- **Profile Only**: Enable for displaying only the current user activities.

- **Resource Id**: User ID. Do not change this as it is default configured for the current logged user.

- **Service Categories**: List of Portal Services to be displayed. Portal Services has associated a Service ID. Look into Oracle Documentation for knowing the exact names for setting up this parameter. For example, oracle.webcenter.doclib is the document service.

- **Portals**: Enter the Portal Names / Portal GUIDs to be streamed within this Activity Stream. If blank it takes the current portal.

Activity Stream Quick View Task Flow

The Activity Stream Quick View is a small version of the Activity Stream Task Flow.
For example, it is used in the Profile – Gallery (Figure 12-81).

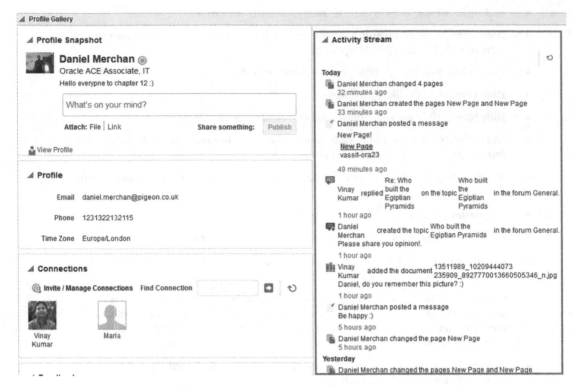

Figure 12-81. *Activity Stream Quick View Task Flow*

The configuration parameters are very similar to the commented ones in the Activity Stream Task Flow.

Notes

Notes is a mechanism that users can use for creating personal reminders.

You may have already noticed, but when we were talking about the Links Service, one of the possibilities is to link a portal activity to a personal Note.

By default, the Notes Task Flow for viewing and managing the notes is not available in the *Default Resource Catalog*. It must be added manually to the Catalog (Figure 12-82).

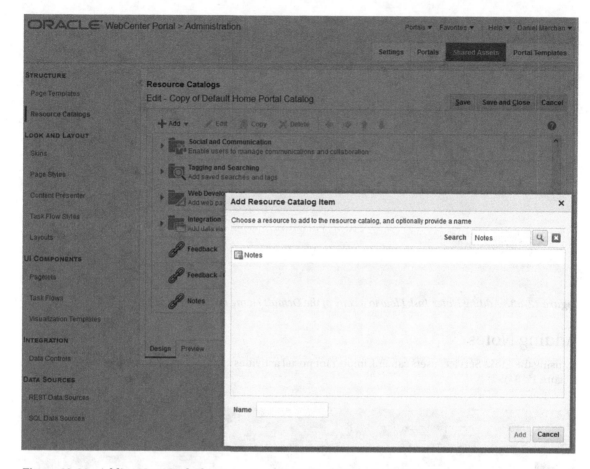

Figure 12-82. *Adding Notes Task Flow to a copy of the Default Home Portal Catalogg*

■ **Tip** Notes are personal. It makes sense to enable them in the Home Portal by a Business Role Page. It can be also added to a Portal if needed.

Notes Task Flow

The Notes Task Flow is a simple component that shows a list with all the Notes that you have created (Figure 12-83). The following options are available:

- ● **Add new Note**: It enable the Add Mode of the Notes Task Flow. For each note you can fill:

  - **Title:** Title of the note:

  - **Detail:** Short description about the reminder.

- ![filter icon] **Filter**: It allows you to filter the list of notes by a given text.

- ![delete icon] **Delete**: Delete the current Note.

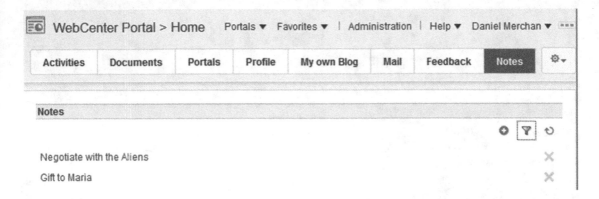

Figure 12-83. *Adding Notes Task Flow to a copy of the Default Home Portal Catalog*

Adding Notes

By using the Links Service, users can link important portal activities such as Discussions to personal Notes (Figure 12-84).

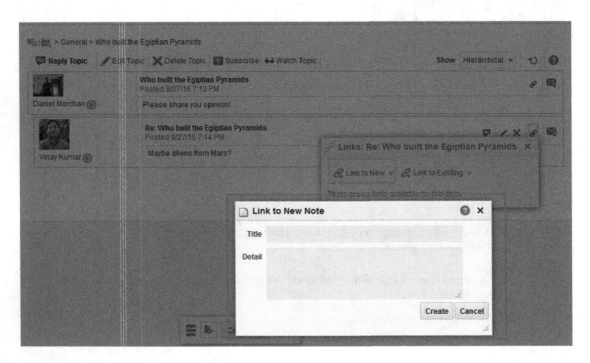

Figure 12-84. *Linking to a Note*

Notifications

Some of the WebCenter Portal Activities can trigger notifications. Users can subscribe to these portal activities in order to be notified when a change has been produced.

The following Table 12-5 displays the possible portal services that can trigger a notification:

Table 12-5. *Activities Tracked*

Tool / Service	Tracked Activities	Level	Where to Subscribe
Connections	When a user sends you an invitation.	Application	User Preferences
Portal Management	When any of your Portal Role changes.	Application	User Preferences
Portal Management	When you are added to a portal as a member.	Application	User Preferences
Portal Management	When your portal membership is removed.	Application	User Preferences
Message Board	User posts a message in your message board. Not by Publisher in Activity Stream.	Application	User Preferences
Message Board	When someone like your message. Receive feedback.	Application	User Preferences
Feedback	When a user posts feedback of you.	Application	User Preferences
Announcement	A new Announcement is created.	Portal	Setup in Portal Subscription Level
Event	When a new Event is created.	Portal	Setup in Portal Subscription Level
Event	When an Event is updated.	Portal	Setup in Portal Subscription Level
Event	When an Event is deleted.	Portal	Setup in Portal Subscription Level
Discussion	A new topic is created in a forum.	Portal	Setup in Portal Subscription Level
Discussion	A new forum is created.	Portal	Setup in Portal Subscription Level
Discussion	User replies to a topic.	Object	A user must subscribe manually to the Topic
Discussion	User comments on a discussion topic.	Object	A user must subscribe manually to the Topic
Discussion	User deletes a discussion topic.	Object	A user must subscribe manually to the Topic

369

■ **Note**   As commented on in Chapter 11, in the 12c version all the Content Management has been moved into Content Manager Task Flow. The Subscriptions and Notifications from documents will come back in future patches and releases of 12c.

About Channels of Notification

As mentioned on the Mail Service topic, WebCenter Portal can be configured for working with a mail server. In addition, WebCenter Portal can be connected with Oracle SOA - BPEL for enabling a multichannel notification via email + sms.

Depending on which one is configured, it will be one of these channels.

- **Mail Server**: For just Email notification.

- **BPEL Connection**: For Email + SMS notification by using SOA - UMS (Unified Message Service). Requires SOA Server.

Application Level – Subscriptions

A user can Subscribe to the application level notifications by:

- Their User Preferences ➤ Subscriptions option (Figure 12-85).

- Adding the Subscription Preferences Task Flow in the Home Portal. This Task Flow is not included by default in the Default Home Portal Catalog. It must be added manually.

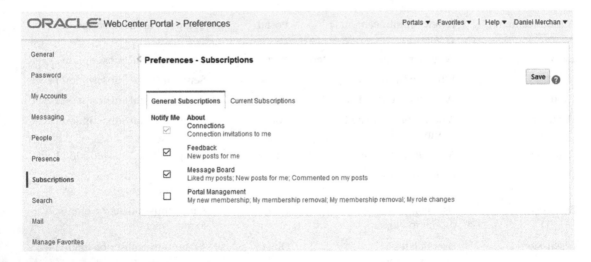

Figure 12-85. *Subcriptions Preferences in Application – Level*

Portal Level – Subscriptions

The portal members can subscribe to the portal service such Discussions, Events etc., by using one of the following approaches:

- In WebCenter Portals List, click ⟳ for displaying the Portal Options. Within the options, click ✉ to access to Contacts options. Here can be found the Subscription properties for that specific Portal (Figure 12-86).

- By adding the Subscription Preferences Task Flow inside of a Portal Page.

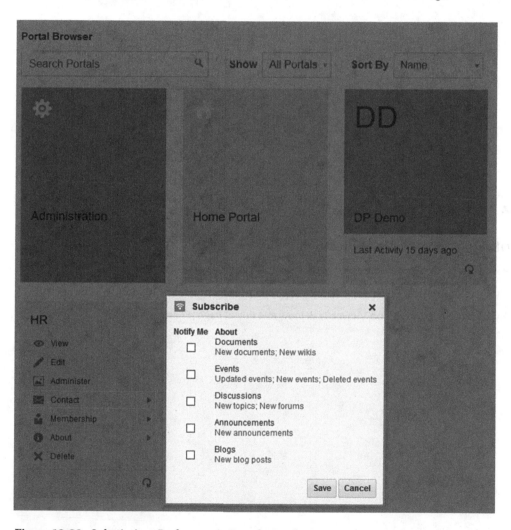

Figure 12-86. *Subcriptions Preferences in Portal – Level*

Object Level – Subscriptions

The object level subscriptions are done by accessing the specific Portal Service component, and then using

the Subscription option displayed ( ). For example, the topics of the discussions displays this option to allow users to track the current topic (Figure 12-87).

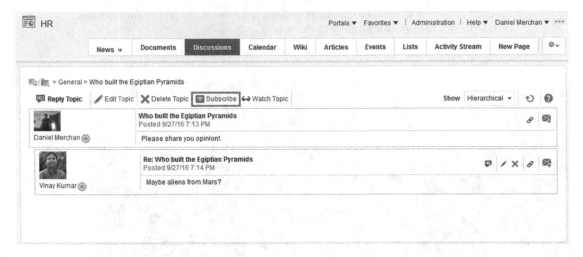

Figure 12-87. *Discussions Task Flow – Topic Subscribe*

Subscriptions Viewer Task Flow

WebCenter Portal offers two ways for checking and managing the current subscriptions:

- By accessing to User Preferences ➤ Subscriptions ➤ Current Subscriptions.
- By adding the Subscription Viewer Task Flow to a Portal Page (Figure 12-88).

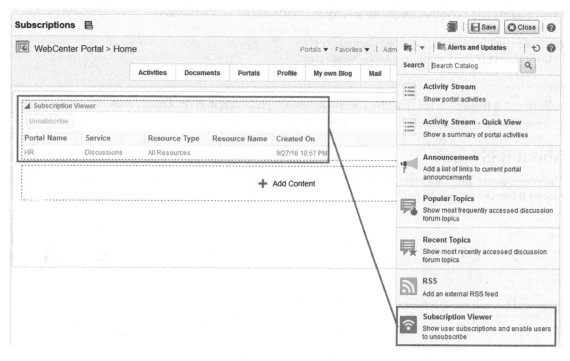

Figure 12-88. *Adding Subscriptions Viewer to Home Portal Personal Page*

This component is simple and allows you to check and unsubscribe from any current subscription.

RSS

WebCenter Portal offers tools for reading RSS feeds and generating RSS (Really Simple Syndication) from some portal services. The three tools offered are:

- **RSS Icon**: An RSS icon is displayed in Announcements, Discussions, and Lists service. It allows you to get the RSS feeds (URL) for that specific service.

- **RSS Manager**: For a quick view of all the RSS that you have access to (depending on the Portals you are part of).

- **RSS Task Flow**: It is used as a Viewer of RSS.

Enable RSS

The RSS Task Flow can be used without any extra configuration. However, if you want to work with the RSS functionalities exposed by the Portal Components then you need to set up a WebCenter Proxy.

A System Administrator can set up a WebCenter Proxy by executing the following WLST Script:

```
setWebCenterProxyConfig(appName='webcenter', proxyHost='www-proxy.example.com',
proxyPort='80')
```

There are also two other scripts for managing WebCenter Proxy connections:

```
getWebCenterProxyConfig(appName='webcenter')
unsetWebCenterProxyConfig(appName='webcenter')
```

■ **Note**   It is required to set up a Proxy Server for enabling RSS Icon in Portal Components.

About RSS Icon

The components: Announcements, Discussions, and Lists allows you to get the content displayed in RSS and Atom 1.0 formats (Figure 12-89).

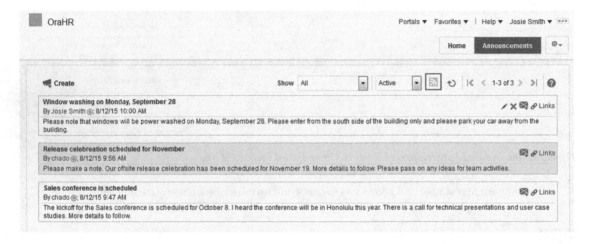

Figure 12-89. *RSS Icon shown in Discussions Forum Task Flow*

You can Drag and Drop the RSS Icon to your favorite RSS Reader. By default, the RSS Icon generates a **RSS 2.0** feed list. If you need it in **Atom 1.0** version, then you can just append to the URL **&format=ATOM1.0**

■ **Caution**   If there is not WebCenter Proxy configured then the RSS Icon will not appear.

RSS Manager

The RSS Manager allows Portal Members to access quickly to all the available RSS Portals they are part of (Figure 12-90).

Figure 12-90. *RSS Manager*

The RSS Manager can be accessed only if the RSS Link is present in the Page Template (Figure 12-91).

Figure 12-91. *RSS Manager Link*

The RSS Link can be added to the Page Template by adding the following snippet of code:

```
<wcdc:spacesAction id="wcRssLink" shortDesc="#{uib_o_w_w_r_WebCenter.GLOBAL_LINK_RSS_DESC}"
text="#{uib_o_w_w_r_WebCenter.GLOBAL_LINK_RSS}" type="rss"/>
```

RSS Task Flow

The RSS Task Flow can be added to any WebCenter Portal Page and configured to consume any RSS 2.0 and Atom 1.0 format RSS feeds (Figure 12-92).

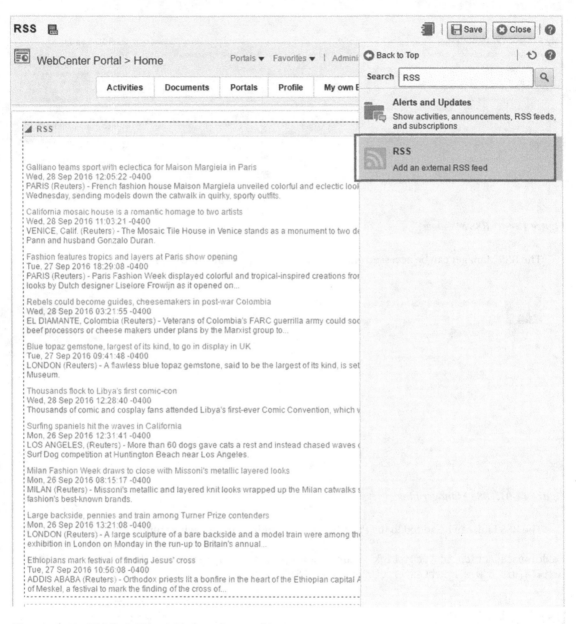

Figure 12-92. *RSS Task Flow Added to a Personal Page*

The configuration parameters of the RSS Task Flow are:

- **External Application ID**: If the RSS requires authentication then it needs to be associated to an External Application.

- **RSS Feed URL**: Enter the RSS URL.

Search

Search services enable the portal members to search for information globally in Oracle WebCenter Portal and in multiple Portals at once.

The Search Services have been changing along the time. The following diagram describes the WebCenter Portal Search Services available (Figure 12-93):

- **Search Live Adapters**: This engine has been deprecated in this version. In addition, Oracle does not offer the steps for enabling it. Live Adapters where a search engine consuming the APIs of the Portal Services for searching information on them.

- **Oracle SES (Secured Enterprise Search)**: SES is the Oracle crawling engine solution that can be integrated with WebCenter Portal.

- **Elastic Search**: In nearly future releases of 12c, Oracle WebCenter Portal will be integrated with Elastic Search for being the core search engine.

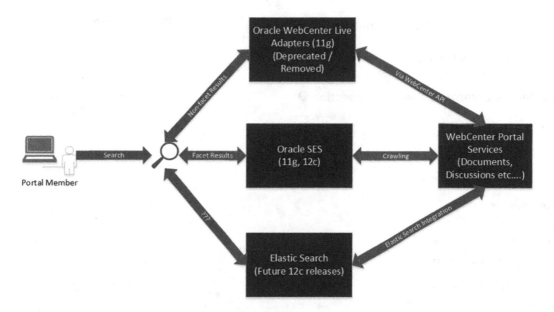

Figure 12-93. Legacy, Present, and Future Search Engines

■ **Note**   In 12.2.1 and 12.2.1.1 versions the only option is Oracle SES. Oracle does not document how to enable Live Adapter in these versions.

Elastic Search will replace and deprecate Oracle SES in future releases of 12c.

About Oracle SES Integration

This book does not cover the Oracle SES installation and how to configure it for crawling the WebCenter Portal Services. To learn about Oracle SES Installation and configuration, refer to official Oracle Documentation.

Once Oracle SES is available and configured, a connection must be configured via Enterprise Manager or WLST (WebLogic Scripting Tools) (Figure 12-94):

Name

- **Connection Name**: Unique connection name for this connection.

- **Active Connection**: Check to use this connection as the default one.

Connection Details

- **SOAP URL**: The base Web Service URL exposed by Oracle SES (usually http://host:port/search/query/OracleSearch).

- **Federated Trusted Entity Name**: Enter the name that you have used when configuring the Federated Trusted entity of Oracle SES.

- **Federation Trusted Entity Password**: Password of the Federated Trusted Entity.

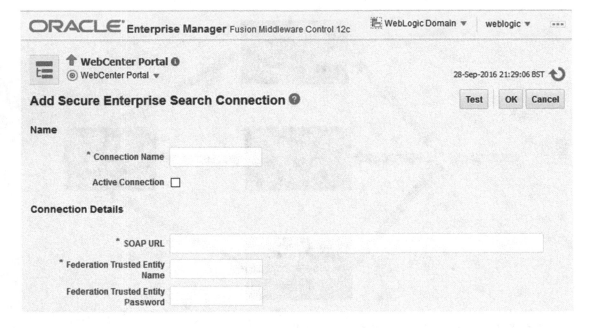

Figure 12-94. *Legacy, Present, and Future Search Engines*

Search Global Settings

As a Portal Administrator, via Administration ➤ Tool and Services there are the following options (Figure 12-95):

- **Use new search task flow with facet support**: It enables to use the Search - Facet Task Flow (Figure 12-96) instead of the old Search - Non-Facet Task Flow.

- **Enable filtering drop-down**: It displays a drop-down for filtering the result over the specific portal services.

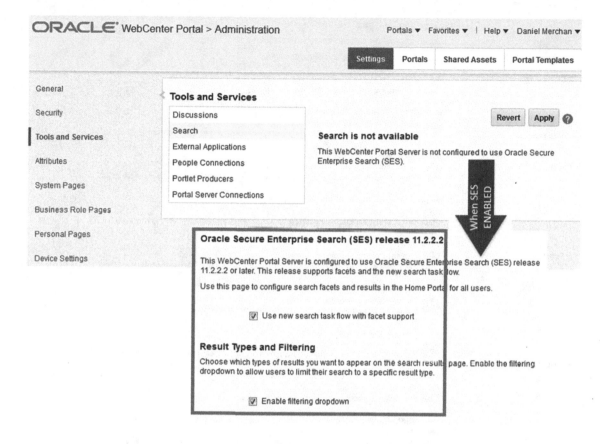

Figure 12-95. *Non SES vs. SES available in Portal Administration Configuration*

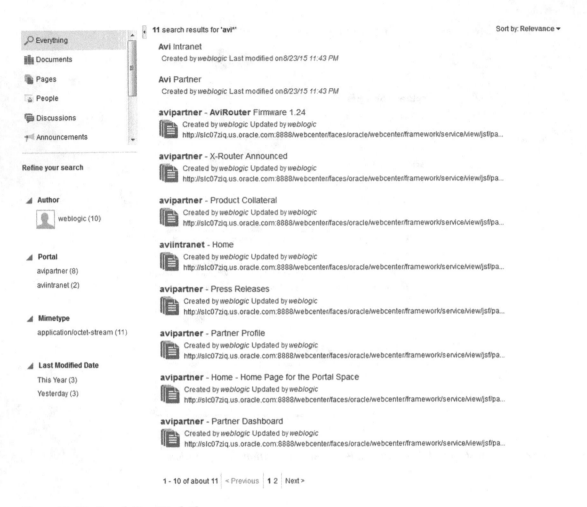

Figure 12-96. *Search Facet Task Flow*

About Search Task Flow and Search Toolbar

The Search Toolbar Task Flow is added Out-of-the-box in the default Oracle WebCenter Portal Templates.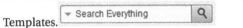

It displays an input text for searching in all WebCenter Portal. In case of *Enable filtering drop-down* then it allows you to also check the filters to be applied before navigating the Search Results Page.

How to know that the Toolbar Search is included? Take a look into the code, and you will find the following snippet:

Page:

```
<af:region id="searchbox" value="#{bindings.localToolbarSearch.regionModel}"/>
```

PageDef:

```
<taskFlow activation="deferred" id="localToolbarSearch" taskFlowId="/oracle/webcenter/
search/controller/taskflows/localToolbarSearch#search-toolbar" xmlns="http://xmlns.oracle.
com/adf/controller/binding">
        <parameters>
            <parameter id="scope" value="#{null}" xmlns="http://xmlns.oracle.com/adfm/
            uimodel"/>
            <parameter id="searchBoxSize" value="20" xmlns="http://xmlns.oracle.com/adfm/
            uimodel"/>
        </parameters>
    </taskFlow>
```

This Task Flow navigates automatically to the System Page – Search. This page displays the Non-Facet or Facet Search Task Flow results depending on the administration settings commented on before. The Task Flow has three parts:

- **Facets** section for filtering the results depending on the portal service they are coming from.

- **Refiners** section for filtering by Author, Portal, Last Modification, and other advanced refiners.

- **Results List**: Single mixed list with the results ordered by relevance.

■ **Note**   Remember from Chapter 11, the Content Manager Task Flow also provides advanced search capabilities for searching documents and files in the content repository.

Tags

WebCenter Portal offers another service for Tagging WebCenter Portal Pages for linking and relating them by similar keywords.

This service does not require extra configuration and is enabled Out-of-the-box in WebCenter Portal.

Tagging a Page

WebCenter Portal pages can be tagged by using the **Tag Icon** . This component must be added by Portal Developers in the Page Template used by the Portal.

The Tag Icon can be added by adding the following snippet into the Page Template / Page Template: Include the following namespace:

```
xmlns:tag=http://xmlns.oracle.com/webcenter/services/tagging
```

Add the following taglib:

```
<tag:taggingButton resourceId="#{facesContext.viewRoot.viewId}" resourceName="#{pageDocBean.
title}" serviceId="oracle.webcenter.page" id="pt_tb1"/>
```

This Tag Icon opens a dialog where multiple tags can be added to a single page (Figure 12-97):

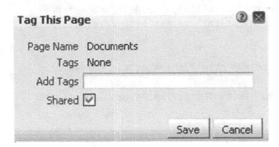

Figure 12-97. *Tagging Dialog*

About Tagging View Task Flows

There are multiple Task Flows for displaying Tags:

- **Similarly, Tagged Items Task Flow**: Displays other pages or documents that have at least one tag in common with the current page. This is very useful for navigating quickly to other related pages.

- **Tag Cloud Related Resources**: Displays the tagged items for a selected tag.

- **Tag Cloud**: Displays a cloud of tags with all the tags created by the users. In case of clicking a tag, it then opens the Tag Cloud Related Resources Task Flow with the tag selected by default (Figure 12-98).

Figure 12-98. *Tag Cloud Task Flow*

- **Tags**: Displays the tags created by the current user. By clicking a specific tag, it will open the Tag Center.

- **Tag Center**: This Task Flow can be accessed from the Home Portal within the Settings ➤ Manage ➤ Tags. It is the main tagging area where a user can search, filter, and manage any tag that he has created or has been created by other users (Figure 12-99).

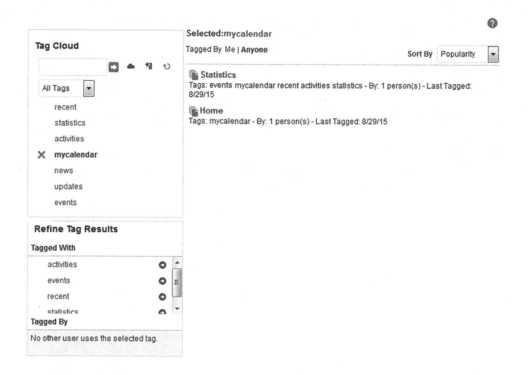

Figure 12-99. *Tag Center Task Flow*

■ **Caution**   WebCenter Tagging Service can be limited and unfriendly for portal members. We recommend that you build your own Add Tag and Tag Cloud Task Flows for enhancing the user experience. For example, add a black list of words that cannot be used as tags.

CHAPTER 13

■ ■ ■

Extending WebCenter Portal

Overview

In all of the other chapters, there have been explanations about contents of WebCenter Portal and development with this framework. This chapter explains extensions with WebCenter Portal. We will talk about WebCenter Portal REST APIs, WebCenter Portal Java APIs, integration with other technologies, and some real-life use cases.

Oracle stack is very wide. While working on big projects, information of different Oracle products in WebCenter Portal is required. Enterprise portal has common challenges with integrating multiple applications. Integration using web services and making new User interfaces while using web services are always valid options. But also consider the costs, development efforts, and time lines. Oracle WebCenter Portal is also used to integrate third-party applications.

In some cases, creating a composite application is a much more viable solution than building a new one or customizing an existing one. For example, integration with E-Business Suite, Siebel, and OBIEE helps to make composite applications.

Integration with OBIEE12c

OBIEE is a great tool for making reports, dashboards, and pages for better a reporting experience. WebCenter Portal leverages BI ADF Integration components. It is part of the ADF stack. Business Intelligence Presentation Service libraries are available on the WebCenter domain by default. Connect between OBIEE and WebCenter Portal/ADF applications using ADF Connection with interface as ***BISoapConnection*** type (HTTP or HTTPS).

Security is always an important factor to consider. It is good to have WebCenter Portal and OBIEE in one WebLogic domain.

Following are some steps to make the integration:

- Create the BIImpersonateUser in the security realm using WebLogic console and Grant Permissions in FMW Control Enterprise Manager.

- Create a SOAP Connection to the BI Server.

- Add the **OBIEE Web Catalog** to the WebCenter Portal Resource Catalog.

- Edit Resource Catalog and On the Add Resource Catalog Item dialog select Connections and then expand **BI Presentation Services** node.

© Vinay Kumar and Daniel Merchán García 2017
V. Kumar and D. M. García, *Beginning Oracle WebCenter Portal 12c*, DOI 10.1007/978-1-4842-2532-5_13

- Under **BI Presentation Services** select the node that has a name that of BI Presentation Service SOAP Connection that was created in Enterprise Manager.

- Add OBIEE objects to WebCenter Portal pages from OBIEE Web Catalog.

■ **Note** The same identity store should be configured to use in OBIEE and WebCenter. If a different identity store is used, then user name should match in both identity stores.

After making a SOAP connection, OBIEE web catalog can be added to WebCenter Page. In the portal page by clicking add content button desired, OBIEE catalog objects can be added in the page.

When BI Content from the Catalog dropped on the page. It is added via the `<adfbi:content>` element:

```
<adfbi:content if="myBIReport" value="#{bindings.biContent}"/>
```

Parameter promptfilterxml allows you to specify prompt values to drill the report. The *biContent* element accepts the *setParameters* contextual event that can be used to pass context from a custom task flow, for example:

```
<event name="setParameters">
<producer region="biparametertaskflow1.parameterFormPageDef.eventBinding">
<consumer handler="biExecBinding1">
<parameters>
<parameter name='Project."Project Name"' value="#{payLoad}"/>
</parameters>
</consumer>
</producer>
</event>
```

OBIEE Integration Best Practices

- BI dashboards typically require a large amount of content on the page. On the ADF/ WebCenter Portal page, the dashboard is rendered in iFrame, which often results in the scrollbars being displayed. To avoid scrollbars you can either work with a BI analyst to change the layout, or use separate reports and link via custom task flows.

- If possible, the author of the BI component should not include the 'Analyze' link because it launches you into the BI Answers interface for slicing and dicing. The problem with this is that when coming from WC, the BIEE chrome is stripped out and you are stranded there.

Integration with Oracle E-Business Suite

E-Business Suite is set of enterprise ERPs (enterprise resource planning), that is, supply change management, financial erp ,and CRM (customer relationship management), etc., developed by Oracle. This is widely used in multiple organizations globally.

Integration with EBS and WebCenter Portal is a common use case. These are ways of integration. Also see Figure 13-1.

- R12 Portlet Generator.

- EBS Integrated SOA Gateway.

- EBS integration using WebCenter Portal Pagelet Producer.

- EBS SDK for Java.

- EBS Integration using Web Services.

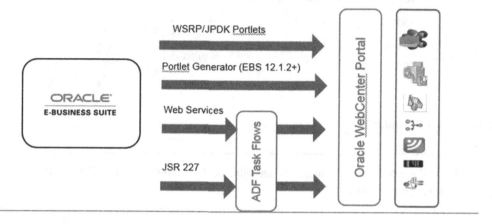

Figure 13-1. *EBS Integration with WebCenter Portal*

Following now are brief explanations for the above-mentioned ways:

R12 Portlet Generator

In EBS release 12, JSR-168/WSRP 1.0-compatible portlets are these:

- **Applications Navigator**: This shows EBS menus based on a user's assigned responsibilities.

- **Applications Worklist**: This shows Oracle Workflow Notifications.

- **Applications Favorites**: This allows users to bookmark menu items for frequently used EBS functions. See Figure 13-2.

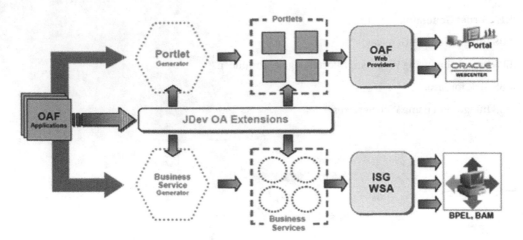

Figure 13-2. *EBS Portlet Generator*

■ **Note**   Oracle WebCenter and Oracle EBS should use the same SSO, for example, Oracle Single Sign-On (OSSO)and Oracle Access Manager (OAM).

The Portlet Generator converts existing stand-alone Oracle Application Framework regions into portlets. It does not require parameters and may be accessed via the EBS Navigator.It does not support all OA Framework regions. It uses the materialized user interface of **FWK_PORTLET_GEN_MV** to verify those regions that can be portletized.

Once a Portlet is available in WebCenter Portal, users can go in a WebCenter Composer, Application Portlets ➤ E-Business Suite WsRP producer ➤ and find the Out-of-the-box portlets that are provided by EBS.

Once a Portlet is available in WebCenter Portal, users can go in a WebCenter Composer, Application Portlets ➤ E-Business Suite WsRP producer ➤ and find the Out-of-the-box portlets that are provided by EBS. See Figure 13-3.

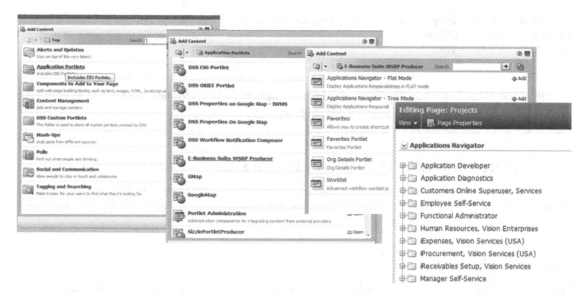

Figure 13-3. *EBS Portlet in Portal Catalog*

EBS Integrated SOA Gateway (ISG)

This enables the service-oriented architecture (SOA) for Oracle EBS. This is an essential part of Oracle E-Business. It provides service-oriented architecture with exposing Out-of-the-box Web services from Oracle E-Business Suite for consumption by standard web service clients. Later these web services can be consumed using SOA in WebCenter Portal. Integration Repository allows you to generate and deploy services for certain interfaces type with a click of a button (Figure 13-4).

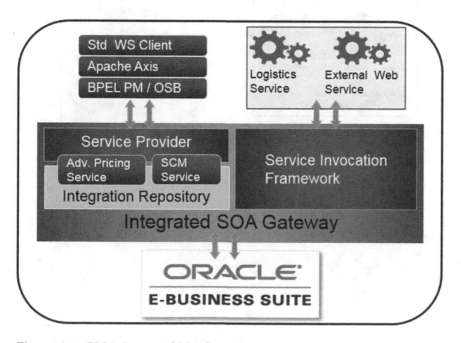

Figure 13-4. *EBS in Integrated SOA Gateway*

389

Integration Repository is a kind of Service Registry. It is a registry for EBS and external WS clients where business users/SOA Analysts can visit the Integration Repo. and identify the Business Objects to be published as a web service.

■ **Note**   Integration Repository: This is an Out-of-the-box catalog that contains more than 1,500 services and integration points of Oracle EBS. It's a central location of all public interfaces.

EBS Integration Using WebCenter Portal Pagelet Producer

Oracle E-Business Suite user interface can be exposed as a pagelet in WebCenter Portal. Pagelet Producer is described in Chapter 9 in more detail. SSO integration can be managed using Pagelet Producer. It operates on HTTP, HTML, and JavaScript layer.

EBS SDK for Java

Using EBS SDK, new applications can be built on EBS sources with any Java EE including ADF task flows and deploys on server. It uses E-Business security via Java Authentication and Authorization Service (**JAAS**). It uses standard AppsDataSource to access the EBS database. And it uses **AppsDataSource** and **AppsXADataSource**. This SDK provides EBS users and responsibilities and manages EBS sessions as well. It also provides error logging, internationalization, and message dictionary APIs. SDK also provides navigation within EBS. Developed ADF task flows can be deployed as shared libraries in the WebCenter Portal.

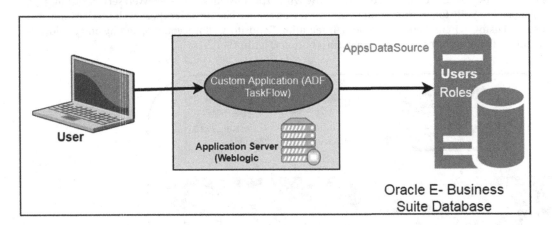

Figure 13-5. *EBS SDK Java Application Architecture*

EBS Integration Using Web Services

Oracle E-Business Integration can also be integrated using standard web services. This can be done by either using SOA gateway or directly accessing web services.

Following are different ways to use web services:

- Web Service Data Control.

- JAX-WS proxy client and POJO Data Control.

- JAX-WS proxy client and programmatic View Objects.

Oracle Web Service Manager (WSM) provides a policy framework to manage and secure Web Services. WSDL can be generated easily by clicking a button from **Integration Repository**. That WSDL can be used to build Web Service Data Control in WebCenter Portal Console (Figure 13-6).

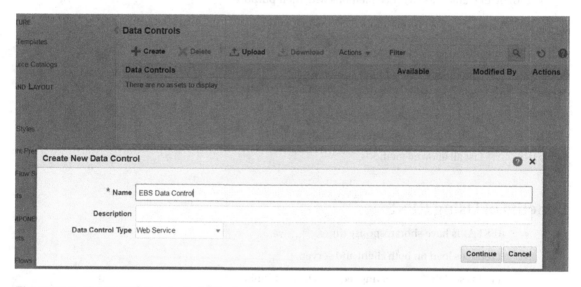

Figure 13-6. *Create Web Service Data Control*

WSDL URL can be provided in **Create New Data Control** Wizard and following information and click save. Later this data control can be used to add content of EBS in the portal page.

EBS Integration Best Practice

- Never use the JAX-WS generated proxy client directly. Always access it through a wrapper bean to avoid code loss problems in cases where the proxy client needs to be regenerated.

- Use the Oracle EBS SDK if the integration requires access to the EBS Tables.

- Use Oracle SOA Suite and Adapter for Oracle Applications if the integration requires services orchestration or control of what data sets are being exposed.

WebCenter Portal REST APIs

REST APIs are an architectural style for native applications to access web services directly using HTTP request. REST stands for Representational State Transfer. REST commands use standard HTTP methods for requests. Every request returns a response with the status of operation.

There are four methods used in REST regarding information:

- GET – method used for retrieving.

- POST – method for creating

- PUT – method for updating

- DELETE – method for removing

The following table lists all HTTP methods with their purpose

Method	Purpose
GET	Used to read. Possibly cached.
POST	Update or create without known ID.
PUT	Update or create with known ID.
DELETE	Used to remove specified resource.
HEAD	Read header, check version changed.
OPTIONS	List all allowed methods.

Benefits of Using REST

- REST APIs have short response times.

- It reduces load on both client and server.

- It helps scalability by serving requests to any number of servers.

- It has various clients interact with the server, without requiring specialized libraries.

- Includes the REST APIs in any development technology.

- Such as JavaScript code.

- Access web services without a WSDL.

- REST API are good for using in mobile and cloud solutions.

In WebCenter, the Resource Index is a starting point for all authenticated access. It provides access to the set of top-level URL entry points. It provides a gateway to all available WebCenter Portal RESTful services. The Resource Index URL is the only URL that you need to know for all your REST API activities.

The URL for WebCenter's Resource Index is:

`http://host:port/rest/api/v1/resourceIndex`

If you hit the above URL in a browser, a pop-up dialog named **Authentication Required** will come on the screen. Provide the web center credentials. See Figure 13-7.

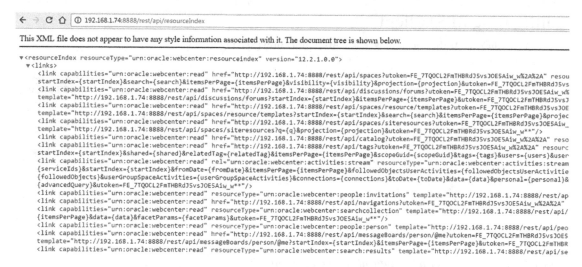

Figure 13-7. *WebCenter Portal Resource Index*

WebCenter Portal tool and services also supports REST APIs. Following is list of those API:

Discussion – It empowers client to read, update, delete, discussion forums, topics, and messages.

Lists – It empowers client to see lists for specific portal .Create, delete, and update lists.

People Connections – It empowers client to manage connection lists, message, and view profile information, etc.

WebCenter Portal – With the API, client can view, update, delete, and create portal list items. It can also bring up portal metadata. Also, a portal member's information can also be seen using this.

Content Management – Using this API, client can have access to the CM VCR (Content Management Virtual Content Repository).

Events - Using this API, calendar events specific to portal can be accessed.

Search - Using API, client can read, update, post searches. Search can be done on basis of keywords.

Tags - Using this API, client can read, update, post, and delete tags and tagged items.

Navigation - Using this API, client can create own interface for displaying navigations.

Feedback- Using this API, client can read, delete, and create feedback in applications.

Read more about these APIs in more detail in Oracle documentations.

For testing these APIs, add Firefox extension in browser named as **RESTCLIENT.** After installing this extension in Firefox, an additional red icon will be added on the top right. See Figure 13-8.

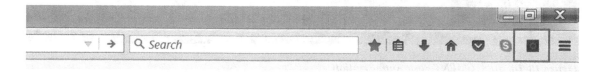

Figure 13–8. *RESTCLIENT Firefox extension*

Open this extension by clicking the red icon.

Configuring RESTClient

1. Clicking Authentication ➤ Basic Authentication (See Figure 13-9).

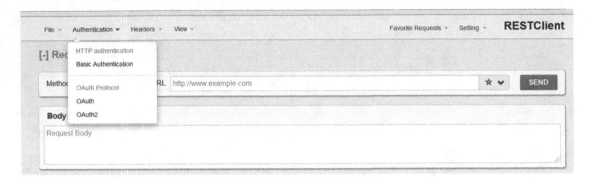

Figure 13-9. *RESTCLIENT Basic Authentication (See Figure 13-10).*

2. Provide username and password for user to access WebCenter API. OAuth and OAuth2 type security can also be configured here.

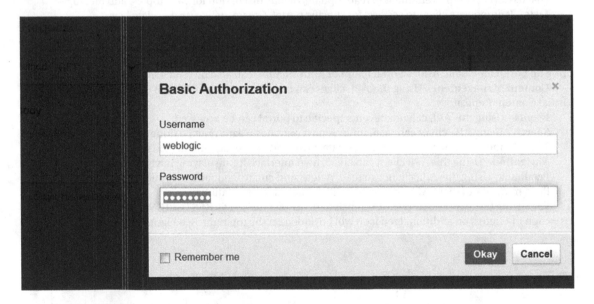

Figure 13-10. *RESTCLIENT Basic Authorization*

3. Click on Headers ➤ Custom Header to configure header setting.

4. Add value of Header as Accept and value as **application/json** and click okay. See Figure 13-11.

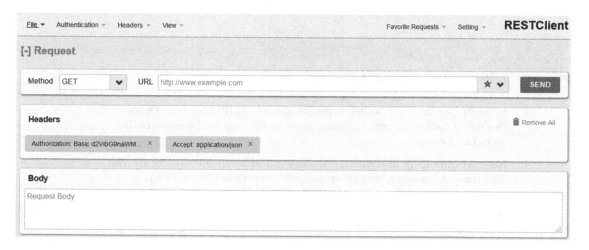

Figure 13-11. RESTCLIENT Request Header

5.   Now RESTCLIENT screen will as Figure 13-12.

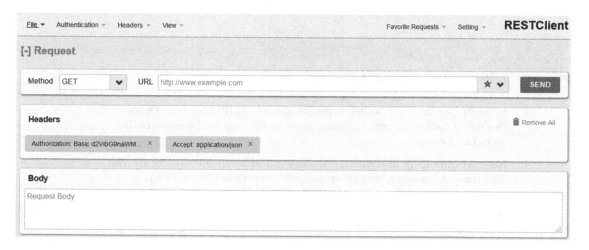

Figure 13-12. RESTCLIENT Header

6.   Provide the Portal **resourceIndex** URL in the URL section of the REST client. Select the GET method and then click SEND.

7.   In the Response section, find the Status Code in the Response Header tab. Confirm that it is 200 OK. It means the authentication is working and the API is accessible (Figure 13-13).

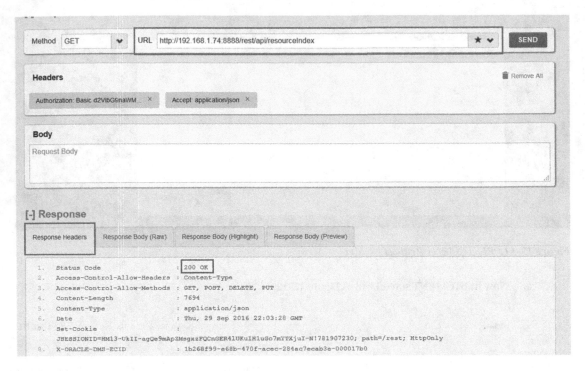

Figure 13-13. RESTCLIENT Request and Response

8. In the Response section, switch to the Response Body (Preview) tab. Observe that it is in the form of json. This page gives the list of all available sources for WebCenter Portal.

9. Note in Figure 13-14 all available resources and what capabilties there are with GET request. For space, read access capabilties are there (Figure 13-14).

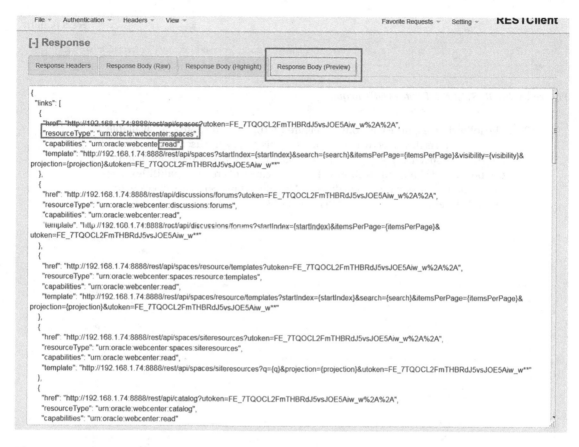

Figure 13-14. *RESTCLIENT Get request Response*

10. For each resource, the Resource Index returns:

   - Resource type URN

   - Resource access point URL

   - Template URL to pass parameters to the resource

   - Capabilities (read, delete, and etc.)

11. If href value of resourceType spaces copied with utoken and send another request using **GET.**URL is as following

   ```
   http://192.168.1.74:8888/rest/api/spaces?utoken=FE_7TQOCL2FmTHBRdJ5v
   sJOE5Aiw_w%2A%2A
   ```

12. Copy above-mentioned URL and send another GET request.

Figure 13-15. *RESTCLIENT Spaces GET Request*

13. The following response will come as Figure 13-16. In the response, all available resourceType is displayed with capabilities. This means the user can get information specific space (portal). New member in space named Documents can be created similar to attributes of space because of create **capabilities**. RESTClient extension is good to dig into API into details. Similarly check with other WebCenter Portal Service APIs (Figure 13-16).

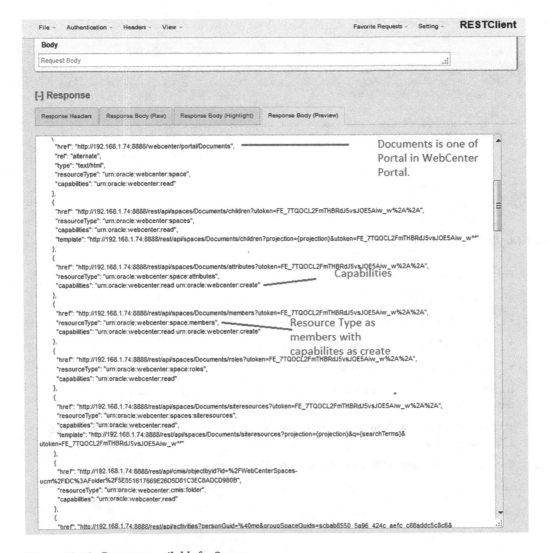

Figure 13-16. *Resource available for Spaces*

WebCenter Portal REST API Authentication

Oracle WebCenter Portal REST API primarily used basic authentication. Basic authentication accepts the user name and password for accessing the resource index. The resource index gives the user the API Token for accessing the portal APIs.

WebCenter Portal REST API can be accessed from the following URL:

```
https://hostname:port/rest/api/
```

For accessing REST API from ADF task flow or any other Java/JEE application, there are various client frameworks. JAX-RS REST client is good as well for this. HTTP header format of Basic authentication is **base64** encoding. Following is snippet of making authentication with WebCenter Portal API.

```java
import static org.junit.Assert.*;

import javax.ws.rs.client.Client;
import javax.ws.rs.client.ClientBuilder;
import javax.ws.rs.client.Entity;
import javax.ws.rs.core.MultivaluedHashMap;
import javax.ws.rs.core.MultivaluedMap;
import javax.ws.rs.core.Response;

import org.junit.Test;

public class BasicAuthenticationTest {

    @Test
    public void VerifyBasicAuthentication() {
        //Define basic authentication credential values
        String user = "user";
        String password = "Password";

        String usernameAndPassword = user + ":" + password
        String authorizationHeaderName = "Authorization";
        String authorizationHeaderValue = "Basic " + java.util.Base64.getEncoder().
        encodeToString( usernameAndPassword.getBytes() );

        // Build the form for a post request
        MultivaluedMap&lt; String, String&gt; formParameters = new MultivaluedHashMap();
        formParameters.add( "field1", "fieldValue1" );
        formParameters.add( "field2", "fieldValue2" );

        // Perform a post request
        String restResource = "https://host:8888/rest/api/";
        Client client = ClientBuilder.newClient();
        Response res = client.target( restResource )
            .path( "login" ) // API Module Path
            .request( "application/json" ) // Expected response mime type
            .header( authorizationHeaderName, authorizationHeaderValue ) // The basic
            authentication header goes here
```

```
        .post( Entity.form( formParameters ) );      // Perform a post with the form
        values

    assertTrue( res.getStatus() == 200 );
    }
}
```

Once authorization is completed and response status is 200, then connect with Spaces API and get information about WebCenter Portal in custom code.

Authentication is also managed by setting identity asserter in Enterprise Manager.

WebCenter Portal Java APIs

WebCenter Portal also offers a Java API for managing common operations with WebCenter Portal. For details and an explanation of the whole API, please read about it in Oracle documentation at `https://docs.oracle.com/middleware/1221/wcp/reference/toc.htm`

There is big list of all packages for each functionalities. Some of the common used packages are the following. Also see Figure 13-17.

- oracle.adf.view.core.component.portlet

- oracle.webcenter.comments

- oracle.webcenter.doclib.view

- oracle.webcenter.generalsettings.model.exception

- oracle.webcenter.likes

- oracle.webcenter.peopleconnections.profile

- oracle.webcenter.peopleconnections.profile.model.crawler

- oracle.webcenter.peopleconnections.profile.security

- oracle.webcenter.peopleconnections.wall

- oracle.webcenter.search

- oracle.webcenter.spaces.beans

- oracle.webcenter.spaces.ws.client

- oracle.webcenter.webcenterapp.application

- oracle.webcenter.webcenterapp.beans

- oracle.webcenter.webcenterapp.context

- oracle.webcenter.page.model

- oracle.webcenter.page.model.config

- oracle.webcenter.peopleconnections.common.settings

- oracle.webcenter.peopleconnections.connections

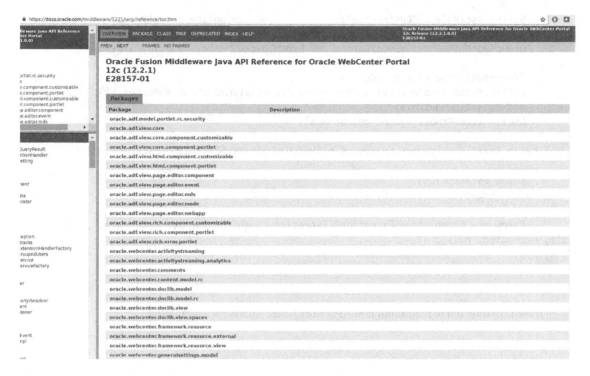

Figure 13-17. *Java API Reference for WebCenter Portal*

This is quite useful to fetch information about space or making custom functionalities in ADF task flows. For example, get a list of all members in one space (portal). Most developers are unaware of this API. Some of the important classes and functions are listed below:

Class	Description
GroupSpaceWSClient	This class provides the utility methods to perform commonly used Group Space operations.
GroupSpaceWSMembers	This class acts as placeholder for storing details of members to be added to the Group Space and to be removed from the Group Space.
GroupSpaceWSMetadata	This class is responsible for providing metadata for given WebCenter Group Space.
ServiceMetadata	This class acts as placeholder for storing the service metadata.

For example, if you want to add a user with a specific role in particular space (Portal), the following code snippet can be used.

```
public void addMemberInSpace(String SpaceName, String userid) throws GroupSpaceWSException {


    try {
        GroupSpaceWSClient Gsclient = new GroupSpaceWSClient(contextData);
```

```
        String userRole = "CustomRole";          // You can define default role as admin,
        viewer, Moderator or some custom role as well
        GroupSpaceWSMembers memberData = new GroupSpaceWSMembers(userid, userRole);

        //Approval code will be added
        List<GroupSpaceWSMembers> addMem = new ArrayList<GroupSpaceWSMembers>();
        addMem.add(memberData);
        Gsclient.addMember(SpaceName, addMem);

    } catch (oracle.webcenter.spaces.ws.client.GroupSpaceWSException gsException) {

        throw gsException;
    } catch (Exception exception) {

        throw new GroupSpaceWSException("Exception caught during addMembership ", null,
null, exception, null);
    }

}
```

Please take time out to read about how APIs work better with WebCenter Portal.

Index

© Vinay Kumar and Daniel Merchán García 2017
V. Kumar and D. M. García, *Beginning Oracle Webcenter Portal 12c*, DOI 10.1007/978-1-4842-2532-5

Get the eBook for only $4.99!

Why limit yourself?

Now you can take the weightless companion with you wherever you go and access your content on your PC, phone, tablet, or reader.

Since you've purchased this print book, we are happy to offer you the eBook for just $4.99.

Convenient and fully searchable, the PDF version enables you to easily find and copy code—or perform examples by quickly toggling between instructions and applications.

To learn more, go to http://www.apress.com/us/shop/companion or contact support@apress.com.

Printed in the United States
By Bookmasters